BEEN THERE, DONE THAT

THROUGH TREACHEROUS SKIES

The Memoirs of

RON BUTCHER

DFC,CD (Ret'd)

carpenter, air navigator, contractor, construction engineer,
association executive, entrepreneur and traveller

Book design, typesetting: Roy Diment VRG
www.members.shaw.ca/vrg
Cover: R. Diment, VRG

Note for Librarians: a cataloguing record for this book is available from Library and Archives
Canada at: www.collectionscanada.ca/amicus/index-e.html
ISBN 1-4120-5797-3

Printed in Victoria, BC, Canada. Printed on paper with minimum 30% recycled fibre. Trafford's print shop
runs on "green energy" from solar, wind and other environmentally-friendly power sources.

Offices in Canada, USA, Ireland and UK
This book was published *on-demand* in cooperation with Trafford Publishing. On-demand
publishing is a unique process and service of making a book available for retail sale to the
public taking advantage of on-demand manufacturing and Internet marketing. On-demand
publishing includes promotions, retail sales, manufacturing, order fulfilment, accounting and
collecting royalties on behalf of the author.

Book sales for North America and international:
Trafford Publishing, 6E–2333 Government St.,
Victoria, BC V8T 4P4 CANADA
phone 250 383 6864 (toll-free 1 888 232 4444)
fax 250 383 6804; email to orders@trafford.com
Book sales in Europe:
Trafford Publishing (UK) Limited, 9 Park End Street, 2nd Floor
Oxford, UK OX1 1HH UNITED KINGDOM
phone 44 (0)1865 722 113 (local rate 0845 230 9601)
facsimile 44 (0)1865 722 868; info.uk@trafford.com
Order online at:
trafford.com/05-0697
10 9 8 7 6 5 4

Dedicated to those aircrew boys
from the Sackville, New Brunswick area
who gave their all in World War II

In Memorium

They shall grow not old as we that are left grow old;
Age shall not weary them nor the years condemn.
At the going down of the sun and in the morning
We will remember them.

CONTENTS

FOREWORD vii

ACKNOWLEDGEMENTS ix

LIST OF TABLES, MAPS AND PHOTOGRAPHS x

1   PROLOGUE... 1

2   THE EARLY YEARS 1921-33 5

3   THE TEEN YEARS 1933-42 15

4   RCAF TRAINING IN CANADA 1942 25

5   ARRIVAL IN ENGLAND 1943 35

6   OPERATIONAL TRAINING 1943 41

7   BOMBER OPERATIONS BEGIN   December 1943 53

8   MORE BOMBER OPERATIONS January-March 1944 65

9   NUREMBERG AND HEAVY LOSSES March 30/31, 1944 79

10 THE TENSION EASES April 1944-June 1945 85

11 SUMMARY AND CONTROVERSY 101

12 OUR CONSTRUCTION COMPANY 1945-51 109

13 BACK IN THE AIR FORCE 1951-1952 115

14 A MOVE TO THE WEST 1952-55 121

15 AND BACK TO THE EAST 1955-59 131

16 MORE YEARS IN THE HEAD-SHED 1959-1963 141

17 FORCES INTEGRATION/UNIFICATION 1963-1971 145

18 FROM ORDERING TO REQUESTING 1971-76 157

19 ENTREPRENEUR AND VOLUNTEER 1976-84 169

20 CHINA, AND ELSEWHERE 1984-2000 177

21 A MOVE, A MARRIAGE, AND MARCHING ON 2001- 2005 191

22 WHAT IT ALL MEANT 197

ANNEX A 203

BIBLIOGRAPHY 205

SELECTED GLOSSARY 207

INDEX 209

FOREWORD

by

Lieutenant-General Bill Carr, CMM, DFC, OStJ, CD, CMLJ, LOM, BSc (Ret)

This book contains the most vivid, uncomplaining and honest descriptions I have ever read of what the WWII Bomber Command aircrews went through during the years 1939 to 1945 when they delivered no less than one-and-a-quarter million tons of bombs on Hitler's empire. From 1943 onward the US Army Air Force added a further three-quarter million tons to this total. And those young aircrew suffered incomparable losses.

Two-thirds of the RAF Bomber Command crews died or became prisoners of war and more than fifty percent of the more than 55,000 deaths occurred before D-Day. One quarter of that number were RCAF aircrew serving with the RCAF's Six Group or in RAF squadrons.

The author is a modest and decorated survivor with a rare gift which allows him to convey to his reader a picture of suppressed and controlled fear which was never allowed to surface or in any way dilute the total dedication and cohesion of 'the crew' of which he was a key member. His accounts of many of the crew's bombing missions told with precision, unemotionally and indeed with wry humour on occasion, cannot fail to help remind the reader how often the human spirit eludes analysis.

But this book tells more than stories about War. It, unintentionally perhaps, paints a picture of an ordinary Canadian from a small town who has very successfully made the most of his God-given talents and opportunities. His duty to others is met with humility and his joy in life is obvious.

The author's biography is fascinating and his ability to build things like houses and scrounge things like warehouses, are almost in contradiction with his rare gift for the written word. This talent came to the fore when, in one of his 'lives' he took on the task as General Manager of the Royal Canadian Air Force Association from 1971 to 1976. Without his personal involvement and initiative at the time, it is doubtful that Canada's leading aviation magazine *Airforce* would exist.

Sprinkled throughout this book are wonderful stories, sometimes sad, sometimes amusing, but always honest. His observations about our changing society and its mores are gems. Who but he could have suggested 'we thought *fast food* was what you ate in Lent' and 'the term *making out* referred to how you did in your exams'!

The author claims at the beginning of his epilogue that it is 'to summarize a most enjoyable life'. Read the book and you'll agree.

Stittsville, Ontario 2005

ACKNOWLEDGEMENTS

Though accuracy, and the views expressed must be my responsibility alone, my gratitude goes to all who have provided inspiration over the years.

Many thanks go to Bill Carr for the *Foreword* and for his excellent and timely advice, and to my wife Veronica, my son-in-law Gary Greenfield, my daughter Brenda Greenfield, and Jim Hanson for reading the manuscript and recommending worthwhile improvements and corrections.

Terry Copp kindly gave permission to use a quotation from his column in *Legion* magazine, as did Jeremy Diamond of the Dominion Institute for the use of the *Memory Project* logo.

In addition to the valuable contributions made by those mentioned in the text, advice, encouragement and reminiscences large and small have been shared with thanks over the years with many folks in all walks of life, including Lorne Andrews, Ron Aumonier, Ron Bailey, Arnie Bauer, Sam Biondo, Hal Brennan, Paul Burden, Tony Cannell, Andy Carswell, Bob Fassold, Al Chute, Bill Cowie, Mike Dooher, Hal Fawcett, Jim Garrity, Julian Guntensperger, Fred Hatch, Don Hepburn, Earl Howard, Norm Hutchings, Alex Jardine, Charlie Konvalinka, Roy Lamont, Len Lapeer, Paul Landrigan, Doug Lewis, Bill Lowry, Jamie MacGregor, Doc Marier, Don Miller, Al Myers, Ron Noel, Bill Owston, Reg Patterson, George Penfold, Tommy Pickard, Dick Plack, David Price, Doug Renton, Joe Romanow, Pete Sandham, Joan Scott, Bill Smith, Wylie Spafford, Nick Stan, George Stoner, and Frank and Jim Wilson.

Roy Diment, of Vivencia Resources Group provided the cover design, maps and much useful advice.

The photos are from the author's collection unless otherwise credited.

Ron Butcher
Saanichton, BC
2005

Tables, Maps and Photographs

Tables:

1- Table of Aircrew Training Progression 29

2- Lancaster Specifications in English Measurements 48

3- Lancaster Specifications in Metric Measurements 49

4- Comparative Rank, RCAF and CF 149

Maps:

Partial map of New Brunswick, Nova Scotia and Prince Edward Island 2

Partial map of England and Europe...66

Partial map of China showing the tour route 179

Photographs:

First flight – 1942 31

Aboard SS Bayano II 36

Derry at the Carlton Hotel entrance...37

DH 82- Tiger Moth 40

Vickers Wellington III 44

High Flight 52

An engine gets attention as S/L Bill Russell watches...54

Waiting for the pub to open 59

Lanc II S-Sugar 59

Our new aircraft..63

WWII Ration Book 64

Changing a prop on K-King, 408 Sqn 64

Bombing-up a Lancaster II 75

Lanc IIs at Linton 80

Ron up in the air during a take-off delay, Suds in the cockpit....................................85

N-Nan near tour's end (also on front cover)..87

The crew at tour's end...90

At the entrance to the 408 Sqn Nav Section 93

Canadian-built Lancaster X 97

Construction Engineering Section, Saskatoon 1953.. 122

Bunny, Brenda and Ron on the doorstep at PMQ.. 123

The beginnings of a chapel, Saskatoon, 1952 124

The greenhouse, Saskatoon 127

The Central Heating Plant, Saskatoon 128

Officer's Mess nearing completion 129

At Assiniboine Park, Winnipeg. 130

The new cantilever hangar at Greenwood.. 131

Canadair Argus 132

The Mobile Home Park, Greenwood 133

Ron, with #2 crew at the fire hall 135

A P2V and a Lanc X at Greenwood 136

Meeting the Governor General, the Hon Roland Michener 152

Nearing retirement in 1971 155

The Governor General speaking at the 1972 convention............................ 162

Ron and Sybil 1973, in a receiving line 164

RCAF D-Day veterans at the 30th Anniversary in 1974 165

From the Catalogue 171

Gift Items Galore..172

A badged carafe set...173

TGIF at the Mess 174

Sgt. Shatterproof 176

The Great Wall through an archway 178

Linked barges on the Grand Canal.. 181

The Temple of Dawn, Bangkok 183

Dancing with Geraldine 184

A traditional view of the Great Wall 189

Trinity Cathedral, Zagorsk, Russia 189

Spanning Highway I-80... 192

Rover's Return Pub, Dunedin, New Zealand... 194

Puerto Vallarta, Mexico harbour 2004... 195

Aboard MS Zaandam at San Juan del Sur... 196

At Waikiki, Hawaii 2004.. 197

Medals 201

On the way to Germany, look who's following us 202

1

PROLOGUE

in which the author's birthplace and forebears are discussed

Middle Sackville, New Brunswick (NB), the village where I was born in 1921, located 2 miles (3.2 km) north-east of its neighbour Sackville, had a population of about 400-500. The Tantramar marshes and Silver Lake (also known as Mortice's Pond) are the main local geographical features, with 400-ft (120-m) Beech Hill as a backdrop.

Founded in 1762, Sackville was a Forge & Frock community with 2,500 inhabitants (now about 5,400). Furnaces and stoves were manufactured at two steel foundries. Mount Allison University (MTA) provided the frock component, and a small harness factory also provided employment. Many workers who lived in Middle Sackville worked at the foundries or MTA. Most folks did not have automobiles, they walked or cycled to and from work daily. The rest of the village revolved around industrial and farming activity.

Middle Sackville had been a busy industrial and farm export community, but in the early 1920s that activity was waning because export markets were disappearing. In common with other areas of Canada and the United States, the advent of the automobile was bringing about major changes. Industries that catered to horse-drawn transportation declined while those related to vehicles gained in stature. For instance, the number of horses on the Eastern Seaboard in Boston and New York declined sharply so less carriages were being built, and less hay and grain exported. This was reflected in firms and individuals changing their products and occupations as time went on. Generally, there was increasing unemployment.

J. L. Black & Sons, Ltd, the leading employer in Middle Sackville, operated a wholesale grocery, flour and feed business on three south-eastern New Brunswick routes; and a retail store which carried groceries, flour and feed, clothing, dry goods, paint and wallpaper. It also had a beef feedlot operation in the village, and an export lumber operation in the Aboushaugan area.

Boots, shoes and moccasins were manufactured from raw hides to finished product at two factories, the A. E. Wry Standard Ltd (the Standard) and Burwash Robinson Ltd. Carriages and sleighs, the primary personal transportation vehicles of the time, were manufactured at the Campbell Carriage Works and were shipped throughout the Eastern areas of Canada and the US.

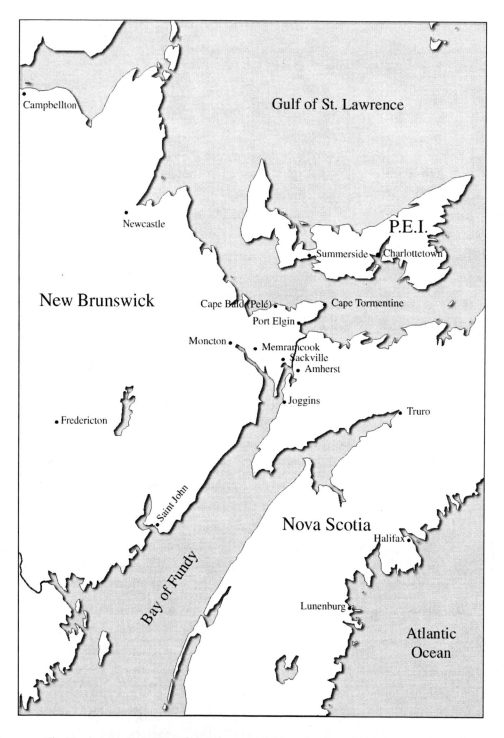

The Home Area- Part Map of New Brunswick, Nova Scotia and Prince Edward Island
(R Diment VRG)

Because this industry was diminishing rapidly, the family became undertakers. They managed to pick a winner, another 'dying' industry, but one that was expanding with the increasing population of the overall area.

William Thomas Butcher, my paternal grandfather, from Titchfield, in the Fareham area near Southampton, England had been trained as a journeyman carpenter. He arrived in Western Canada in 1898, with his wife and six children. My father, Arthur Freeborn Butcher was the youngest at six years of age. The family homesteaded in the area of Cardston, Magrath and Standoff, Alberta near the Blood Indian Reserve. Little is known about their farm life on the prairies but in our childhood, we children were regaled with stories of chuck wagons and cattle drives. Although most of the time was spent farming and ranching, Granddad also worked on the Reserve from time to time as a carpenter.

In 1916, Granddad and family arrived in the Sackville area and bought a farm near the Red Bridge on the Walker Road, about 1 mile (1.6 km) from Middle Sackville. They moved there because Grandma suffered from acute bronchitis, and it was thought that the local environment would help her back to good health. Apparently it was not the answer because she died of emphysema before I was born. Later, Granddad went back to England for a year, married Grandma's sister and they returned to Canada. Sometime during the intervening years Dad had also achieved status as a journeyman carpenter.

In July 1920, he married Stella Pearl Brundage, daughter of Harry and Gertrude Brundage, descendants of United Empire Loyalists who originated in New York State. The family had farmed at Upper Greenwich on the Saint John River for many years, then Grandpa Harry operated a grocery store on Waterloo Street in Saint John, NB. My mother had gone to a small rural school, by canoe in summer and over a river ice road in winter. Upon graduation from high school, she attended the Provincial Normal School (Teacher's College) in Fredericton, and then taught at Middle Sackville Superior School.

She boarded with Mrs. Arnold Smith about 1 mile (1.6 km) from the school. Her contract with the school board stipulated her clothing and habits: that she wear clothes that concealed the ankles, arms and neck, and wear her hair in a bun on top of her head. She was forbidden any boy friends. Nothing is known of my parent's dating habits; however, because they married, it must be assumed that some sort of a courtship took place.

Upon marriage my parents bought a house in Middle Sackville which became the family home until 1946. It was a substantial house with lower and upper front verandas, had running water but lacked electricity, and was heated by a coal furnace.

The house was located on a 2-acre (0.75-ha) plot, without any outbuildings. A wood stove, with a tank for heating water, was used for cooking. Notwithstanding that toilet facilities were available and, probably harking back to earlier accommodation, there was a thunder jug under each bed. With the move from the Red Bridge area Granddad, his wife and my spinster Aunt Marion joined the newlyweds in their new home, and the farm was sold to Roy Estabrooks.

The local doctors in those days led hard lives. They covered the territory from the Nova Scotia (NS) border to Midgic, NB on house calls in a radius of about 15 miles (24 km). They travelled by horse and buggy in the summer, and horse and sleigh in the winter, in all kinds of weather. It was well-known that most babies did not cooperate, generally picking the midnight hours to arrive in a howling snow storm. And many times the doctor was unable to get through!

Each doctor had a driver to get him to his patient and tend the horse while he was making his house call. There was no shelter for horse and driver at many homes so, often during my younger years, I saw the driver pacing back and forth in the dark and cold, trying to keep warm. Sometimes this continued for hours. We children were very suspicious of what we perceived as a connection between the horse waiting in the snow and the arrival of a new baby in the village. We remained very sceptical, and didn't buy the 'stork' story.

The closest hospital was in Amherst, NS 10 miles (16 km) away, so babies were usually born at home. As what must have been a prelude to my cooperative and adapting personality it came to pass, with my mother attended by Dr. Knapp of Sackville and a village midwife, ... I was born May 19,1921 on a nice, sunny spring Thursday during daylight hours, and began growing up in a 1920s New Brunswick village.

2

THE EARLY YEARS
1921-33

in which growing up in the village is outlined

Employment for carpenters was scarce in the Sackville area in the early 1920s, but was available at the Blood Indian Reserve near Cardston, Alberta in the area where Dad had previously lived. With no job immediately in sight when I was about 18 months old, he departed for the West and was employed in Cardston until I was three years old.

Upon his return, it was decided he would operate as a self-employed contractor. His first contract was the renovation of a farmhouse home in Frosty Hollow, 5 miles (8 km) from Middle Sackville, for the President of the Enterprise Foundry Company, Fred Fisher. He travelled by bicycle, transporting his tools as necessary. It must have taken some forethought, because tools that far away when needed are of little use, and you can't haul much on a bicycle.

Other contracts followed, and he earned a solid reputation. He was seldom without work, and never looked back. During evenings and weekends, he worked at building a 24-ft x 60-ft (7.3m x 18.3m) 2-storey building to house both a workshop and headquarters for his business. He had the assistance of his son who liked nothing better than pounding nails. The only problem at the time was Dad's penchant for perfection, everything had to fit just right. It did enable me to learn quickly, and to undertake construction of advanced articles at a very young age.

Pounding nails became a vocation in itself. Dad found it difficult to keep any on hand, so an arrangement (through admonishment) was made that my brother Charles, born in 1924, and I would reuse as many as possible. Any project that appeared worthless when completed was stripped down, the wood saved, and the nails straightened, our first lesson in recycling! While Dad worked out in the community, Granddad looked after a vegetable garden, a few fruit trees, and a front lawn and flower garden.

The early 1920s were the years of the big snows. One picture in Mom's album showed Granddad, who was the village Postmaster, holding me in his arms in the snow 'tunnel' leading into the post office.

Snow drifts built up to the level of the electric lines through the rock cut that levelled the road at Mabel Read's house. Automobiles and teams of horses travelled on top of the snow all winter. When break-up came in the spring, men went out with shovels, and dug through the cut. Otherwise there was no communication with Sackville except by a long detour, and that was a mud road across the marshes. The first year that the provincial government snow blower came from Moncton to do the job you could almost hear the sighs of relief.

Fresh fruit was non-existent in winter, so Granddad brought in rhubarb roots and placed them on the earth floor under the basement stairs, where very fine, pink stalks resulted, and they tasted great when cooked. When spring came, the roots went back out to the garden. He taught we children much about care of the soil, plants and planting.

Our entertainment outdoors was stilts, hopscotch, softball, fishing, and weeding the garden in the summer. In the winter we had sleds with which to slide down the hills, and skates to go skating on the lake. Indoors, we had board games such as snakes and ladders, tiddlywinks and cribbage, but no playing cards as they were considered to be a pastime of the Devil, as was dancing. We also had a Meccano set. We became quite adept at building wooden stilts and wagons, although the early editions were always doomed to short-term failure for one reason or another.

Weekly allowances for small children in those days were a pittance. Each was given two cents weekly, with the caution that one of them must be saved. If we could not account for our savings the next week, there was no allowance for two weeks. The desire for at least a cent's worth of rock candy was enough to keep the savings growing. Summer brought a special allowance of five cents each week for ice cream, provided we were very, very good. Visiting relatives usually gave each child in the family money as a gift, from a low of one cent, to a high of a nickel. All in all there wasn't much chance of us getting fat from too much in the way of sweets.

Upon starting school, it was most pleasing to see that gold and silver stars were handed out for excellence. I became competitive and gathered as many as possible, being quite successful in the lower grades. A little souvenir booklet given to me by the Grade 1 teacher, Joyce Murray at Christmas 1927 for *highest average* has an entry, 'Memory like the ivy clings to olden times and ways and things'. Little did she, nor I, realize that it would be read 77 years later, and recognized as most apt in preparation for writing my memoirs.

Our school was about one-half mile (0.8 km) distance from home and I enjoyed the early school years very much, but was a small child and seemed to attract the bully in the class. I reasoned that I would need some assistance to keep him at bay so it was contrived, when his next onslaught happened, to be close to the concrete step at the old town hall, half way home, and ensured his head got bashed on the step. No more problem, he ignored me after that!!

Very few homes in the village had electricity. We became one of the early families to live in a wired house. Art Wry was the electrician who came daily from Fairfield Road, 5 miles (8 km) away on foot, accompanied by his trusty little flask of rum which, he assured us, was for medicinal purposes. He was usually glassy-eyed before noon but, surprisingly to we children, the lights he installed worked.

Wiring opened up a whole new social whirl, and with electricity came a radio. Every Saturday night a select group of local young men, who were hockey fans and players, came to huddle around the dining room table to listen to Foster Hewitt broadcasting the National Hockey League games. Small children could listen, but had to be very quiet. From these Saturday night huddles the idea developed of the village having a skating rink. With Dad's leadership, it was a reality within years.

Lawson Smith was a neighbour who owned a 2-door 1926 Chevrolet. One day in 1927 he and his wife, a large, rotund Newfoundland lady invited our then family of four for a Sunday afternoon drive over primitive country roads. We can now go to Singapore for three months or longer, with less preparation than we went through that day to go on a 25-mile (40-km) round trip to Rockport. The outing was very nice, chugging along at about 12 mph (20 kph) until Mr. Smith misjudged a pole culvert in the road, and the car bounced violently, so much so that Mrs. Smith's head, accompanied by her large hat, went between the wooden structural ribs and through the canvas roof. We boys had the temerity to laugh, and that in itself probably precluded further invitations.

A highlight occurred when I was eight years old, a trip to visit Aunt Olive, Mom's sister, in Saint John, NB, 120 miles (192 km) to the west, during the summer holidays. I travelled alone by train, and by city bus to the stop at the New Brunswick Museum on Douglas Avenue. From there it was a short walk down to her house on Wilmot St. As Olive and her husband, Ron Seely both worked in their attached grocery store, I was allowed to explore on my own, visiting the Reversing Falls, Rockwood Park Zoo and other local attractions within the city bus routes.

Burwash Robinson was our neighbour in the village. He owned the smaller of the two tanning and shoe manufacturing establishments. With the downturn in the boot and shoe trade, he was searching for an appropriate replacement endeavour. He had a small general store and the first gasoline pump in the village, and had taken over the post office when my Granddad returned to England a second time.

He soon bought a 1½ ton 1929 Chevrolet truck chassis. Dad had the contract to build a wooden cab and a stake body on the truck, and it had been agreed that, because of the low price quoted, Dad could work on it evenings. No speedy finishing of this job, and an indication of the laid-back sense of the community. This suited we boys very well because we were allowed to put on the stakes and rails, boring holes and inserting bolts after school, and painting it when it was finished .... child labour first hand, and cheap!

Driver's licenses were still not required in the area. If you could drive, you drove! I remember when they were first available in Sackville. They were obtained from one of the undertakers, Fred Jones, who had added this mandated item to his services. Instruction, what instruction. You passed over a two-dollar bill and you got a license.

When the truck went into service, it was first used to go into the surrounding countryside with relatively fresh fish to sell to the local population. Robinson asked me to go with him during the summer school holidays. Having been taught to drive by another neighbour, Robbie Estabrooks, it was immediately found that he was parking on the road, and making me walk long farm lanes lugging a big shad, sometimes both ways if there was no sale. Luckily, he admitted he was afraid to attempt turning the truck around, and allowed me to do it for him (at about 9 years old), even though it was necessary to sit on the very edge of the seat to reach the pedals, and usually use both hands to shift gears. In order for him to save face, he talked to the people we were visiting while I turned around. Before the summer was over, he allowed me to drive if we were on a straight road with no hills. The local marsh country fitted very well into this permission.

Mrs. Robinson was also a character well worth knowing. She was very interested in art, and had run out of walls. There was an outhouse at the end of a long hall in the mostly unused barn behind their house. She proceeded to hang prints along this hall, and we children would make any pretext possible to use the outhouse, in order to see the art gallery.

We liked to visit around the community, mostly to homes where our school friends lived. We always enjoyed going to Mack Legere's and to Bride Ayer's, but we got short shrift at Becky Long's house. Generally speaking it was a warm, nurturing community environment in which to grow up.

It was in 1930 that Dad became the proud owner of his first car, a new 2-door Ford ($684, cash on the table). The first thing he did was to make a rear outside trunk, contoured to match the back of the car, mainly to carry tools back and forth to work, and covered it with black leatherette. Cars were in their very early stages, so we were among the first generation of little passengers to repeat 'Are we there yet?' By this time Albert (1928) and Evelyn (1930) had joined the family, making us capable of a lot of noise, parents and surroundings permitting.

There was always lots of excitement in the spring and fall when young cattle were moved to and from their summer grazing grounds. They went through the village, seemingly under control. But there were times it didn't go quite that well, like the day Granddad, back from England and now retired, tried stubbornly to protect his chicken run from a rampaging yearling. He ended up taking a few days off, with the octagon outline marks of chicken wire showing clearly on his bald head, face and neck.

Meanwhile, all my spare time was devoted to learning carpentry .... and pounding more nails. By the time 10 years of age was reached, there was sufficient proficiency that Dad allowed me to work the summer holidays with his crew renovating Dr. Gass's house in Sackville. I did all kinds of things, including laying strip hardwood flooring. The strips were toe-nailed to the sub-floor and a miss with the hammer could ruin the floor. The only remedy would be removal and replacement, and probably the immediate loss of the job. One of the senior carpenters, Irving Wheaton commented that, in most jurisdictions, I would be considered a journeyman. I knew better though. I wasn't big or strong enough at that time for many of the carpentry tasks.

Also, about then, visits to nearby farms began, where work was done for pin money: weeding turnips, picking strawberries at one cent a box, getting the cows from pasture for milking, hoeing carrots and other little chores. Some farms were so interesting that my chums and I visited, ... and worked for nothing. This was unique with Levi Lerette, and a couple of others of we children of about the same age. We must have been different, the others seemed to be happy doing little or nothing to while away their time.

Donald Harper's farm was one such place. He had graduated from the Agricultural College in Truro, NS and lived at the farm with his widowed mother, later marrying one of my favorite school teachers, Gretchen Hansen, and serving as a Member of Parliament in Ottawa. He used modern farming methods learned at college, and had almost everything running on electricity, a first for the local area. He raised Holstein cattle and later experimented with crossbreeding to a Shorthorn bull in an attempt to produce an advanced strain of dairy/meat animals. Donald had three horses, Tom, Sandy and Queenie, all of mixed parentage, and we always tried to find an excuse to drive them.

One of my early experiences with Queenie was hauling turnips to the barn cellar in a dump cart. Another was harrowing a field with a spike-toothed harrow. All went well until leaving the field with the spikes turned up. Queenie moved quickly in a direction that had not been expected, and I ended up sitting on top of the harrow. Two spikes had pierced .... you know where. On arrival home, and not daring to report the incident because I would probably be denied access to the farm, iodine was put on liberally while resisting the temptation to yell out in pain. There are still scars to prove it, and a vivid memory of the pain to go with them.

In the winter each farmer went to his wood lot to cut stove and furnace wood for the coming year, and also some saw logs for additional income. Morice's did custom sawing for many small producers. The lumber was used in the local building industry, and also exported. We would spend some of the Christmas school vacation accompanying Donald into the woods, 3 miles (5 km) away at Mount View, where one of his wood lots was located. There were no chain saws in those days. Either Donald or his hired man, Sam White, would get on one end of a crosscut saw, with two boys on the other.

The crunch of sled runners on the hard snow as we returned in the frosty, waning light of late afternoon with loads of wood will never be forgotten. The wood was piled behind Donald's house, and would be sawed into firewood later during the spring thaw period. Some days saw logs would be substituted, and they would be placed on Donald's pile at Morice's Mill, and sawed into lumber in the spring, when the water was in freshet and maximum power was available to run the water-driven saw.

During an Easter break we went with Donald and Sam to one of the back pastures where they were clearing a new piece of land. We marvelled at how the horses pulled out stumps, sometimes with the use of a triangular pole arrangement to multiply leverage. On occasion dynamite was used if a big, stubborn stump was encountered. Later, we helped seed the newly prepared land with buckwheat.

The scene at Grey Prescott's farm was much different. That's where we learned about the birds and bees. We always knew when something interesting was going on at Grey's because he was loud and didn't abhor profanity. He was mainly involved in importing Western horses by the freight car load, and breaking them to harness. He was always selling and bartering, and had a varied collection of horses on hand at any given time.

One day we went over to see what was going on. Grey was attempting to breed a thoroughbred mare with a little piebald Western stallion. As the stallion had shorter legs than the mare, she was backed up to a slope so that the stallion would be higher, but Grey didn't comprehend that the footing was wet and very, very slippery. The result was that the stallion lost his footing when mounting, and slipped under the mare's back legs, so that she was tripped up. The situation became a screaming, neighing mess with hooves flailing in all directions. Grey was swearing a blue streak and the assembled children were trying not to giggle, or they would have been shooed off home. The heat was out of the situation and the horses went to separate corners of the barnyard to sulk, refusing to perform again. Eventually, on another day, the breeding was successful and a cute, long-legged and perfectly-marked piebald filly was born.

Abner Smith, who always wore a soiled suit and tie, no matter what the surroundings or event, had been involved as a shareholder in the Standard. He also had a hog operation housed in the basement of a bank barn. As the basement was obviously too dark to be suited to this purpose, he built a modern pig barn which had a massive steamer for boiling potatoes, thus using cheap cull potatoes from the local area for pig feed. The local children liked nothing better than to visit on a cold winter day because it was the warmest place in the village. Even today, every time potatoes are boiled with the skins on, I get the smell and immediately remember that place and its warmth.

The salt marshes of the Maritimes are composed of very heavy saturated clay. To build and repair dykes a very narrow dyking spade is required. Blacksmith Leonard Estabrooks was well known for the dyking spades he manufactured. He shipped them throughout the Eastern Seaboard to areas that had clay marshes. Sometimes we helped him to make them. When we children arrived to pester him on our frequent meanderings, he would put us to work, filing and smoothing handles or putting on varnish. He always seemed to stop at a certain stage, apparently because he knew we would show up before long.

Hay was cut on the marshes in July and August and stored in the many barns that dotted the landscape, then baled in the winter months and shipped in railway carloads to Newfoundland, Boston and New York. A selected few of us were allowed to go haying. The village teams would stream off to the marshes early in the morning, each with two empty hay carts. We took our lunch, worked putting hay in the marsh barns all day, and went home late in the evening, each team of horses hauling two carts loaded with hay which would be put into the home barns, before leaving for the marsh again the next day. If any mares in the teams had young colts, they were tagging along throughout the day, and by the time they were old enough to work required little training.

Potatoes were another local crop which was exported. Deliveries were made to a building called the *Potato House*, at the railway siding next to the school. There they were sorted, bagged and loaded into railway freight cars for shipment throughout the Eastern Seaboard.

One place which often attracted us was the picnic grounds at Silver Lake. We could wander the woods, fish, and eat the sandwiches that various mothers had provided. We were prohibited, however, from going into the water, an admonishment that was to prove a problem in later years, because the art of swimming was never learned, sinking like lead on every attempt.

Morice's had a giant ice warehouse near the picnic grounds. Ice cut on the lake during the winter months was stored in sawdust for delivery on the 'ice route' in the Summer. This endeavour lasted until refrigerators became standard in all local homes.

About 1932 it was decided that we would raise chickens, so a chicken house was built at the rear of the property to house about 100 Leghorns and Plymouth Rocks, and the chickens became my responsibility.

The tanneries/shoe factories run by the Standard and Burwash Robinson were very interesting places where we spent quite a bit of time. The tanneries had boiling vats of chemicals and hides, and were separated by narrow walkways. The hides were immersed in rotation through the vats for pre-determined periods, and then scraped to remove the hair. Rinsing through more vats completed the process, after which the hides were scraped, dried and went to the upper floors where moccasins and boots were made. We got great pleasure from talking to the shoemakers. They were marvellous storytellers.

About 1933, Dad bought a brindle cow and we kept a pig to be butchered in the fall. The cow was pastured at Morice's field near the sawmill, and we children took turns bringing her home, milking and returning her to pasture, a round trip of about three quarters of a mile (1.2 km), morning and night. Later a second cow was added, a purebred Jersey from the Dominion Experimental Farm at Nappan, NS .... and there were visions of a Jersey dairy herd in the future! An addition to the back of the house was completed as a mud room, with space for the cream separator and butter churn. A little later, Dad bought some acreage on the Beech Hill Road to use as pasture.

We now had a 1½-mile (2.4-km) return trip morning and night with the cows. We also built a lean-to addition at the rear of the shop to serve as a stable. This allowed Dad to increase the size of his carpenter shop, to include the area where the animals had previously been housed. In the meantime, our flock of chickens had increased to the point where we had to double the size of the chicken houses. With about 125 Barred Plymouth Rocks and 175 White Leghorns in residence, both white and brown eggs were weighed, candled and sold.

The next year Brownie, a retired race horse arrived and this gave me the opportunity to start an egg route. Now farming in earnest, equipment and a second horse were borrowed when necessary. Any wooden farm equipment required was built, including a hay rig. Ironwork for these items was manufactured by my blacksmith friend.

As we went on, further buildings were built and we were still pounding nails. I was so busy in the mornings that one day as I arrived at school slightly late the teacher said, during roll call, 'I know Ronald is here, I can smell him'. The farm smell permeates clothing almost as badly as tobacco does. There is no doubt that I was farming very busily and, in this down-to-earth climate, would carry on in similar fashion into my teen years!

3

THE TEEN YEARS
1933-42

in which school, hobby farming, graduation, a full-time job and marriage are covered

Weather in the Sackville area is generally temperate with mean temperatures in January-March of about -5 dC (23 dF); June-August about 16 dC (60 dF); and October-December about 2.5 dC (36.5 dF). The annual snowfall averages 94.5 ins (240 cm) and rainfall is about 43.3 ins (1,100 mm). The air is not uncomfortably humid, and there are many clear and sunny days. If the weather was watched reasonably closely, it was not difficult to program the many activities in which a person was involved, without surprises. Especially in July when haying was in full swing, the weather usually cooperated. There could be the odd thunderstorm but, otherwise, it was usually clear sunny days and good drying conditions. Again in the late fall period of Indian Summer, conditions were good for the harvesting of root vegetables and corn.

I suppose I acted like a normal teenager, consistently difficult; however, Dad seemed to have problems with the father/son relationship, and treated me more like a brother than a son. Although there was yearning for fatherly love and a better relationship, it seemed to me that he was incapable of it. It was there, but he didn't know how to show it; however, there was an inherent benefit: I was allowed to do things that were well beyond my age. In discussion, brother Albert felt the same; however, we did know, because we had comments from the neighbours, that Dad bragged to them about his children and how proud he was of us and our achievements. Our siblings had different, and warmer, memories. Could it have been because Albert and I were masters at mis-compliance, looking for adventure when we should have been acting more like model children of the era?

Of course, being a teenager, some things were done that Dad didn't know about or, should it be said, it was thought he didn't know about? One such experience was when an old Harley Davidson motorcycle was purchased with the intention of making it roadworthy, and driving it. It was stored in Robbie Estabrooks' garage, but no matter how hard I worked on it, it was impossible to get it to run, always coming so close to achievement. Eventually, it was sold for ten dollars more than the purchase price. Nothing was lost, and a lot of practice attended tinkering with it. It was many years later that it was finally figured out there must have been an arrangement with Robbie that it would never run, at least until an older age!

We teenagers found the veterans of WWI most interesting. We could not get many stories out of them, but a scar or two would be shown on demand. And we thought they were really old .... at forty some years!

Graduation from grade 8 into high school occurred in 1934, into the last room in the school. Our school had a stone-and-brick basement, and was a two-storey clap-boarded wooden structure of four rooms, each home to three grades, except the first room, which housed grades one and two. The school principal was male, and taught high school, the other three teachers were female. Total enrolment was about 100 students, a few of which were from surrounding villages and boarded with relatives, usually because there was no high school available near their homes. This was before school buses, and it was difficult for parents to make provision for their children to attend the higher grades. For instance, my cousin Kathleen who lived in Port Elgin, 18 miles (29 km) East, stayed with our family throughout her high school grades, go-ing home only on weekends and for the summer holidays.

In the meantime, work continued at my various farming endeavours, my school grades were deteriorating, but they did remain passable, and enough was done to preclude failure. With my farming operations becoming more demanding, sitting in school rather than exploring the great outdoors seemed very limiting, and it was hard to keep my mind on algebra and Latin.

Brownie, the horse, was used for all manner of activities. I had a Western saddle and no one else was so equipped, at least no one among those who were that way inspired, so I always led the July 1 Dominion (now Canada) Day parade in Sackville. Brownie liked to dance to the band, a good reason for volunteering, and it was also a big thrill for me.

In the summer of 1936 an investment was made in my first property, nine acres (3.6 ha) of marshland; however, because of being underage, Dad had to hold the deed. A garden on that property didn't do so well, but the marsh soil grew a magnifi-cent hay crop. To do the haying a big, rangy old horse was borrowed from a second blacksmith friend who lived and worked in Sackville, and a mower and rake were borrowed from a close neighbour who had finished his haying.

All went well until, on the way home from the marsh property one day, a freight train travelling on the rail line from Prince Edward Island (PEI) went by shortly after the team had left the crossing. Its whistle blew for the crossing, and Blackie took off, dragging the big horse (Sam), the mower and me along with him. He would not go far; he had acted in similar fashion before. As soon as the noise of the train was gone he settled down, but not before a nosey neighbour had reported to my mother on our newly-installed telephone that my team had run away. This led to a long discussion on safety, and my protests that nothing unsafe had happened remained unheard until very late in the conversation, when reason prevailed.

Hay was transported by wagon with a hay rack that had cut-outs, so that the front wheels could turn on a short radius. It also had side racks to keep the hay from obstructing the wheels. In the winter, this same body was used with a pair of bobsleds. When baled hay was hauled, the side racks were removed, and the bales placed on the floor of the rack. The hay from the marsh property was built into two haystacks on site. It was later transported to the home barn in winter, once the majority of the hay already stored there had been used.

Now we had to build another addition on the shop because Sam was given to me. There were also three cows, two calves, and a yearling Jersey bull, at that time assumed to be the potential future sire of our dairy herd. There were three pigs housed, and 350 laying hens in the chicken pens. I was really into farming, and learning how to do all kinds of operations, including hand broadcast seeding, and how to use a scythe to cut hay and weeds.

It was about this time that we were treated to some rather different entertainment. Charles was helping me clean out the pig sty and Mom was hanging the washing on the line in the yard. A rat was dislodged, it ran out into the yard and up Mom's leg. She danced a cute little jig and made more than a lot of noise, to our great amusement.

My involvement in building a house was a new experience. In the Maritimes in those days, basements were dug using hand labour, picks and shovels. The excavated material was moved out of the basement area using a horse-drawn scoop. Forms for basement walls were prepared using wooden studs and tongued-and-grooved sheathing. Cement and gravel were mixed into concrete by hand, and poured from wheelbarrows using ramps and a staging around the top of the basement perimeter. Framing was done using the material that had been in the forms, augmented by more of the same type. Joists and rafters were usually dimensioned wooden planks. Sheathing was used for boarding-in, and roofing was usually asphalt shingles. Side cladding was almost always wood clapboards, painted when application was complete.

Road work was similarly primitive, gravel was hauled on horse-drawn wagons using loose planks as bottoms and sides. It was quite easy to unload. A man on each end merely lifted the planks in sequence and the gravel fell to the ground, where it was levelled by other men using shovels. Residents were allowed to use their road work efforts as credit against their taxes.

It was one of the children's chores to keep a watchful eye out for droppings for the garden when any horses went by, and before the neighbour's children realized they were there. There were no paved roads in the local area, and the roads were tended spring and fall using gravel levelled by a horse-drawn grader. Through railways and paved roads to today's trucks: no beneficial droppings of manure for fertilizer there now!

I was looking forward to going to Army summer camp in Sussex, NB with the VIII Canadian Hussars (Princess Louise's) in the summer of 1937, the year I turned 16. The regiment was a cavalry unit, and I would be able to use Blackie as my mount .... and get paid as well! Alas, the regiment became a tank unit that year, and cars were required for manoeuvres. The idea had to be given up because there was no way my father was going to allow his car to be used as a tank: I knew enough not to ask. It was probably for the best; otherwise, I might have gravitated to the army, and not had an air force career.

What did happen leading up to my sixteenth birthday was the violent loss of all my teeth. We had a hockey team in the Sackville Town League, and it usually either won, or came second in the annual finals. On the way to practice for our junior team one Saturday, on opening the door to gain access to the rink a hockey puck hit me full in the face .... broken jaw, severe lacerations and, two hours later, after the dentist's activities (no permission asked) and the ether worn off, it was realized there were no teeth left.

As it was going to take some time for my face and jaw to heal it was decided to visit my mother's home village at Upper Greenwich and help out at Uncle Ronald Brundage's (the source of my given names) mink farm, while surviving on soup. Charles was not too happy about my departure, because he would have to look after the farm animals in my absence.

Uncle Ronald was a bachelor Anglican priest who had the mink farm and a blueberry farm as hobbies. My job while at the farm was to feed the mink, using fish (shiners and perch) that we caught in the Saint John River, which was not yet frozen over. Safety procedures were a must, because mink have very sharp teeth and offensive action comes to them naturally. A shelter was also built where frozen meat could be kept over the winter months. Still pounding nails! When I went home, dentures were fitted and I never leave home without them or, more properly, their successors.

Now back at school, high school finals were looming. I studied hard for the few remaining months and passed the Provincial exams, but couldn't feel very proud of myself, because of just barely passing with a mark of 60.9% when the passing grade was 60. Hardly a demonstration of brilliance! It was a much different picture than in my younger years when I was invariably at the head of the class. Some will question the wisdom of foregoing learning in school for the questionable advantages of working hard outside of school. My conclusion is that school should have been a priority, but a working career was started with much more knowledge than most of my peers, and a much easier time was had picking up additional 'street smarts'.

Dad counselled that my farming efforts should probably be abandoned, and something should be learned about the mercantile world. He also knew that Fred Ayer was retiring at J. L. Black & Sons, Limited. So, with cap in hand, I went to see Lieutenant-Colonel (LCol) Laurie Black, an Army reserve officer and President of the company, and became the new employee. My hobby farming days were finished, and Charles took over.

Work was commenced at Black's with starting wages of $1 per day, 11-hour days (start at 0700 hrs, ½-hr lunch, quit at 1830 hrs), and a 6-day week, at 16 years of age in the fall of 1937 just before my youngest sister Elizabeth (Betty) was born, only to find that I would be going to work at Black's forestry operation for the winter. One of the teamsters was seriously ill and had to miss the season, and my experience with horses provided a background. So much for the mercantile business! It would have to wait, giving place to driving a team of black Percherons in the lumber camp, even though it was necessary to stand on a stool to harness them.

The camp comprised a logging operation and saw mill some 15 miles (24 km) north of our village. A Foreman oversaw a Woods Boss who was responsible for felling, cutting into logs, and yarding; a Camp Boss who was responsible for the Cook and those tree-fellers who rotated to sharpen saws and axes; and a Haul Boss who was responsible for moving the logs to the sawmill, and the sawed lumber to the railhead.

There were eight teams in the camp. Selective cutting was practised; no clear cutting allowed. Felling was done with crosscut saws and double-bitted axes. Each team, in rotation, took the fellers into the woods. On arrival at the felling area, the team was broken up, providing two horses for yarding logs.

The rest of the teams were either hauling logs to the mill, or moving lumber to the rail head at Upper Sackville, chores in which they were rotated weekly. Lumber was piled at the railhead and air-dried for a year, then loaded onto railway flat cars for delivery, and was in high demand, mainly along the US Eastern seaboard. All loading and unloading was done by hand. The food in camp, though basic staples, was the very best quality, thanks to a good cook. Life was enjoyable, but getting up at 0500 hrs was not what had been expected. Encountering the forestry culture was wonderful, the experience deeply appreciated.

When that winter was over, my place was finally taken among the employees at the store. My initial duties were mostly in cleaning-up and refilling bins. Gradually I was allowed to serve customers and price items. After about six months, responsibility was undertaken for reordering grocery items.

During this period Dad had a contract to build a large new unheated one-storey warehouse 70 ft (21 m) behind the store. This made space to increase the amount of goods in bags and cartons, not requiring protection from frost, that could be held in inventory.

Every time a railway box car of goods arrived at the Middle Sackville railway siding one-half mile (0.8 km) away, three of us were required to unload it, and bring the materials to the warehouse by truck. There were no hand trolleys. All contents had to be carried from the location in the boxcar to the truck. From the far end of the box car to the front end of the truck body was an awfully long way, especially late in the day.

While then only 5' 4" (162.5 cm) tall and weighing 119 lbs (54 kg) soaking wet, the coarse salt bags weighed 140 lbs (63.5 kg), and flour weighed 98 lbs (44.5 kg). On occasion, we also had to unload molasses puncheons which weighed about 350 lbs (158 kg). Those days were strictly eat, sleep, work, and wonder if we could make it through the day. There was no residual energy with which to get into any trouble after work.

Black's had both retail and wholesale grocery components in its business. In earlier days, wholesale orders had come in by mail and were dispatched by freight train, using the less-than-carload (LCL) rate. As vehicles became more widely used, a detail salesman went out for orders on the different routes in rotation on Monday, Wednesday and Friday. Local detail sales were done weekly on a part-time basis by one of the in-store employees. Deliveries were made by truck the day following the sales trip.

By the fall of 1938, I had graduated to driving the large truck on the wholesale routes but, on the days in between, still had to unload boxcars and make local deliveries. For the route deliveries there was no helper, although a friend would go along for the ride occasionally, and to assist. There was help by the store staff in filling and boxing the orders and loading, which had to be completed by 1000 hrs. Then it was off to delivery mode. Again, no loading or unloading devices.

Tuesday was Dorchester/Memramcook delivery day, with Sackville deliveries on the way if there was enough space available on the truck. Otherwise someone else would deliver there with a pickup truck. Prominent delivery points on this route were MTA in Sackville, the Convent and St. Joseph's Seminary in St. Joseph, and

Leblanc's General Store in Memramcook. On occasion I have facetiously taken credit for attending the School of Hard Knocks: the rear doors of MTA, the Seminary and the Convent.

Thursday deliveries were on the Port Elgin/Cape Tormentine route. Russell Ward in Port Elgin was a storekeeper to watch. After his goods were unloaded, he insisted the driver go into the office to get the delivery bills signed. He always had a few teen-agers hanging around, and was not averse to arranging for them to sneak things off the truck when a back was turned. It was essential that a scan be done before leaving the truck, so that you knew which items to reload. He thought it was a real nice game, and never said a word when you put items back on the truck. There was no way I was going to get caught, because you either had to pay for items lost or leave employment.

Saturday was the day for the Port Elgin/Shemogue/Cape Bald route, in part through a relatively poor farming and fishing area. After deliveries were finished on that run during the fall months, we picked up cattle that had been assigned to stores in payment for goods, by a store's individual customers. The cattle were loaded and brought back to home base. Great pains were taken by Blacks to ensure that store owners on the other routes did not find out about this arrangement. It was good for the people in the area, but hell for the driver!

There was always the possibility that the cattle would break the weak side racks on the truck and escape. Upon return, the cattle had to be unloaded and put into an enclosure next to the feedlot barns. They would enter the barns, be fed over winter, and sold in the spring. The truck had to be thoroughly washed down before the day's work was considered finished, on Monday it would be hauling foodstuffs again!

On one occasion, a puncheon of molasses was being unloaded at the Shemogue Post Office & General Store. Puncheons were very difficult to handle because they were hauled in a vertical position, but had to be tipped onto their sides, to be rolled off on two stout planks. It was relatively easy if you could rock them just right, and tilt them at the right moment, especially if you held your mouth right! That time it must have been held wrong, the puncheon crashed and broke. People, pans, cans, dippers and pails appeared from all directions. The locals got enough molasses to last a while, but must have had to strain out the gravel. It was noticed on later deliveries that there always seemed to be a lookout, ... in case it happened again?

In the winter, deliveries to the logging camp were made when required. Usually the trip was uneventful and a hearty dinner in camp was always welcome; however, on one trip school chum Charles Ayer was with me, mainly for the free dinner. When we were about a mile from camp a yearling moose came charging out of the bush, collided with the truck, and ended up dead on the hood against the windshield. We considered delivering the moose to camp, but the windshield was broken and vision obscured. It was not possible to see ahead with the moose there. After contemplation, it was decided that Charles would back up along the road to guide me. We had to be sure that we stayed on the compressed sled tracks, otherwise we would probably be stuck. We arrived in camp, and the cook looked very pleased. It didn't take long to butcher the moose, but it was not aged long. We quickly settled down to enjoy a moose dinner with my lumber camp associates of the previous winter.

Sometime during this rather hectic period, a promotion was received to the position of part-time wholesale detail salesman, using a 1936 Chevy 2-door car. This gave me a raise in pay of $2 per week but required that a $40 suit be bought on credit, and interest had to be paid to the company. At the time, Eaton's catalogue listed 3-piece suits at $9.98, but one had to be bought from the company or my promotion would surely have been jeopardized.

The detail sales days produced some strange situations, one was the weekly audience at the convent with Mother Superior, in a small room furnished only with an unpainted well-washed wooden table and two simple wooden chairs. She had a list of goods for me to copy into my sales book, then I had to sign her copy and give it back to her, and leave with her cold, 'Bless you', but never a smile, as goodbye. The atmosphere was much different down the road at the seminary. The purchasing agent there was an Irish priest with a heavy brogue, who was a happy-go-lucky purveyor of a good joke during each visit. Where did a priest get stories like that?

On my truck deliveries, I had become friendly with the proprietor's son at LeBlanc's, a store owned by an Acadian French proprietor. When I showed up as a salesman, the son's welcome was, 'Hi, Ron, where you go wit' da good pant on your h'ass?'

One fall night I came back from Shemogue with ten cattle for the winter barns. After unloading and hosing it down, the truck was put in the garage. As I turned from closing the door, I noticed a glow in the store window next to the rear door, a glow that should not have been there. After glancing around to see where a reflection might be coming from, it was realized that the store was afire. A few seconds later there was an explosion, probably caused by a barrel of gas in the basement. The back wall was blown out and molasses splashed on me from the retail puncheon which had been located by the door, and the store was truly ablaze. In a short time it was totally demolished. The only structures left standing were the new warehouse (its asphalt siding was scorched) and the adjacent barn which housed the truck.

Of course there was an investigation and, at Laurie Black's behest, I was questioned strenuously about why I was there at that time of night. It was explained that Black's policy of a person working on the truck without a helper, and having routes and activities that would not allow return before late at night, was at fault. Harassment on the subject only ceased when it was stated that, ' I knew where I was at the time and why, but I didn't know where Laurie had been, or why'. Although I remained friendly with other members of the firm, relations with Laurie never recovered.

Hasty arrangements were made to re-establish the store. The empty Standard store building, ½ mile (.8 km) away, and of identical size and design as the store that burned, was purchased. Dad was the contractor for the alterations required to adapt the new site. He engaged Charles Raworth, a building mover, to relocate the warehouse.

After the building was loaded on skids, and rollers were placed between the skids and a track made of planking, the move began. In those days the moving method was the use of a device called a capstan used to wind cable on an upright drum, powered by a horse travelling around the capstan. As the cable was wound the building drew closer, then the capstan was moved farther away and pegged, the cable extended, and the process continued. Luckily there was a clear route but it involved two right-angle turns which made tracking difficult. All the warehouse contents had been moved into the basement of the new store, and then moved back into the warehouse upon its arrival. The store itself was modernized, and restocking of inventory proceeded quickly.

The next few months involved alternating between working in the store, selling on the routes and occasionally driving the truck. Becoming very disenchanted with the low pay and long hours, consideration was given to returning to carpentry, where wages would be 75 cents an hour. It was also theorized that there would be 8-hour days and 5-day weeks. It couldn't be disputed that I was as fit as I would ever be throughout my early working life but, after attempting unsuccessfully to get a pay raise to $16 per week, and willing to settle for $14, I went back to work with Dad as a carpenter in Spring 1940 and then, with overtime, almost tripling my pay package. Pounding nails again!

With the large volume of work Dad had on hand, it would turn out that overtime was involved most weeks. I was fortunate to be able to return to work on a decision made by me alone, in isolation from any other factors. The tail end of the Great Depression was still having its effect. Most of the fellows who were joining up to go to war were doing so because jobs were not available. At the same time we couldn't get enough carpenters because potential employees were untrained. At the time Dad had two apprentices and could not handle more. The Depression had not affected our family very much, other than Dad having to go West to work during my early life, but there were others in our community who went through such hard times that they would never forget it.

During this period there must have been some spare time because my girl friend, Doris Oulton, and I eloped July 30, 1940 and started married life in a rented upstairs room in Sackville.

It was not difficult going back to work with Dad's crews, working on house construction and small industrial contracts. In late Summer 1941, Dad was awarded the contract to install the glass in the new CNR shops in Moncton, 30 miles (48 km) away. This established a connection with Hobbs Glass (now Pittsburgh Glass) Canadian office, based in Montreal, which would produce other work, such as storefronts, during the later wartime years, and even closer connections afterwards. He established a crew of 20 employees in Moncton to install the wire-armoured glass, and expected the job to last about 6-8 months. It was left to me to look after the operations in Sackville, and that role was continued until leaving for the Royal Canadian Air Force (RCAF) in January 1942.

4

RCAF TRAINING IN CANADA
1942

in which Ron joins the RCAF and trains as an air navigator

As days and weeks went by in late 1941, and with World War II in full swing, most of my contemporaries were in the Services, many of them overseas. It was felt that I should be doing more toward the war effort. Joining the armed forces would be explored, and Dad agreed to make arrangements for my position to be taken over by one of my fellow tradesmen. Considering among the Services was not difficult: wading in the mud with the Army was not enticing, neither was convoy duty on the stormy Atlantic, so it was the Air Force or nothing. And there were no pretensions about what I would do, thinking I would be lucky to be put in uniform as a carpenter.

At age 20, in early December 1941 the recruiting office in Moncton was visited, where the interviewer convinced me that my sights should be set higher, recruiting me as potential aircrew. They didn't want carpenters anyway, unless it was the result of failing an aircrew or other course! The entry examinations and the medical were passed, and I was sworn in as a member of the RCAF with the rank of Aircrafts-man Second Class (AC2), as low as you could get on the totem pole, and expected to be trained through the auspices of the British Commonwealth Air Training Plan (BCATP).

Then it was home and back to work, subsequently receiving a very official-looking envelope with a letter that said 'pleased to inform you that you have been accepted for aircrew training'. On January 20, 1942, it was off to No.1 RCAF Manning Depot, Toronto for recruit training. I was issued an ID card and a set of 'dog tags' that advertised me as 'R138942', my name and religion, and I gained access to wages at the princely rate of seventy-five cents per day.

At its wartime peak, the RCAF had a strength of 215,200 serving personnel, including 15,153 women. There were 78 operational squadrons: 43 on the home front and 35 overseas.

The BCATP was inaugurated early in WWII, a most ambitious undertaking for a country with Canada's small population. By the end of the war it had completed the training of almost 200,000 aircrew, about 50,000 of which were pilots. The remainder were observers, navigators, flight engineers, bomb aimers, wireless-operator air gunners, and air gunners. Most were Canadians included in the RCAF strengths shown previously, but the Royal Air Force, Royal Australian Air Force, Royal New Zealand Air Force, and the Royal Navy Fleet Air Arm were well represented. Large numbers of ground crew were also trained in a broad range of trades.

Nationals of occupied countries who had left their homelands to take part in the struggle on the side of the Allies were represented by Free French, Czechs, Norwegians, Belgians and Dutch. Also included were many United States citizens who chose to enter the war before their country did so, and came to Canada to enlist.

The manning depot occupied buildings at the Canadian National Exhibition grounds on the shores of Lake Ontario, and nearly 100,000 airmen would be processed through it during the war. We were billeted in what was known as the Bull Pen, an area where cattle were housed during prewar agricultural exhibitions, and the aroma of the space lived up to its previous use and its air force reputation. The beds were in long rows of double-decked bunks and the billets were energetically patrolled by acting, unpaid corporals. Even at that lowly rank new entrants looked upon them as God almighty, and they attempted to lord it over recruits in every way they could. They seemed to enjoy yelling at any of us who were within range of their voices but, when encountered later in their careers, they would pay for these indiscretions through shunning and slurs.

All 'other ranks' recruits, regardless of potential future employment, attended the depot for indoctrination and basic training, and got at least one, but more likely several, of the famous recruit haircuts, shorn-to-the-cranium hair cuts were *de rigueur*. We learned the basics of drill in accordance with the *Manual of RCAF Drill & Ceremonial*. We learned to fall-in, march to music and look ramrod-stiff on parade and in our marches through High Park, next to the depot. The subjects of a puritanical upbringing in a small village had to get with it, and learn a much broader approach to life, and we will never forget the distances we had to march, in both good and bad weather.

Lectures were given, ranging from aircraft recognition to venereal disease. We did our share of physical training and we learned what it was like to wait in endless queues. In fact, our life became one of waiting: for a place at the sink, for breakfast, for short arm inspection, for pay, and for almost anything else possible. *They also serve who stand and wait!* We were up daily at 0600 hrs, made the bed to inspection standards and began daily activity in Training Wing where we were scheduled to spend 21 days.

Having a uniform, even though the fit (one size: too big) was less than perfect, brought new trials and tribulations: shoes had to be polished and buttons shone. We soon learned how to shine our cap badge, belt buckle and use a button stick to do our buttons: apply Brasso and rub, rub, rub, almost forever but usually much less than an hour. We learned how to look after, use and clean a rifle. The end result was a reasonably fit group of young airmen. 36-hour passes were granted at one stage of our stay but most recruits could not go home in the time available because of distance, and finances kept us from doing much in the way of other diversions.

We were also given plenty of inoculations for many diseases. These must have ignored the possibility of scarlet fever because, in a short time, I reported to the Medical Inspection Room under the Grandstand. I was there three or four days in a ward before it was decided that, yes, it was scarlet fever.

It is not now medical practice to quarantine for scarlet fever, but in 1942 penicillin was not available, so off to Riverdale Isolation Hospital where patients were not allowed out of bed for 28 days. This played havoc with muscles and they soon atrophied, so much for fitness!

Once my hospitalization was over, my billet for rehabilitation was with a family located next to the posh district of Rosedale. And so began the long and tortuous process of rebuilding my leg muscles. Every morning, and again in the afternoon I walked, and walked, and walked. Needless to say, the early days were filled with pain .... to say the least. At first it was sheer torture to put one foot ahead of the other, but there was considerable incentive in knowing that the first day back at the depot would include resumption of route marches in High Park, and one had better be ready.

Upon finishing rehabilitation, with about six weeks lost, and returning to the depot, an intake was joined that had been in place for about the same length of time I had been, prior to reporting sick. The training period finished and having reported to Disposal Wing, my posting was to 1 Technical Training School (TTS), St. Thomas, Ontario for guard duty. The first lesson in keeping above water in the military had been learned: *Non Illegitimus Carborundum- Don't let the bastards grind you down!*

Preparations for travel were rather short but demanding, in the time available. First we had to visit every section on site, except the barber, to get a clearance signature. All of our possessions went into one kitbag and we struggled with it in a comical way, part carrying, part towing, part dragging it to a truck, and then on to the train. This was the first move in this manner, many more were ahead. And it got even worse when a kitbag of flying clothing was added to the load.

1 TTS was the predominant RCAF ground training school, and the largest organization in the BCATP. The school property covered 487 acres (195 ha). Its 25 buildings were of stone, and it had a maze of tunnels joining them together. Maybe there are still ghosts there, airmen who became lost in wartime? Before the war was over the school would train about 45,000 tradesmen. The buildings had been a former Provincial mental hospital and evidence of that use surrounded us, including barred windows. Our duties there were to man guard towers to keep spies from infiltrating, and running away with the buildings or the students, or so it seemed at the time. The pupils insisted we were there to prevent their escape.

The strength of the personnel who were there for security duty was twice the requirement, effectively creating 'make-work' employment to waste time, because our future schools were filled with intakes and there was currently no unfilled spaces to accept us.

We found our stay in St. Thomas long and very boring. We could go to Port Stanley, a lakeside resort area, or to London, the quiet mercantile centre for a large farming district. A couple of visits to these on days off gave us our only respite from the RCAF community. The only other excitement through the whole stay was the night one of my compatriots shot himself in the leg, climbing down from a watch tower with his supposedly empty rifle. In our minds this whole period was lost to the war effort .... would we ever get to aircrew training?

Subsequently, 50 or so other aircrew trainees and myself were posted to No. 6 Initial Training School (ITS) in downtown Toronto, where we were all promoted to Leading Aircraftsman (LAC) and were privileged to wear the white flashes of aircrew trainees in the fronts of our wedge caps.

The school was located in what had been the first Normal School for aspiring school teachers in Ontario. In the postwar period it would be used for retraining veterans of World War II, then become the Ryerson Institute of Technology, and later Ryerson University. Here we were given aptitude tests, including a night vision test, and studied in all ground school subjects involved in the operation and guidance of aircraft: navigation, airmanship, morse code, trigonometry, and spent time at, guess what: physical training and sports.

The results of our studies, along with more psychological testing, would be guiding factors in selection for further training as a pilot, navigator, or one of the other aircrew trades. Failure to meet the minimum requirements for aircrew would result in one being allotted to a ground crew trade.

A pupil would attempt training in the most demanding trade, or a trade with current shortages. Trainees were re-mustered progressively to down-stream trades as courses were failed, or until the trainee could find his niche. And, as a last resort, the war could even be fought peeling potatoes in a mess at one or another of the many RCAF stations then in existence. The usual training syllabus for aircrew is shown in Table 1; however, at times there were variations to the sequences shown.

A lot of dependence was placed on a Classification Test which supposedly found a person's level of 'basic intellectual status, mechanical aptitude, perception, numbers, following directions, verbal, reasoning, etc.'

Table 1- Table of Aircrew Training Progression

Pilot	Navigator	Bomb Aimer	WOP/AG	Air Gunner	Flight Engineer*
Manning Depot **					
Guard, or other duty					
Initial Training School					
Elementary Flying School	Air Observers School	Bombing & Gunnery School	Wireless School	Gunnery School	Flight Engineer Course
Service Flying Training School			Gunnery School		
Pilot Advanced Flying Unit	Observer Advanced Flying Unit				
Assembly, Crew Formation and Training at an Operational Training Unit					
Heavy Conversion Unit					
Posted to Operational Squadron					
* Usually volunteers from similar ground crew trades.					
** Shaded area, within Canada. Clear area, usually in operational theatre					

A lot of hard study was ahead because of my weakness in mathematics. Fortunately we had good teachers who would provide extra help when required. I still marvelled at even being there, let alone aimed at being a pilot; however, my nemesis was the Link Trainer, an early flight simulator that tested a potential pilot's reflexes and ability to adjust instantaneously, and with the right reaction, to the movements inherent in aircraft handling. The trainer was crashed three times within a very short time one morning. The die was cast .... I would not be trained as a pilot! But .... I have always wondered, did the instructor help me crash? After all, everyone wanted to be a pilot, ... there was a surplus of wannabe pilots and a shortage of personnel wishing to be navigator trainees at the time!

Once it was decided that a trainee would not be acceptable as a pilot, he appeared before an Aircrew Selection Board. As a result of this Board, they reassigned me to attempt training as a navigator. Marks on math and the other subjects had been much better than expected, but there was still a long hard road ahead to finish navigation training. My marks placed me in the top 7% of the ITS course, so possibly there was a 50/50 chance at the next level. After going through the station clearance process again, we were finished at ITS and the graduates selected for navigation training left for London, Ontario.

I was now entering the period of my career when wages would be augmented by flying pay of $30 per month This added to the pay package, but only provided for a very austere lifestyle, even by 1942 standards.

August 4, we arrived in London, then a city of 87,000 (now 336,500) on the Thames River in Southern Ontario, and our group reported to No. 4 Air Observer School (AOS) at RCAF Crumlin, at what is now London International Airport. We who would manage to graduate, would do so on November 20, 1942, after sixteen weeks training, without the bomb-aimer portion of training previously given to Observers. The previous work of an observer was being divided among two crew members: a Navigator and a Bomb Aimer, in the larger crews for the newer 4-engined aircraft in Bomber Command.

The Observer Schools were operated by civilian companies. Most of them had been civilian flying clubs and had expanded to cope with far more students. Most instructors, mechanics and ground support staff were civilian. There were some instructors who had either been involved in civil flying before the war, or had been trained by the RCAF and released to their civilian role with the schools. The only military personnel were the students and the administrative staff to look after us. There were several courses running concurrently, at different stages of their training.

Except for an early tomato stain on my new summer khaki uniform, which then always showed a dark patch, life at AOS was very good. Early in the course I volunteered to assist with woodwork instruction at the station craft shop and met a wide cross-section of personnel, many of whom were pounding nails there.

Our training consisted of ground school subjects, and air flights for practice. The early training was entirely in ground school with math, maps, meteorology and celestial navigation being paramount. Ground school went well and we prepared for the day we would leave the ground, if even for a short flip. The first flight, on August 7 as second navigator, was in Anson #6161 with Mr. Saarup as pilot.

The remaining days of the course would be divided between ground school and flying. Our first day flights were cross-country trips using map reading and radio, usually on a three-leg journey from town to town, we would marvel at the scenery and try to convince ourselves that, yes, there really was a phenomenon called aerodynamics, and that was why we stayed aloft.

Those Anson aircraft had a rather distinctive odour, almost bad enough to create a bout of air sickness. They were slow, but even the landing speed of 70 mph (113 kph) over the airfield boundary was much faster than we had ever moved before. Many navigators would suffer from the smell, but carried on even though they made sure they kept air sickness bags available, and would probably suffer this malady on every one of their later operational trips. Fortunately for me, sickness was never a real problem, but I was nauseous and close to it on a few early occasions.

First flight – 1942

The basic method of navigation was dead reckoning, in which course and speed formed two sides of a triangle, with the wind providing the third. It was easy enough to plot these, but finding the actual wind was often an enigma. And this basically was the navigator's prime duty: to discover the direction and force of the wind.

Our principal tools were the Dalton computer, a good mechanical device conceived well before the days of digital capability, and the Douglas protractor. The navigator's tool bag with its pencils, rulers, maps and other tools of the trade was cumbersome. Add a sextant and parachute and any navigator felt that all he was doing was lugging heavy parcels around.

In the meantime our course experienced one of those bitter realities of air training, attending a crash site, and then a funeral for two trainee navigators from an earlier course. Their pilot's body had been returned to his family in Manitoba for burial.

Our early day trips usually lasted about three hours, with two embryo navigators forming a team, to alternate at first and second navigator duties during the course. The first navigator was responsible for keeping the dead-reckoning track up to date, and informing the pilot of the courses and speeds to fly to get to each turning point on a triangular trip, and back to base. He also undertook to give the pilot any other information he needed, related to weather and other factors. The second navigator sat in the right hand seat beside the pilot. His duties were to wind the undercarriage up and down, using his left hand to make 140 turns with a crank beside the pilot. This was very tiring indeed. He also was tasked, in his spare time, to do the map reading.

The pilot, incidentally, was supposed to be aware of his location, and salvage the situation if the navigators became hopelessly lost. This was fine as long as an experienced pilot was involved, but occasionally a young pilot showed up who could get lost just as easily as the navigators. The navigation instructors reacted quickly to such a situation, and made sure they sent the navigators who showed most promise with the pilots who didn't. And some pilots never did graduate to night flying. Of course, there were also some navigators who didn't graduate, and went on down the line to other jobs.

Generally the pilots, and particularly those who had been recent RCAF graduates, were more interested in flying for flying's sake than in attempting to make the flight beneficial for the trainees. This showed in laxity in flying the compass courses given, wandering off course to see something that looked interesting, or just plain 'stooging around'.

We started night flying September 28, again on cross-countries, but now using a combination of radio and astro-navigation. Each time we flew at night we had the privilege of taking the next morning off. I was lucky. I drew the duty of first navigator for my first night flight, and found this a very challenging experience. The world looked a lot different from up there, groups of lights all over the place, just begging to be identified.

Whenever we did astro shots in the air we had to open the upper hatch. We noticed that the pilot always looked around to see if the navigator had connected his safety cable. The last thing he wanted to do was to lose a navigator in a sudden downdraft .... perhaps one had!

We were required to concentrate on star shots both on the ground and in the air. It looked rather comical to see a group of rookie navigators on the ground with their sextants, trying to get a fix on where they were actually standing. Some found that they were in another province, but diligence paid off and we got closer to where we were standing with each passing evening.

The total time on this course was 102:45 hrs: daytime, 64:50 hrs and night, 37:55 hrs. Relatively good weather had been experienced and there were few equipment failures.

About halfway through the training, Doris arrived and we could live in London for the remainder of the course. We obtained a room on Central Avenue, a tree-lined street on the park near City Hall, where she went to work on a temporary basis, and we were able to spend time together most days.

Why did I worry about failing? On graduation day, it was a relief to find that there had been better success on my part than some of my fellow trainees who had far more schooling. I had worked hard, but had been unnecessarily concerned on first exposure to the mathematics one had to absorb. In addition, the presence of a college professor, two school teachers and a mining engineer in the classroom as pupils was intimidating to someone who was deficient in math.

Graduation found me among the top ten and we were briefed to attend the Wings Parade 'in best blues', but the powers-that-be should have realized we only had one blue uniform, whether 'best' or not. Each graduating member of our class was presented the Air Observer wing (an 'O' with a single wing attached on the right-hand side, usually called the 'flying arsehole'). I was promoted to Sergeant (Sgt) effective November 20,1942. The next day I was commissioned as a Pilot Officer (P/O), retroactive to the previous day, so I could hardly say I had been a Sgt. There was also a new serial number: J20961.

After saying goodbye to new friends in London, Doris and I boarded the train for home, and I had a 30-day embarkation leave. This time would mostly be spent resting and studying booklet *AFP4- Notes for the Guidance of Officers*, which those of us who graduated as officers were given on departure. It was also necessary to go to a tailor to be fitted for a uniform, for which officers were reimbursed at a standard rate. At the first opportunity there was a trip to Moncton to order it, and it was worn after a two-week wait.

It would take some time to become accustomed to this new status, and the prospect of having to return a salute was abhorring. It was even worse that the first instance was when I met Charles Ayer, also home on leave. I had seen him in Toronto, where he was on a course in Hart Hall at the University of Toronto, to become a signals (radar) technician. And it showed how unfair the system was, he had completed a one-year course which was much more technical, complicated, and secret than mine, and was graduated as a LAC, whereas a commission was given me, only because of my course marks and the traditional status accorded aircrew.

Getting used to the uniform was gradual, because of feeling most conspicuous walking around in it, especially as it looked so new! Every new P/O tried his best to make his uniform look somewhat used. I also felt really humble, like, 'Whatever is this carpenter doing here!'

While on leave, the old vets who were met all gave the impression that they were thinking, "You poor bastard, you don't know what you're in for." They had been through it all in WWI. Too naive to understand at the time, I would recognize and appreciate their attitude later on when the going got tough.

Reporting December 21,1942, when leave was over, to RCAF Y Depot at Halifax, NS, the holding unit for overseas postings, ... I was prepared for a new cultural experience, and the next phase of aircrew training. It appeared at that time that the only possible obstacle might be in getting there. German U-boats were plentiful in the Atlantic.

5

ARRIVAL IN ENGLAND
1943

in which overseas duty is started

There certainly was not much delay once we arrived at Halifax. After kitting for overseas, including a mandatory gas mask and helmet, we boarded the SS Bayano II. We didn't know it at the time, but that lucky ship made more Atlantic crossings in convoy than any other merchant ship. On this occasion it sailed December 23, 1942 from Pier 21 in a large, slow 10-knot convoy, just in time for an onboard Christmas dinner. We had no idea where we were going, no one was telling; however, anyone's guess was probably the right one, because almost everything at the time was headed for Britain.

The Bayano was a converted fruit ship, so Christmas on a cruise ship it was not!! As we departed, we certainly had mixed feelings standing on deck and looking back at Halifax, as it disappeared over the horizon in the early dusk of a winter evening. Here we were, going overseas with no idea what fate would serve up to us. Would we come back to this part of the world safely, or would we ever see it again? Unfortunately, many who viewed that sight didn't!

German U-boats operated in wolf packs to sink ships attempting to deliver goods and personnel to Britain. They were plentiful in the North Atlantic, having reached their peak in 1942-43. The Navy provided escort vessels and directed the ships on the protocol for operation of convoys and, despite heavy losses the convoy system worked, and enough essential supplies eventually got through to complete the build-up for the invasion of Normandy in 1944.

The cargo on our ship for this voyage was high explosives, along with we 45 RCAF officers and one Knights of Columbus (KofC) welfare officer. He was on his way overseas to provide recreation and games support for a Canadian Army regiment. His immediate intention was to assist us to pass the voyage in an active way with games, books and other items. We had only just cleared port when the first signs of seasickness began to appear. Luckily, throwing up was forestalled in my case but, for a few days, it felt uncomfortably close. The KofC officer was the worst hit. We didn't see him again until he was taken off on a stretcher when the ship arrived at Milford Haven, Wales seventeen days later.

We were quartered in private cabins, a luxury we did not expect. My cabin was about 80 sq ft (7.4 sq m), and was situated immediately above sea level. Meals were served in a dining room and, in spite of wartime conditions, were very good; however, we were soon aware that the ship had not been built for the North Atlantic. We hit one of that ocean's famous winter storms, said to be the worst of the season! It was most comical to see the way the waiters were able to manoeuvre about on the moving deck with trays loaded to the extreme. Although tables and chairs were connected by chains to their allotted spots on the deck, there was one occasion in heavy seas when the chains broke at our table and most everyone landed in the corner, along with the soup of the day, the tablecloth, all the cutlery and, of course, the table and most chairs. Only Mike Derry was left sitting in his chair with his napkin in place and his spoon at the ready. The direction of movement had been away from him.

One night my cabin porthole went missing, flooding the floor and most of my kit. I had to bunk down in a storage room (thankfully, without a port-hole) and it took most of the rest of the journey to get my kit dried out, living in clothes borrowed from the captain and crew in the meantime. We were told that the ship was capable of righting itself from a 46-degree roll, and that we had been close to that on several occasions.

Aboard SS Bayano II with, left, Ray Daly of Ottawa, and centre, John Duke of New York City, decked out with tin hat and gas mask

The swells were so high that very few ships in the convoy could be seen at any one time, and often none. It was a continually moving vista in which it was difficult to keep the convoy together. In some ways that was good because it took a U-boat commander seven minutes to get in a position to aim his torpedoes. The convoy was continually running an evasive course, changing direction frequently to make it more difficult to line us up as a target.

Evasion took us all over the ocean: East, North, then South-east, then North-east, forever changing in direction. Eventually, we reached Milford Haven January 9, 1943. At last we were sure of our destination.

Next was the culture shock. Here we were boarding trains which were much smaller than those in Canada. They looked almost like toys to us. And they had separate seating compartments, accessed by doors along either side.

Initially, it was difficult to walk on dry land. We must have looked like a group of drunken sailors as we staggered along the railway platform to the train which would take us to Bournemouth, England, the location of the RCAF Reception Depot. That would be our home location for about four months, but it seemed to us more like years. We had expected to go to advanced training units almost immediately on arrival, but aircrew were arriving faster than required by losses in the squadrons, so a monumental backlog had developed.

The first thing that struck us in England was the completeness of the blackout. It was energetically policed, and any trace of light brought a hasty reprimand. Poles were erected in any large field, which included golf courses, to deter any would-be enemy glider and parachute landings. We recognized that we were now in a war zone. Almost the entire population was employed in an essential capacity on farms, in factories, and in the Forces.

There were shortages evident in almost every commodity. There were wailing sirens many nights, and most civilians and Service people were required to go to air raid shelters when an alert was sounded; however, I managed to keep out of them most of the time, even with alerts sounding. All windows were taped, and doors sandbagged. There were queues for almost everything, but we had been well-trained for that at Manning Depot. There were many posters displayed on a myriad of subjects: save food, lessen travel, keep secrets, talk about not talking, security. We also had to carry the gas mask everywhere we went, but the country didn't appear to be as battered as we had expected.

Bournemouth is an English south coast seaside city with a mild climate. In peacetime it was one of Britain's leading holiday resorts, but most of the hotels had now been taken over for other purposes. Mike Derry and I ended up in a room at the Carlton Hotel on the cliff edge, where we were housed two to a room on iron cots with unbelievably hard mattresses that had many lumpy areas.

Derry at the Carlton Hotel entrance

We got a rather quick introduction to English customs which were much different than those in Canada. Rather than batmen, we had bat-women, but they were still called batmen, members of the Women's Auxiliary Air Force (WAAF).

37

The WAAF was a subordinate organization of the Royal Air Force (RAF), composed of women members. It was intended to free men for combat, and women appeared mostly in administrative, catering, hospital and housekeeping roles, but there were many in jobs such as flight mechanics (engines), parachute packers, flying control assistants and plotters.

The batmen made our beds, cleaned the rooms and 'knocked us up' each morning by knocking on the door to tell us it was time to get up, and leaving a cup of strong, hot tea to rouse us. We went to the Officer's Mess, about half-a-mile away (0.8 km), for our meals. Breakfast normally was farina, toast with margarine, ersatz eggs and lots of tea. Lunch was usually sandwiches and tea. At 1500 hrs we had 'afternoon tea', complete with a string quartet and linen table settings. Where was the war? Later on we had supper, and more tea. Meals were generally good; however, we got lots of kale and Brussels sprouts, and they were almost cooked to destruction, even though there were RCAF senior cooks in charge of the kitchens.

The Mess was a popular spot in the evenings, the focal point of activity; however, the distance from our billets prompted us to stay away on many occasions. It was located in the Bath Hotel at the town centre, and fondly called 'The Bath Tap'. We were able to read there, and listen on the radio to all the current songs by Vera Lynn, the Andrews Sisters and others. Our lounge (bar room) was located in the very large reception area on the ground floor, in the centre of the building. Liquor was sometimes in short supply but there was always lots of English beer available. 'Mild' was a light golden brown in colour whereas 'Bitter' was dark brown. 'Mild and bitter', a mixture of the two, was most popular. Again English customs surprised us, for instance, we were unfamiliar with beer served at room temperature, without refrigeration.

We quickly became bored with our situation as a reservoir of aircrew waiting to go somewhere .... anywhere, ... literally stockpiled against an expected future need. It was a problem to keep everyone occupied in these conditions. There were refresher training courses, parades, organized walks, a library, and lots of long walks by individuals.

The walk along the promenade on the cliff was enjoyable, rain or shine. The only thing we had to watch for was sneak raids by Focke Wolfe 190 fighters. They would sneak over every so often and fire off a few rounds to make sure we didn't get complacent. Shortly after such a raid Lord Haw Haw, on German propaganda radio, would tell us that the clock on the Metropole Hotel was two minutes slow.

He would also tell us that our being killed was being delayed, because squadron personnel were going as far as the middle of the North Sea, flying to and fro and then coming back, they weren't going into Germany where they most certainly would not survive. The Luftwaffe would soon shoot them down, in which case *we* could go and be killed. We took it for what it was, using exaggerations in an attempt to break our morale. It was also found that a person could get killed in Bournemouth, as a casualty of the German fighter raids.

The powers that be tried, but failed to keep us busy. There were lots of volunteer jobs offered …….. you, you and you!!! For exercise and to reduce boredom, several of us took up golf, although it was far from casual because we had to wear our uniforms, not having much in the way of civilian clothing with us. We all had bicycles to get to the golf course and found our time there relaxing, even though the course had the omnipresent poles scattered about. We also had to religiously recite the route to the course, because anti-invasion needs had dictated that the street signs be taken down.

Our bicycles also took us to visit places like Wimburne Minster, Ferndown, Hurn, Poole and Christchurch, and it was not long before a camera was purchased, a very large, old Kodak 616. We also frequented the dance hall in Christchurch on occasion.

When leave was granted the mandatory initial trip to London was undertaken. It might seem an illogical choice with the bombing going on, but this was 1943 and the Germans had mounted their concentrated attacks in 1940. By now the raids were still a danger but less often than before, however, they did continue intermittently throughout the war. We still had to contend with the V-1 and V-2 offensives when they developed.

Shows were seen, pubs were visited, museums looked at, the Hammersmith Palais was visited for dancing, we gawked at Buckingham Palace, explored the London Underground and took in all the other things tourists of the time were expected to do. During this visit, local people were met at a pub near Euston Station. They would remain friends until most of them were killed by a V-2 missile in 1945, along with most of their community.

After being at Bournemouth for about 3 months, I was sent to No.6 Elementary Flying Training School (EFTS), at RAF Sywell, near Northampton March 19-April 6 for what was called a 3-week, 13-hour flying and 'map reading course'. Billetted with a family in Northampton, I commuted to work by city bus. This was an opportunity for both a pilot and a navigator to get refresher training, and to keep from going cabin crazy.

The aircraft we used were deHavilland DH 82 Tiger Moths, small biplanes with front and rear open cockpits, and we could pick our routes to fly. One selection was a trip to Old Sarum airfield on Salisbury Plain near Salisbury Cathedral. Another was

DH 82 Tiger Moth

to Boscombe Down, in the same general area .... we would fly to an airfield, land and have lunch at the Officer's Mess, then return in time for tea at our home Mess. Almost as good as Snoopy in WWI, it was a most welcome diversion during a very boring period. The only problem was that the staid old RAF officers at some of the sites did not often see trainees from the colonies, and showed that they did not appreciate their otherwise quiet messes being invaded.

The next leave was spent on a visit with Aunt Marion (Dad's sister who had lived with us) at 73 West Hill, in the village of Titchfield, near Southampton. She and my elderly great-aunt, Elizabeth Foot, were soldiering on in this large house, going to the Anderson air raid shelter in the garden as necessary, waiting for the war to end. This was a duty visit without excitement of any kind and it became rather boring, but it was much better than being in Bournemouth, and long hikes in the countryside were enjoyable.

The next posting was as an Air Liaison Officer April 20-June 3 with the 2nd Battalion South Lancashire Regiment at Dover Castle. Our days were spent sloshing around in the hedgerows on infantry training, and evenings trying to get a fire going to warm up the billet at the Officer's Mess in the castle, a magnificent stone ring and bailey fortress high above the English Channel at the closest point to Europe.

Built, modified, rebuilt and expanded over two thousand years, it certainly was uninsulated. There was a fireplace and a bucket of coal in the bedroom, but no kindling. In desperation, it was necessary to have several 'gin and tonic' drinks at the bar, and go to bed with every bit of fabric on hand as covers. This turned out to be very interesting employment but was not such a welcome diversion as the Sywell experience. What it had to do with air liaison remains unknown, not one aircraft was seen throughout the sojourn there.

On return to Bournemouth, it was clearly demonstrated how difficult communication was in those days, and how the delays involved crept into everyday life. There was a telegram among the accumulated mail that my son Roderick (Rod) had been born April 22, 1943, and that both mother and baby were doing well. There was also a posting waiting, to No. 4 (Observer) Advanced Flying Unit (AFU) at West Freugh near Stranraer, Scotland. Back to the promise of action at last!

6

OPERATIONAL TRAINING
1943

in which training in England for bomber operations is described

On May 15, 1943 a group of 19 navigators boarded the train in Bournemouth with the feeling that, at last, they were on their way. After the relative doldrums of life at the Reception Centre for most of the time we were on strength, it was a relief to anticipate busy days again.

Unfortunately, it was a sad fact of Bomber Command life that one in seven trainees became casualties at its training units. A person had to be trained, so one had to ignore it, with the hope that only others were prone to disaster. About 70% of the trainees who boarded the train that day would lose their lives while in training, or later in combat.

In due course we arrived in Stranraer, a port town on the Mull of Galloway opposite Ireland. Its redeeming grace was a large McEwen's Brewery where McEwen's Old Strong dark ale was brewed. There was an Open House and sampling session for air force trainees each Saturday morning, and everyone who was not on duty showed up with alacrity. Each participant who was not already a Scottish native, was made an Honorary Scotsman.

Bordering on a swamp near Stoneykirk village, West Freugh was a grass field where we were housed in Nissen huts, arched metal buildings with potbellied stoves designed to burn coke .... but we spent a lot of time scrounging enough coal to maintain a semblance of warmth. Even with the stove pipe crimson with heat, little of it could be felt.

The navigation refresher course we were attending was intended to review what we had studied in Canada, and to allow navigators to gain familiarity with the geography, weather and atmospheric conditions of the British Isles. Flying there in twin-engined Anson aircraft would be fraught with mist and rain, and lots of cloud.

The experience would prepare us for an upcoming course at an operational training unit. We had heard recent stories of heavy losses, and we also realized that the output from West Freugh was destined for Bomber Command squadrons. At the time any navigator, given a choice, would rather be in an environment other than

Bomber Command, but that destiny had been established when our names came up for the posting to the course.

When the weather was fit and we had time off, we cycled down the Mull of Galloway to Port Logan for tea. The area was hauntingly serene with rural scenery, fishing boats, the smell of the sea, gravel roads and sun drenched shores (when the sun shone). In really bad weather, training would be cancelled and there was not much to do other than go to the mess, or listen to the rain on the Nissen hut roof.

Soon after takeoff one night on a cross-country exercise, our radio became unserviceable. We proceeded on our briefed exercise but, obviously, at the end of the exercise we would have to descend, and land. We were above solid cloud and there had been no success in repairing the radio. Our only clue as to where we were was our dead-reckoning position near the Irish Sea, which was only as good as the computations of two embryo navigators.

A course of action was determined and the pilot was directed to 'let down on a heading of 315 degrees, and don't run into Ailsa Craig'. It was hoped that we were descending in this north-westerly direction over open water. If the assumption was correct, the only obstacle would be Ailsa Craig a 220 acre (89-hectare) mound shaped like a giant tea cosy which rises to a height of 1,114 ft (340 m). This great bunch of rock weighed heavily on our minds as we let down through cloud, which broke at about 800 ft (244 m) and the first thing we saw was the pundit, a coded red signal light normally located at airfields, which flashed its three-letter identity in Morse code from Turnberry Airfield, 11 miles (18 km) from Ailsa Craig .... saved!

We stayed at West Freugh for five weeks and flew 39:00 hrs, involving 30:50 day, and 8:50 night flying. We were all granted end-of-course leave which was spent in London. On return from leave, we departed for Operational Training Unit (OTU) June 22, 1943.

From the time I left West Freugh, the site was not heard of again until 2004, when it was learned from an RAF Association newsletter that the site had survived until at least 1978. Its use at that time had been as a base for two DC3s used by the Royal Aircraft Establishment, in research involving sonobuoys and forward-looking radar for the British TSR2, an aircraft that did not get beyond the prototype stage because of political obstruction.

Our arrival at No.23 OTU, Pershore, near Evesham, England was to attend a 9-week course. It opened with an Assembly and the selection of 5-member crews, in a procedure called 'crewing up', the gathering together of a crew which would be trained to fly together on twin-engined bombers. The making-up of the crew was a significant moment in our lives. In our case Clive Boulton and I met up and decided to find a pilot. Norman (Suds) Sutherland was standing alone, apparently reluctant to take the plunge, but he succumbed to Clive's overtures because he did not relish being a wallflower. Then we went to collect the remaining members. Each person's joining the crew was sealed with hand shakes all round, before we reported to the registration desk for Suds to have 'his' crew officially entered into personnel records.

The first loyalty was to the crew you flew with, everything else was secondary. Happily our crew turned out to be skilful and congenial; however, there were other crews who lived to regret picking wrong matches. They could not be blamed because the only knowledge they had was the visual picture they formed when they met. With the formation of the crew, we largely ceased to exist as individuals, and the crew was now the entity.

Included were: Pilot Sgt N. 'Norm' or 'Suds' Sutherland, 21, La Fleche, Saskatchewan, a very nice fellow, shy and retiring but very effective; Navigator Pilot Officer (P/O) R. W. 'Ron' Butcher, 22, Middle Sackville, NB, somewhat shy and retiring; Bomb Aimer/Air Gunner Sgt C. A. 'Clive' or 'Prof' Boulton, BA, 20, Russell, Manitoba, a recent university graduate who was very outgoing and cheerful; Wireless Operator/Air Gunner Sgt R.K. 'Roy' Hobbs, 19, Luton, Bedfordshire, England, exceedingly efficient but sometimes a bit nervous and panicky; and Rear Gunner, Sgt A. E. 'Al' or 'Gramps' Demille, 42, Boissevin, Manitoba, a sage and serious, but gregarious grandfather.

Once crewed up, we departed for training at a nearby satellite airfield, Atherstone-on-Stour near Stratford-on-Avon, where the accommodation was in Nissen huts which were again, extremely cold, damp and drafty. The officer's mess, also a Nissen hut complex, was on a hilltop and the roadway up to it was bordered by a bramble hedge. That hedge was almost as dangerous as air training, traversing it downhill by bicycle sent many to the hospital with bramble cuts and scratches and, on occasion broken bones.

Atherstone could also claim one of the lowest standards of meals, the worst food ever, overcooked and bland: memories of tough mutton and Brussels sprouts (mush), boiled potatoes (mush), must have been just as bad as reported by crews who remained at Pershore. And we never got used to breakfasts of ersatz eggs and greasy, oversized sausages.

Our training aircraft was the Wellington III, a bomber of geodetic construction which had been Britain's most successful twin-engined bomber before the advent of four-engined aircraft. Naturally most of these aircraft had been redirected from squadrons because they were older, or had been damaged. But they still were quite good, even though they suffered from visits by gremlins, exasperating pixies who raised hell with aircraft from time to time: why won't the petrol gauge read, where is the ruler, the oxygen can't be turned off. The strangest things would happen with no known cause.

Vickers Wellington III (RAF photo)

We did our fair share of ground training. It included going to a pool in Stratford-on-Avon for dinghy drill which was considered essential if you were to fly over the North Sea. A new concern now arose, how was a non-swimmer to meet the requirement? An easy solution appeared, a jump into the water and one of the crew would always save me. We carried it off successfully, with none of us concerned that we had used this ruse. We all felt that, if there ever was a ditching in the North Sea in winter, a person would not last long. Being able to swim was not, in our opinion, a major factor in such an instance, because we would each be wearing a Mae West flotation device.

Our air training consisted of standard cross-countries, and 'Bullseye' exercises where we did night manoeuvres in conjunction with searchlights at selected English cities, as well as gunnery and fighter affiliation. Some flights were sent over occupied France on leaflet drops or other activity, but our crew was not tasked to this duty while on the course, where we flew 41:20 hours day and 51:40 hours night for a total of 92 hours.

Naturally we visited the pubs in Stratford-on-Avon by bicycle in the evenings when possible. We managed to find trouble driving along in a gaggle without front and aft hooded lights, and the police responded to this action as a result. One night a bobby chased us on his bicycle but, somehow, got forced off the towpath and into the canal. His loudly-voiced words on impact were, 'Oh, you blooody Can-eye-dians!' The next morning he was unable to identify his assailants on parade. We didn't know who did it either! Was it self-inflicted? But we managed to lie low for several days, just in case.

When we left OTU, contact was lost with those navigators who had been with me at West Freugh because our crew was selected to go direct to a squadron, rather than to a heavy aircraft conversion course, as was usual. We seemed to be always parting company with recent acquaintances!

Our crew was granted leave August 30. For me it included a 6-day visit with my uncle Ronald, now a Captain and the Protestant staff padre at an Army Group headquarters in Godalming, Surrey. A very quiet leave ensued and a lot of army officers were met, while getting an appreciation of that part of England.

It might now be useful to recap some of the development of the bombing campaign and Canadian participation in it. From the early period of World War II, a German bombing offensive lasting for more than two years was directed at Britain. This, and other military activity in Europe, Africa and Russia gave Germany and its Axis the ascendancy until late 1942. Britain had been threatened with invasion, and had little with which to fight back. U-boats were wreaking havoc against the supply lines on the high seas, and the people of Europe were suffering from German occupation. Japan had entered the war.

Air bombing early on was hit-and-miss at best. Because of heavy losses in daylight, Bomber Command had been forced into night bombing. There were few precedents to go by, and the strategies and tactics had to be learned by trial and error. Air Marshal (A/M) Sir Arthur Harris took over in February 1942 and was promoted to Air Chief Marshal (ACM). Twin-engined bombers were already being replaced by 4-engined aircraft, the renowned Lancaster was beginning to make its presence felt, and more effective navigation aids were appearing on the scene. However, the dismal fact remained that, in 1943, even in its developing state of readiness and effectiveness, the Command was the only force among Allied commands in the European area with the means of carrying offensive operations to the enemy in any meaningful way.

The British bomber force had been built up to several hundred heavy night bombers and Harris's leadership was such that morale was high. New strategies and tactics were improving the situation for crews, and getting more bombs on target. The force used more than 50 airfields in England, in the general area from Cambridge to Darlington, County Durham. The Command was then joined by Flying Fortress day bombers from the 8th Air Force of the United States Army Air Force (USAAF). Together, the effort was slowly becoming a major offensive. For this and many other reasons, the balance of power then slowly changed.

The Bombing Offensive was aimed at destroying German industry and reducing the ability to fight on several fronts. An increased level of bombing would lower German morale, force the enemy to build fighters rather than bombers, and spread out a 'proportionate defensive organization' of about one million personnel against the bombers. This would greatly reduce German offensive capability and lead Hitler's armaments minister, Albert Speer to declare the effort to be 'the greatest battle that we lost'.

Having been trained to twin-engine bomber standards, we were now about to join the sharp end of Bomber Command. Avro Lancasters, Short Stirlings and Handley-Page Halifaxes were the principal delivery vehicles employed at that time, although the Vickers Wellingtons remained in use. Thousands of tons of bombs cascaded on German targets.

Canadian politicians and senior RCAF officers had worked tirelessly to have a Canadian bomber group established. Finally on January 1, 1943, 6 (RCAF) Group (Gp) came to fruition in RAF Bomber Command, a satisfying symbol of Canada's independence. Initially the RAF view had been that the Group was a colonial exercise that would fail. It was initially commanded by Air Vice Marshal (A/V/M) George E. Brookes, OBE, CD, a most personable fellow who would become a mentor in later years. Unfortunately he was considered a mediocre commander, looked upon as a fatherly figure rather than a dynamic leader; however, he was very successful in getting the Group up and running in the short time available. Operationally, the Group was reputed to be slow in developing, in other words it appears he had done all the spade work to set up ready for sustained action, but the recognition of success remained for one who followed him.

It would be up to A/V/M C. M. 'Black Mike' McEwen, CB, MC, DFC, who took over February 29, 1944 to bring the Group to a high state of operational effectiveness. A fighter ace in World War I with 22 kills, he would develop the Group to the point that, in the end, Bomber Harris would say it was 'among the very best'. The Group grew eventually to 14 squadrons, and became the largest single component of the RCAF, by then the fourth largest air force in the world.

In normal circumstances a crew would go from OTU to a Heavy Conversion Unit (HCU). Our posting was direct to 408 (Goose) Squadron (Sqn) at, RCAF Linton-on-Ouse, Yorkshire, part of No.62 Base, 6 Gp. We arrived September 14 to find that we had just missed A/C/M Harris, who had been there earlier that day on one of his exceedingly rare station visits.

6 Gp stations were located in what is now commonly known as James Herriott country, a very pleasant area indeed. Linton-on-Ouse was immediately west of the city of York at the south end in the Vale of York, most of the others were farther up the Vale, and the remainder in County Durham immediately to the north. It was the most northern area of Bomber Command, which meant that every sortie flown by a 6 Group crew was at least an hour longer than those of 3 Group, at the southern end near Cambridge.

Many Canadian aircrew were on the strength at RAF squadrons, in fact one-fifth of the squadron aircrew in Bomber Command were Canadians, and the probabilities of us going to an RAF squadron had been great. We felt particularly fortunate that we ended up at a Canadian squadron.

408 and 426 squadrons at Linton and 432 at Skipton-on-Swale, were just receiving, and converting to the comparatively rare Lancaster Mark II. The period when 408 had Lancaster IIs, Fall 1943 to Fall 1944, would closely parallel the period of our

crew's time at the squadron. Our first flight in a Lanc II was September 22, and we fell in love with the type on the first flight.

It had been thought that building the Mark II was necessary as a safeguard against a possible shortage of Merlin engines, but only 301 (4%) were built out of a total 7,375 Lancs manufactured. It is little wonder that few people, even among ex-Bomber Command personnel, knew that they existed.

Arriving when we did made us just one more crew being converted at Linton-on-Ouse, but from twin-engined Wellingtons rather than the four-engined Halifax IIs the squadron had previously used. The training we would undertake here would help us gain a working knowledge of the aircraft; further individual trade training for each individual in the crew; bombing, gunnery, Bullseye exercises and fighter affiliation with Hurricane fighters.

There were almost 40,000 workers building the Lancaster [1], a heavy bomber of all-metal stressed-skin construction, with a crew of seven (408 Sqn later had eight). Avro Type 683 was the maker's designation. A. V. Roe & Co. Ltd (Avro), of Manchester, England was the originator. It was manufactured by The Lancaster Group, comprising Roe and several subcontractors. Most Lancasters were equipped with inline liquid-cooled engines; however, the Mark IIs, from subcontractor Armstrong Whitworth, had 14-cylinder 1,650-hp Bristol Hercules XVI radial (air-cooled) engines, for a total of 66,000 hp. They also had an enlarged and lengthened bomb bay to carry 8,000 lb. blockbuster bombs; however, this did not leave room for the installation of H2S, a major navigation aid. Most surviving Lancasters would be scrapped at the end of the war but one of the Mark IIs managed to make it into the jet age. It survived for a time, in use at Farnborough as a flying test bed for early jet engines.

The performance of the Mark II Lancaster differed from the Marks I and III, generally being advertised as marginally inferior because of the additional drag of the radial engines, but our crew considered this a myth. Each of the aircraft in which we flew performed on a par with the advertised performance of the other marks, and in some areas was marginally better.

Moving about the interior of a Lancaster presented difficulty. By the time you were bundled up in a flying suit, wearing flying boots and helmet, carrying a nav bag, sextant and parachute, there was a lot of you no matter how small you were. How did the heavier fellows manage it?

A WWII bomber base resembled a small town, but with camouflaged buildings. It had many of its own amenities. The messes had bars similar to pubs but many, both

---

1   Specifications for the Lancaster are shown on page 48 in English measurements, and on page 49 in Metric measurements

air and ground crews, preferred the companionship and culture of the local pub. At Linton many officers were housed in their Mess building, others in what had been Permanent Married Quarters (PMQ) before the war; however, the aircrew NCOs were billetted at Beningbrough Hall, to the south of Newton-on-Ouse some 3 miles (5 km) from the station.

Table 2- Lancaster Specifications in English Measurements

> *The Lancaster wing span was 102 ft, length 69 ft-6 in, height 20 ft. The wing area was 1,297 sq ft. The aircraft weighed 36,900 lbs empty and 68,000 lbs loaded. Its range was 1,660 miles with 14,000 lbs of bombs and its service ceiling was 24,500 ft. Its armament was twin 0.303 guns in each of nose and dorsal turrets, plus four 0.303 guns in a tail turret (later 408 Sqn added one 0.5 ventral gun). It could carry a large variety of bomb loads, ranging from one of 16-1,000 lb bombs to another of one 8,000 lb bomb and five cans of incendiaries; however, loads were generally one-4000 lb bomb with incendiaries. The maximum speed of the Marks I and III was 287 mph at 11,500 ft. The cruising speed was 210 mph and the climb to 20,000 ft took 41.6 minutes.*
>
> *Special modifications to the Lancasters used by 617 Sqn allowed them to carry the 12,000 lb deep penetration 'Tallboy' bomb. Dropped from 20,000 ft it made an 80 ft deep crater, 100 ft across and could go through 16 ft of concrete. The Grand Slam bomb, at 22,000 lbs, and first used in 1945, compares with the recently-developed USAF Massive Ordnance Air Blast Bomb (MOAB)*

Conditions there were not good, and we railed about the lesser treatment that differences in rank produced. Notwithstanding, officers and NCOs in a crew would meet at Beningbrough to share the contents of parcels from home and spent as much time together as they could, the officers from a couple of crews would just naturally gravitate together on our bicycles over to see the NCOs, so when we got there we would find that others had done the same, and several crews would socialize together. From there, we also went to the Alice Hawthorne pub close by.

Many bomber stations were of temporary construction; however, Linton-on-Ouse, our home away from home until June 1944, had been an RAF station between the wars and had many permanent peacetime buildings.

On arrival we joined 1679 Conversion Flight for training purposes and formed the typical heavy bomber crew by picking up two additional RAF lads as crew members, Sgt A. 'Artie' Hampson, 20, from Wakefield, Yorkshire, tall and gregarious and the jokester in the crew as our Mid-upper Gunner, and Sgt S. H. R. 'Les' Bore, 21, from Chelmsford, Essex, a short, serious guy, as the Flight Engineer. His duties were to monitor engine performance, watch oil temperatures and fuel consumption, manage the fuel tanks and generally assist the pilot. On takeoff, when the aircraft started down the runway at maximum engine revolutions, the engineer held down the throttle locks leaving the pilot free to use both hands for lift-off. Once airborne he monitored engine performance, and kept a lookout in his quadrant of the sky.

Our standard Lancaster crew was now complete; however, we would add a Mid-under Gunner later when the enemy shot at bombers from underneath with *Schrage Musik* upward-firing cannons.

Table 3- Lancaster Specifications in Metric Measurements

The Lancaster wing span was 31 m, length 21.3 m, height 6 m. The wing area was 120.5 sq m. The aircraft weighed 16,737 kg empty and 30,845 kg loaded. Its armament was twin 0.303 guns in each of nose and dorsal turrets, plus four 0.303 guns in a tail turret (later 408 Sqn added one 0.5 ventral gun). It could carry a large variety of bomb loads, ranging from one of 16-454 kg bombs to another of one 3,636 kg bomb (composed of two-1,818 kg bombs bolted together) and five cans of incendiaries; however, loads were generally one 1,818 kg bomb with incendiaries. The maximum speed of the Marks I and III was 462 kph at 3,505 m. Its range was 2,656 km with 6,350 kg of bombs and its service ceiling was 7,468 m. It cruised at 338 kph and it took 41.6 minutes to climb to 6,096 m.

Special modifications to the Lancasters used by 617 Sqn allowed them to carry the 5,443 kg deep penetration 'Tallboy' bomb. Dropped from 6,096m it made a 24m-deep crater, 30m across and could go through 4.88m of concrete. The Grand Slam bomb, first used in 1945 at 9,979 kg compares with the recently-developed USAF Massive Ordnance Air Blast Bomb (MOAB).

We heard on the BBC every day the number of losses from raids the night before, but not knowing how many aircraft in total were involved in an attack, we had insufficient information with which to assess the magnitude of the losses. Only on arrival at the squadron did we become privy to this information. It was quite a shock to realize what the losses actually were.

In the Lancaster all of the crew, except the rear gunner, was grouped in the front portion of the aircraft and they could move around as required. The rear gunner, however, was stuck in his turret throughout an entire trip. There were electri-cally-heated suits for warmth but these sometimes malfunctioned, either through mechanical failure, or enemy action which cut electrical or hydraulic power. Then the gunner arrived back at base half-frozen. His main role was to warn the pilot of an attacking fighter so that evasive action could be taken to thwart the fighter's aim.

In our crew, they were to keep their guns silent except when we or a nearby air-craft suffered an attack. The credo was, *'Be quiet and inconspicuous.'*

'Suds' Sutherland, who had been promoted to Flight Sergeant (F/S) in October was probably the most laid-back and stable low-experience pilot on the squadron. No fancy aerobatic manoeuvres for him, just logical thinking, sound flying and the atti-tude, *'Lets learn all we can, and be sensible in applying it!'* When many other crews were partying, we were busy figuring out what strategies and tactics experienced squadron aircrews were using. We wanted to elevate our continued existence somewhat above pure chance.

Discipline was always foremost in our minds in these discussions. We knew that several factors could be involved in an accident, or in casualties: mechanical failure, which the ground crews did their best to preclude; bad weather over which we had no control but could ameliorate to some degree by knowledge of weather patterns and local tendencies; and human error which we could overcome by keeping ourselves fit, responsible and continually train, train, train. After that we knew that we were at the mercy of enemy action, and the enemy's ability relative to our own. Primarily, we knew we had to be vigilant and very, very careful.

One of the aids installed in the aircraft was G-H, which we practised on dili-gently. It was an instrument that worked with a two-station radio direction-finding system. The aircraft was tracked over the target by measurement from one station, and determined its bomb release point by its distance from the other. Unlike OBOE, which was an aid for Pathfinder target marking aircraft (two at a time), G-H could be employed by up to 80 aircraft from one pair of stations and thus could be used simul-taneously by many aircraft for direct bombing, without the aid of target markers.

As the operations phase drew closer, our training included day and night naviga-tion exercises conducted at 20,000 ft (6,096 m), the normal height for operations, G-H blind bombing practice, and low level practise in the valleys of Northern Ire-land. The Women's Land Army girls doing the harvest there, threw potatoes down hill at our aircraft, which was skimming the tree tops. It was never revealed to us why we were tasked to do the low-level practice.

On the high-level day trips in good weather, the view of the landscape from height was staggering, there below us was a postage stamp with intricate designs of streams, railways, trees, streets, houses. The English countryside, miniature compared to Canada, was laid out almost at the scale of the map being used.

My promotion to F/O was announced November 20, 1943 and, because of my construction background, the CO took that as an opportunity to volunteer my services as a member of the standby runway bomb repair crew. This was a function that was never practised and, significantly, never needed.

Our biggest drawback in flying was the weather. The winter of 1943-44 produced the worst weather England had experienced in 100 years. And it was consistent, usually dull and gray, and certainly wet and cold. The common flying term was *clag*. Some of the poor conditions could be blamed on industrial cities to the west, which seemed to funnel their residue into our area. In winter, air temperatures were close to freezing, most everything bordered on discomfort and some was truly so, the wind raw, cold and generally uninviting. Flying in such conditions generated a lot of icing, and aircraft could quickly gather more ice than they could bear unless corrective action was taken.

During our conversion training two things occurred which would have an effect on our tour: one, WINDOW, a primary aid, had first been used against Hamburg on July 24/25, 1943 and two, the Battle of Berlin started on November 18/19, and would continue until March 31 the next year.

WINDOW was used by the main force, but also by spoof groups of aircraft to make it look like we were going to a city other than the actual target. It gave the appearance on radar of an armada of aircraft where only a few existed, a formation headed for a target of importance other than the one which was intended by the real force. It was composed of myriads of aluminium strips cut to the length of the German radar frequency and taken aboard in boxes of bales, each bale dropped in the chute in turn, then the bails separated in the wind stream and the chaff floated earthward. Initially, it had totally frustrated the German defences. Use of this tactic kept them at bay for a short period but may actually have been of more benefit to the enemy than to us because it forced a change in enemy defence architecture, to our disadvantage.

Before we graduated to do our first operational trip, our squadron's Commanding Officer (CO), Wing Commander (W/C) W. D. (Tiny) Ferris, DFC finished his tour of operations and was replaced by another pilot beginning his second tour, Acting W/C A.C. Mair, DFC, with us only four short weeks when he was killed in action (KIA) in a raid on Berlin, November 26/27 and whose name is inscribed on the Runnymede Memorial as one who has no known grave. His replacement was W/C D. S. Jacobs, DFC, another pilot who was beginning his second tour.

Our arrival at the squadron direct from OTU was probably a blessing in disguise. We had the opportunity to live within an operational environment while doing our conversion, and soon observed that aircrews were not exposed to much discipline, not much in the way of extra duties, and had adequate leisure time when not flying. Because we mingled daily with crews that were currently operational, we started our air force sharp-end career with a lot more knowledge than those crews who arrived at a squadron after training at HCU, and went on their first operational flight almost immediately thereafter.

High Flight and other Plaques: [2]

High Flight

Oh! I have slipped the surly bonds of earth
And danced the skies on laughter-silvered wings;
Sunward I've climbed, and joined the tumbling mirth
Of sun-split clouds - and done a hundred things
You have not dreamed of - wheeled and soared and swung
High in the sunlit silence. Hov'ring there
I've chased the shouting wind along, and flung
My eager craft through footless halls of air.

Up, up the long, delirious, burning blue
I've tapped the wind-swept heights with easy grace
Where never lark, nor even eagle flew.
And, while with silent lifting mind I've trod
The high untrespassed sanctity of space
Put out my hand and touched the face of God.

- Pilot Officer John Gillespie Magee, Jr., RCAF

---

2   *Poems are included where space is available. They are discussed as Unique Decor products at page 172. The badge with the one shown above is the Canadian Forces (CF) Air Operations Branch badge*

7

BOMBER OPERATIONS BEGIN
December 1943

in which the crew undertakes bomber operations Nos.1-3

So our crew was ready to be put on the Battle Order and expected to be 'under fire' shortly. There is little doubt that we were still very naive, but would soon know the full horror and reality of war. In the meantime, the crew went on leave together in London, and we joined together in many activities.

The comradeship of crews was recalled in words by Hal Jackman, a former Lieutenant-Governor of Ontario, who said in a warmly valid statement: 'There is a mystique, a fundamental ethos in a regiment that captures the mind, the heart, the very soul of all who have the privilege and honour to serve in it.' The same occurs in a squadron, and was doubly true in the smaller unit: a bomber crew! As we embarked on our tour of operations, destined to fight in the bloodiest air battles ever fought, our commitment as a crew was to become the most professional of the squadron. We worked as a team that took nothing for granted, and we were prepared for the work ahead, which would involve, in part, deep penetration trips to Berlin and south-east Germany.

The tides of war were now turning in favour of the Allies, but the German fighters were overcoming their tactical problems and gaining ascendancy over our bombers.

Astro-navigation was used extensively because radio aids were subject to jamming; however, an aircraft was unstable as a platform, and this made precise plots very difficult. The route was often in or near cumulus cloud with its inherent updrafts and instability. Star sights on three stars were preferable to plot a triangle, but most often only two were possible to attempt a cross. The centre of the triangle or cross was used to fix the position of the aircraft, sometimes relatively close to its actual position, sometimes not.

Often we had to resort to less celestial possibilities: dead reckoning using drifts (when the sea was visible), the assistance of loop bearings when the radio was not jammed (seldom), pinpoints if land was visible (not often). If 20 minutes had gone by without a fix being available by normal means, one was taken using searchlight and anti-aircraft fire (FLAK) bearings of the known major defensive areas. They were not the best, but Clive kept a watch and we could treat his track sense among them as fairly reliable.

The Germans used FLAK and fighters for defence, both guided to the bomber stream with radar or sometimes, moonlight or vapour trails. At one time Bomber Command would have the means to counter them, then the enemy would achieve a breakthrough. This would be succeeded by a breakthrough on our side, and so on throughout the later years of the war.

An engine gets attention as S/L Bill Russell watches

GEE was an airborne navigation aid with a transmitter to interrogate two ground stations in England, and could be used by an unlimited number of aircraft. The responses showed as lines on a cathode ray tube at the navigator's table and these related to a chart overlaid with a grid. The fixes obtained were very accurate until you ran out of range at about 400 miles (640 km), then there was nothing but snow, and almost the only thing you had from there to distant targets was astro shots and informed guesses.

Aircraft from the squadrons in our area became airborne at about one-minute intervals, and orbited as they climbed to their starting height. Then, at their allotted times, each aircraft flew independently over a defined point. By the allocation at briefing of times, heights and speeds, each wave of the operation developed and the 'bomber stream' for the trip became a reality.

The practice was to provide each crew with a 9-day leave every six weeks. This gave us a good chance to continue exploring the local culture. Once we became familiar with the Yorkshire brand of the English language we, especially those Canadians who originated in country areas, really got friendly with the locals. There were farms abutting the airfield and we took many opportunities to help the farm families with their seasonal chores. After all, these were the people we met at the pubs in Little Ouseburn and Green Hammerton.

The city of York was closer to what we experienced in the cities back home than was London, and we went there often on non-flying days, particularly to the small family-run White Horse Hotel, in the shadow of York-minster.

So, back to December 3, 1943 .... on a typical day for a crew, everyone got up at the normal time about 0630 hrs (6:30 am), and prepared for an uneventful day, but wondered whether or not operations might be on for that night. If there had not been notification by noon that an operation was planned, training of some sort would be undertaken. Suds had already been on his 'second dickey' trip to a target with an experienced crew and we were considered ready for action. But today an Ops Order for that evening was posted in the messes at noon with Suds' name included, and everything went from neutral to high gear. I felt that the most appropriate phrase to express my feelings then was 'innocents abroad'. We had been prepared for operations but were innocent of that actual state. By the next morning, however, we would be fully indoctrinated. As has been said, some boys became men overnight!

Meanwhile, with receipt of the Ops Order the ground crews were doing all the necessary aircraft checks, the aircraft were being fuelled-up to the level required for the length of the flight, and the armourers were busy bringing the specified bomb load from the bomb dump, and loading it into those aircraft slated for the trip. During this period petrol bowsers were moving to and fro, and bomb trailer trains were passing by with bombs while, it seemed, everyone was checking everything.

We were to report to the briefing room at 1800 hrs (6 pm), so the process for our first bombing operation had started. We visited the crew room before briefing to ensure that all our personal equipment was ready, and that nothing we needed was missing. Our crew arrived at briefing with some trepidation. There had been several Berlin trips recently and we would not have been surprised to find another for this occasion. The first item on the agenda was roll call, then we smoked as we sat waiting for the station CO, the squadron CO, and the briefing entourage to arrive, wondering what was hidden by the map curtain. We had now arrived in the 'front lines'.

We would be flying in S-Sugar, usually used by Doug Harvey's crew, on our Trip No.1 among a total force of 524 aircraft. The roll was called, each skipper replied 'Yes' to indicate his crew was present and accounted for at his table. The air in the room was expectant and a pin dropping would have been a din. The CO said, 'Gentlemen, your target for tonight is .... Leipzig!' as the appointed briefing officer pulled back the curtain to show the map with its red splotches for danger areas, and the route to and from the target displayed, our first glance at reality. This action was accompanied by moans and groans from the assembled crews, but on occasion there would be cheers if the assembly thought it might be an easy target. The scene reminded us of movies we had seen, but this was no movie house.

The choice of routes for the planners was difficult at this stage in the attacks on Germany. They were severely limited, mostly because of where the concentrations of FLAK guns existed. Briefings were given by Intelligence, Met, Navigation, Gunnery, Bombing, Signals, and Engineering. The importance of the city, the target and its designated aiming point, and the industry and military installations in the area were detailed.

We were given information concerning defences, diversionary raids, radio codes, pathfinder marking methods, which wave involved squadron crews, the designated time on target, what sort of weather to expect throughout the trip, and engine handling/fuel conservation procedures.

This night the route would be generally straight in toward Berlin, then south to the target at Leipzig. Special features along the proposed route were described. And while this was going on I marvelled at how everyone, including the senior officers, looked to be so young.

After synchronization of our watches and completion of the briefing, Clive and I remained behind to complete the charts and finish the planning section of the flight plan, while the others went to the aircraft to start preparation there. Clive and I were the last to leave the room, then we joined the rest of the crew for a very good dinner which included real eggs and bacon. 'The condemned man enjoyed a hearty breakfast' came to mind. It was no surprise to find that the crews called it the *last supper*.

It was also necessary to abstain from eating anything gaseous because, although there was an Elsan toilet in the aircraft, using it would have required taking off all those clothes and putting all of them on again. Or was it because we didn't wish to take a chance on a fighter attacking us with our pants down? We also stayed away from anything diuretic, using the pee tube was a real nuisance, and sometimes the updraft in it unceremoniously spewed liquids back to the donor, seemingly more than discarded.

Then it was off to the crew room to empty our pockets into small bags which were gathered into a larger crew bag and deposited, to be picked up on return. Drawing our parachutes and escape kits was next, then we got suited up and ready to go. We boarded the Bedford crew truck with another crew. As we progressed along our route, that other crew was dropped at their dispersal and my thought was, 'Carpenters build, but here we go with plans to tear down'.

We disembarked from the truck at the S-Sugar dispersal to prepare for departure into a milieu where there were 1 million personnel, 20,625 guns, 6,680 searchlights, many of them radar-controlled, forming a formidable barrier for us to get through, and possibly upwards of 400 fighters were en route, all having the prime purpose of frustrating our efforts to bomb, killing us being their preferred outcome. Everyone carried out their aircraft checks in preparation for takeoff and, because we finished early, lounged around for a last cigarette, and wished that time would pass quickly. We boarded and, at the appointed time, Suds swung S-Sugar onto the taxiway and we worked our way into the line of aircraft taxiing line astern to the takeoff point.

When our turn came, Suds taxied onto the runway, and aligned with its flare path stretching out ahead for 6,000 ft (1,829 m). At the threshold he did a brake check, opened the throttles and ran the engines to full bore against the brakes. It seemed that every aluminium panel and rivet was vibrating as though the aircraft would come apart at the seams, but both the engines and the airframe passed the test. Then, when the aircraft ahead of us was three-quarters of the way down the runway, the Aldis lamp flashed a 'green' to us from the control hut at the end of the runway.

Suds released the brakes and we were off, racing past the many well-wishers assembled alongside the runway. With the aircraft heavily laden with bombs and fuel, we held our breath as the weight shifted from the wheels to the wings and they flexed to support it, with everyone hoping we would get into the air without mishap. Soon all the tension was released, both in the aircraft and the crew, and we were away .... to what we did not know. However, this is why we had done all that training, so we could go off to face the enemy. Now we had no alternative but to visit Germany, hopefully only in the air.

One aircraft departed each minute or less until the station's (408 and 426 Sqns) contribution of aircraft got airborne. We circled for height and, at an altitude of 10,000 ft (3,048 m), I gave Suds the first course on our route toward the point where the aircraft would assemble into a concentrated bomber stream headed toward the target. We were now in the company of those who 'pressed on regardless .... whatever the cost!'

Each aircraft had its own navigator who worked toward maintaining the course, height and times given at briefing. The pilot relied on the navigator to stay on track and in turn, he relied on the pilot to follow courses and heights religiously, or to inform him to update his plot if the pilot had to deviate.

Half an hour later we were at 14,000 ft (4,267 m) prepared to set course, and begin a timed period to find the first wind. We had to position our aircraft by speed and height so that there was separation between aircraft, and so that we could reach the target at the time allotted. The stream could be up to 10 miles (16 km) wide and 15 or more miles (24 km) long, depending on the number of aircraft involved, and whether everyone had figured out the true wind.

A navigator's chore was simply to find out where the aircraft was being blown, and use that wind to correct to the intended path. That included getting a fix every ten minutes, plotting the wind and correcting course or revising speed if necessary to be on time at the next turning point, and to do as much forward navigation steps as possible.

We felt that we should always practice undulating flight, weaving up, down, left, right about the course we were on and always being at a high altitude, as far from the ground as was practical. Other bombers were usually so near but so far away. If one got into trouble there was no way anyone else could help it.

All members of the crew except the navigator continuously kept watch for any sign of enemy activity, such as fighter planes, FLAK and searchlights, so they could warn the pilot. The navigator worked at a desk in a closed compartment, so that his work light could not be seen outside. He seldom left his seat during a flight but on occasion, with his current work done, he would spend time standing behind the pilot and engineer watching the sights and providing another pair of eyes. There were puffs of FLAK all around us. Scarecrows were bursting in front of us. They were very similar to sky rocket bursts, and scattered bright stars to illuminate the bombers. Intelligence had assured us there was no such thing, but we and other crews swore they were there. They were never explained to our satisfaction.

Target timing had been planned in 4-minute waves between 19,000 and 23,000 ft (5,791 and 7,010 m), but waves would be shortened in later months to two minutes in order to saturate the defences. As we approached to bomb, Suds and Clive prepared for the bombing run, and the rest of the crew waited in suspense for the 'Bombs away' from Clive and the thump as they went. The aircraft then surged upward from the sudden loss of weight.

Fortunately, target marking was perfect. We bombed as briefed while FLAK shells burst harmlessly at a distance around us. Each spent FLAK shell produced black smoke so there was lots of it in the sky: almost appearing that you could walk on it.

But then, S-Sugar was hit by predicted (radar-controlled) FLAK on the way out of the target area. The entrance door was blasted open and severed, and several lines were cut, including the communication and power lines to the rear turret. Al was then exposed to cold and silence, without contact all the way back to base, getting out half-frozen with icicles dangling profusely from his moustache, but he cheered up a bit when we all laughed at his appearance.

Fighter flares were exploding above us, and we were almost in daylight conditions. This made us much more visible to enemy fighter aircraft. Below, there were thousands of little red dots where fires were burning. Otherwise the 8-hour trip was uneventful, but 24 aircraft were lost, 4.6% of the attacking force, representing about 168 crew members[3].

Little attention seems to have been paid to the significant number of aircrew personnel represented in losses. To speak of the number of aircraft lost sometimes seems

---

3   To give an idea of the number of personnel losses involved in the raids, a figure is cited for selected operational trips. This should not be considered precise, it is merely the number of aircraft that FTR multiplied by seven, the usual number of crew members in a heavy bomber.

a horrendous figure, but to recognize the number of men removed from action provides the human element and the true cost of the raids. Moreover, in the system used to count aircraft that failed to return, those that crashed in England were not counted because it was known. where they were; however, there were usually such losses.

Lanc II S-Sugar

The raid on Leipzig was categorized as a success with much damage to industrial sites, and we had been indoctrinated in the work we would be doing until our trip count was thirty, or we went missing, whichever came first.

On return our maps and parachutes had to be returned for storage, our personal belongings retrieved, and we went back to the briefing room for debriefing. During interrogation, the padres took charge of refreshments, being there in an unobtrusive manner in case someone needed them. There were plenty of sandwiches available and lots of tea, laced with rum for those so inclined. Then, we had eggs and bacon for breakfast and thankfully, off to bed and a much needed rest.

The sympathetic contribution of the padres must be recognized with gratitude and much thanks. In the aftermath of such a raid they were certainly overworked, but their considerable impact on the morale of aircrew in normal circumstances was often overlooked. One such was S/L Wilf Butcher, no relation, the senior Protestant padre on the base who, after the war, was in Quebec City fairly high in the hierarchy of the Presbyterian Church of Canada.

Waiting for the pub to open, l to r, Butcher, Hampson, Boulton and DeMille

The padres put their hearts into their work and always seemed to be here, there and everywhere on their trusty bicycles in sunshine or the worst of rain storms. Another well-known padre was Norm Gallagher, a Roman Catholic with an Army unit in wartime, who carried over into the postwar RCAF and was later the Bishop of North Bay.

There was a full moon early in the next period, and bad weather leading up to December 16. Our activities during this period consisted of G-H practice in J-Johnnie on December 5 at Ely Cathedral, where we emerged from dense cloud into bright sunshine and a vivid blue sky, somewhat scarce in England. There were very tall anvils of cumulonimbus clouds that rose to dizzying heights. We took pictures, having disregarded that we were not supposed to have a camera with us on flights.

On December 9/10 a 3-hour cross-country exercise and bombing practice was done in E-Eddie. Then, on December 10/11 we took off in G-George to do a Bullseye but did not complete it, because the aircraft became unserviceable. On December 12 it was back to Ely Cathedral in E-Eddie for another 3 hours G-H blind-bombing practice. On December 13 we changed targets, and went to Lincoln Cathedral for more G-H practice. By now the crew members were entitled to, and had been awarded the Aircrew Europe Star.

A WWII bomber was not the streamlined and cosy passenger aircraft we know today. They vibrated and were drafty and very cold. Attempts had been made to improve crew comfort, but with only partial success.

We were now more aware than ever that these trips could be long and very boring as well as exceedingly dangerous, and the biggest difficulty was to place the bombs within a reasonable distance of the aiming point. We kept close watch on the Mess notice board each day. If we were listed for an operation, someone hied out to the aircraft allotted to us on the roster, and queried ground crew about the fuel load. A part load would mean a short trip such as one to the Ruhr valley, whereas a full load signified a much longer trip, probably Berlin or somewhere in south-east Germany. We watched the weather for conditions that would stop operations, good weather and no moon kept things most active: we were largely dependent on weather cycles and moon phases.

The Battle of Berlin was the longest and most persistent air offensive against any one city in WWII. Berlin was also the hardest of the German cities to bomb because it was so spread out, it was most frequently cloud-covered, making pinpoints on the lakes seldom possible. It had very poor radar characteristics on the Pathfinder's H2S, an airborne radar set, the first capable of providing a map of the ground below an aircraft. It was a high speed scanner housed in a ventral blister behind the bomb bay, with a screen in the nav compartment which showed a radar image of the ground below. H2S was not subject to jamming or distance limitations but, unfortunately, effective identification of the images required a lot of concentrated practise, and enemy fighters could home in on the sets when they were turned on.

While the battle would continue until March 31, 1944, our crew did its first raid to Berlin, flying G-George on our Trip No.2, December 16/17 when 483 Lancasters and 15 Mosquitoes departed England. At briefing we were given a straight route in to the target and a circuitous route, north over Denmark, on the way back and there would be moonlight. No matter how varied our route and tactics, the enemy controllers were seldom deceived for long. We were briefed that bad weather might develop at the target and there might be fog over England on return. Weather, often forbidding, would be almost as much of a problem as the defences throughout the Berlin campaign.

Takeoff time would be shortly after 1600 hrs (4 pm) and, for the first time, we would have assistance over the target by Serrate Mosquitos, able to home onto the radar transmissions of enemy fighters.

It was expected that the trip would be scrubbed because of poor conditions; however, there was much surprise when it went ahead, with the takeoff time advanced by 20 minutes. During this 7:35 hr trip we experienced severe icing and had to adjust altitude accordingly. We ran the gauntlet of fighter flares from the coast in, to well beyond Hannover. There were many fighters en route, and it was found that Berlin was strongly defended when we neared it.

The FLAK defences, which provided a heavy and sustained barrage, were in a ring 40 miles (64 km) across and the searchlight belt stretched out much farther. Berlin was well protected .... no wonder it was called 'the Big City'. It was a place that, because of the defences, could be tremendously hot at operational height in the coldest of weather. There were also up to 15 decoy sites to draw bombers away from the city. It turned out that there was cloud over the target, which prevented effective activity by the searchlights. Bombing was done blind on accurate sky markers which had been dropped by Mosquito pathfinder aircraft using OBOE, an aid with a pulse repeater which picked up transmissions from a ground station. Bombs were dropped when an intersecting signal from another ground station was reached. Unfortunately OBOE was limited by distance and only two aircraft could be handled simultaneously.

On this occasion fair bomb concentration was achieved, and there was little enemy activity on the return voyage. Back over England on return there was the grimmest of weather: extremely low cloud was in place and heavy fog was prevalent in each low-lying vale, by coincidence, the usual areas where airfields are built. Although anticipated, the fog had arrived earlier than expected and our aircraft was very low on fuel. We were diverted to our neighbouring bomber station, Tholthorpe and priority landing was granted, but fuel had been totally depleted by the time we touched down. The engines having quit, we were left stranded on the runway, and had to be towed off while the meat wagon stood by in case of crisis. Meanwhile, other crews had worse problems ranging from fatal crashes, to crash landings and bailouts.

Losses en route were 25 aircraft, or 5.2%. The crashes and abandonments over England added 30 more losses, and brought the night's toll to 55 or 11.04% of the force (probably approaching 385 aircrew), the heaviest rate so far in the bomber war, and sufficiently disturbing for the day to be given the moniker *Black Thursday*. When we landed we were certainly glad to be safely back on planet Earth, a very thankful crew. The raid was categorized as moderately successful.

At debriefing someone made the first mention of an encounter he saw, where the fighter appeared to fire straight up .... *Schrage Musik* had arrived! It had recently been introduced by the enemy along with the new SN-2 air-borne radar.

This raid demonstrated to us why aircrew got 'twitchy' after several difficult ops. Challenges to the senses could be thrown at you from several directions, seemingly with great rapidity. Those afflicted would gaze around nervously and tics would show in their faces, their hands would shake, any sudden sharp noise would keep them alarmed for some time, and they would have poor appetites. Good leaders sensed this affliction in the crews and juggled leave for a crew to give an appropriate rest period. Unnoticed, it was possible for a crew member to become a medical casualty, and it could be catching.

When an Ops Order was posted, the impending operation made a great difference in the life of both service personnel and local inhabitants. Everyone on the station was at their busiest, the guard house was on high alert, and the village was practically closed down as far as traffic was concerned. This situation applied on December 20, as preparations were made for an incursion that night by 650 aircraft, our Trip No. 3 to Frankfurt, spending 6:10 hrs in G-George. It was a relatively quiet trip to a target covered by 8/10 cloud. The relative quiet was disconcerting. We knew that the defences were all intent on shooting us out of the sky; we were intent on getting through to the target to drop our bombs. Where were they? So this operation ended without incident to us, but a JU-88 showed up dead-centre in our aiming point picture, showing that the fighters had been there, but they just happened to be most prevalent at a time other than when we were in the area. Although we were unharmed, there were 41 a/c, or 6.3% FTR, comprising about 287 personnel.

There was massive opposition from both ground and air defences over some targets, and practically none at others. Different waves of a raid could go through hell while crews in other waves just stooged to the target and back, unmolested. This raid demonstrated the latter for our crew and was a welcome change. The routine involved was to cross the coast, run the gauntlet through the light and heavy FLAK by trying to follow a track where there were few guns. Also included were the fighters, they could only be countered by vigilance on the part of the gunners, and the searchlights which were the most disconcerting. Getting coned by searchlights made a crew feel, in the intense light, that they were nude on a public stage. We were fortunate, only coned once during our tour, and that was short-lived. Suds' ability got us out of it.

Like a gift from home, we had snow at Linton on Christmas day, and all Canadians were immensely cheered by this memory of home. The rest of the station personnel thought it a great inconvenience.

There had been news that my brother Charles, fresh from air gunner training, was newly arrived in Bournemouth. Being granted leave on December 27, several crew members joined to travel with me to meet him. We had an opportunity to assist in Charles' introduction to the culture and help him find his way around. He would eventually be posted to Burma, where he would fly in Liberators with 356 Sqn, complete a bombing tour there, and finish up as a gunnery instructor with the rank of Warrant Officer, First Class (WO1).

On January 14, Suds told us we would be getting a new factory-fresh Lancaster and we should be at the flight line the next morning about 1000 hrs (10 am) for its arrival. It taxied up at about 1045 hrs, but what happened next was not quite what Suds had in mind.

Our new aircraft

The door opened, and a diminutive female pilot of the Air Transport Auxiliary (ATA) descended the aircraft ladder, ... and no one followed her, not even a flight engineer. Talk about a deflated pilot: Suds needed six persons to crew with him and here was a woman flying a Lancaster by herself! But we had our new aircraft and were very pleased.

The ATA was a paramilitary organization of civilian pilots who ferried military aircraft within Great Britain, wherever and whenever required, among factories, and maintenance units and squadrons. The ferry folks were always quick to point out that they only needed enough knowledge to fly the aircraft safely, and that our pilots had, in addition, a crew to look after, strategies and tactics to learn, and more weather knowledge to absorb.

We did an acceptance check and air test on the new arrival. The factory number was LL722 and she got the designation letters of the squadron: EQ, with the code N (for Nan). We immediately named her 'Lady be Good' and created artwork for her nose. Painted the standard black and green camouflage colour, she looked obviously new. She also had that new aircraft smell. In my experience all Lancasters smelled reasonably good, new ones smelled even better. A rookie crew getting its own Lanc after three trips was unheard of; usually more experienced crews were given that courtesy. As each new aircraft replaced one recently lost, this gave a good indication that experienced crews were becoming scarce.

WWII Ration Book

One of the benefits of 'owning' an aircraft was that we could now ally ourselves with one particular ground crew; however, we were kidding ourselves to think that we owned it. In truth, it belonged to the ground crew that had inhabited the dispersal site since the squadron moved to Linton. They were permanent, but they would let us call it ours if we wished. Even the dispersal shack appeared inviting, it was clean and was kept neat and tidy. It had lettering, *Hell's Paradise* and a distinctive sign, *The only tool we loan belongs to our tom cat, he always brings it back.* The 'N' dispersal was located close to a farm where we could buy goose eggs, a rarity not included in rationing arrangements. The rapport between our ground crew and the farm folks was marvellous .... and they also seemed to like the members of our aircrew.

Changing a prop on K-King, 408 Sqn

There were a lot of shortages of essential foodstuffs, not just luxuries. Supplies started to dwindle and some items were impossible to obtain, especially imports such as tea, bananas, oranges, grapes and other fruit. Most of these were not seen again until the late 1940s. Butter, lard, sweets, cakes, flour and sugar became hard to get too, followed by meat and fish. All were subject to rationing, which was sustained throughout and after the war, covering most products in one way or another. Tokens in ration books were the authority for each person to obtain food stuffs. Tokens could be saved up, or used at the owner's discretion. Meals at the mess also reflected these shortages, with the exception of aircrew getting eggs with meals associated with operations. We did not have individual ration books, except when we went on leave. Rations were issued on the basis of a Messing Register. It has been jokingly said that the only commodity not rationed was 'love', and that would appear to be borne out by the fact that 44,886 war brides came to Canada at war's end.

8

MORE BOMBER OPERATIONS
January-March 1944

in which bomber operations Nos.4 to 17 are described

The response to WINDOW had been a reorganization of the German defences. This led to two aptly-named tactics: *Wilde Sau* (Wild Boar) and *Zahme Sau* (Tame Boar). The Wild Boar aircraft were freelance fighters set loose in the target area to pick off bombers in the ambient light provided by German flares, and that from the target itself. The Tame Boar tactics involved the radar controlled night fighters.

On occasion there were now Tame Boar interceptions for 150 miles (240 km) before and after the target, but enemy attacks were not pressed over the target as much as had been expected. The deep penetration to reach Berlin, and the time allotted for an attack, allowed for fighters to be brought in from some distance away. The German defences were able to come back into their own through the use of these strategies.

During this period the RAF created the position of Master Bomber to control activity at the target by assessing the marking done by the Pathfinders, and broadcasting to the participating main force aircraft any commentary concerning where to bomb among the TIs to improve effectiveness.

A pattern had now been established for us on days when we were not scheduled for operations. If we were not slated for ground studies, we would be doing air tests, bombing practice, SBA and GEE homings, G-H practice at Ely or Lincoln Cathedrals, circuit practice and homing or bombing practice at the local range. There were fighter affiliation exercises to be done, and often ferrying to get back aircraft that had landed away from home base after a raid.

Trip No.4 was a raid to Brunswick on January 14/15 by 498 aircraft. We were airborne 5:50 hrs. Our Nan was getting her letters painted and some minor local upgrades, so we had to use B-Baker. By now we had established our crew ritual to perform before takeoff. After completing our checks, we would all leave the aircraft, have a smoke, pee on the tail wheel as a group (real kid stuff, eh!) then board in the order in which we sat in the aircraft, Clive leading because he was in the nose compartment.

Map 2- Part map of England and Europe (R. Diment, VRG)

On this occasion, we were late getting away because there had been an aircraft malfunction in B-Baker that required correction. Course was set for the first leg of the trip as soon as we were clear of the runway, in an effort to catch up. German fighters hounded the stream even before it reached the Dutch coast on the outward leg, and were active throughout, until we passed that coast again on the way home. Other than seeing bombers go down, this was a relatively quiet trip but the raid was not a success, most bombs falling in open countryside. On most attacks, if we didn't hit the target, cows were killed in open pastoral settings. 41 a/c FTR, 7.6%, and about 287 aircrew.

A crew was cohesive and sacrosanct to each of its members. Its comradeship was important, and it paid off. In the air: rigid discipline on board, no chatter on the intercom, safety in the stream, and total vigilance. After a raid it was always nice to be back in England rather than shot down and on the run, or stuck in a police station in the Lowlands or Germany, or even dead.

Our ground crews were among the best. They were always there for us, daytime maintenance and servicing, takeoff, return, and they were always busy, and creative too. They worked in all kinds of weather conditions, mostly cold under a tarp, and their standard of maintenance was excellent. They were devoted to their jobs and to their aircrew. It was often wondered how many times they had grieved over lost aircraft and crews during their time at the 'N' dispersal.

In fact, ground crews were the unsung heroes of Bomber Command. Their contributions have not received adequate recognition: without their dedication the aircrews would not have had much chance of success.

Almost anything could go wrong with the plans made at briefing. The result could be a loose gaggle of bombers spread out widely. The gaggle would get in closer as navigators found the true direction and strength of the wind, then it would separate again with a new wind change. It was always improving, then getting worse again, a very fluid situation; however, by the time of arrival at the target most aircraft were in their time and height slot, unless it was one of those nights when the correct wind could not be found by any means with the navigation tools we had.

Then, when the Pathfinders marked the target, all the aircraft which were off course and time could see it, and headed for it from all directions. This added danger which we could have done without. It was remarkable there were many fewer collisions than would be expected. It didn't take much for a crew to find themselves staring death in the face. With luck a crew got through the target and, at last, finally home to bed. We always slept before showering, probably because of exhaustion from the strain we went through. The sleep, and then the shave and shower in the morning always revitalized us, and we were ready to go again when called upon.

On January 20/21 we did Trip No.5, the first in our new aircraft. This operation in Nan took us back to Berlin via a circuitous northern route in a force comprising 769 aircraft. The time on target for which we were briefed on this occasion, was in waves within a short span of 20 minutes beginning at 1953 hrs (7:53 pm). This required a daylight takeoff which, for the first time, enabled us to actually see the development of the bomber stream over England. Now we knew why the local population was so excited about seeing bombers assemble. Previously we had been in the dark, literally, about the emotions brought out by the vista of hundreds of aircraft spread out around us. It also made us wonder how close some had come to us in the dark!

After crossing the North Sea, we found that the German controllers had managed to insert fighters into the stream rather early on. They were successful in shooting down bombers throughout the outward route, and as we approached the target from the north. We bombed, but fighters were still in the stream on the way home. After we reached a point well out from the Dutch coast we felt safe enough to break out the coffee thermos and enjoy the contents, but there was no chance to relax until the 7:08 hour trip was finished. 35 a/c FTR, a rate of 4.6% and approximately 245 crew members.

The next night, January 21/22, we went to Magdeburg, for operational Trip No.6, using T-Tommy in a raid by 648 aircraft. One aircraft did not clear the boundary fence, so the crew took a long section of Paige wire fence to Germany and back.

We created vapour trails in the damp air and prayed for a change in air conditions. On arrival we saw the target open before zero hour. Some Pathfinder navigator had goofed. Red TIs, then green, went down, but there were also many decoy fires. Chandelier flares were placed to assist the enemy fighters and waving searchlights were disconcerting, as were the 'scarecrows'. And the enemy fighters had ignored the spoof raid on Berlin.

We managed to escape the many fighters that showed up, but on occasion I found myself floating almost to the ceiling in sudden turbulence. We were in hotly defended country and managed to get hit by FLAK but it was not serious. We had been airborne 5.35 hrs when we landed at the USAAF Bomber Base at Newmarket with hydraulics problems, no doubt caused by the FLAK hits. Losses had been 57 aircraft (8.8%) representing about 399 crew members. Of particular concern to Bomber Command staff after this trip was the 15.6% loss rate suffered by the Halifaxes involved. It would lead to the older Halifaxes being removed forever from main force duties.

Flying has always been portrayed as glamourous, but consider this analogy .... we were in the long haul air cargo business, specializing in hazardous products on very dangerous routes, generally with the weather most decidedly against us, and definitely no glamour.

40% of losses occurred in a crew's first five operational trips, when crews were inexperienced. We had now beaten those first odds. After that, danger seemed to lessen until a crew was near the end of a tour when, in a period of incessant tension, the loss rates went up again. Lots of experience, but less luck! Nothing could replace bad luck, but in our crew we had the blessing of a well-behaved and efficient crew working with an unflappable pilot, and this made us feel protected.

At HQ it was believed that the way to lessen risk was to have the Pathfinders on target precisely on time, and for the main force aircraft to be well concentrated, to shorten drastically the time which the target was open and thus reduce the risk .... if only all this were possible! In 1943/44 it certainly was not.

Our 7:45 hour foray, Trip No.7 to raid Berlin in Nan January 27/28 would involve 530 aircraft. Time on target would be 2028 hrs (8:28 pm) for a 14-minute bombing period. We were briefed for an outbound route with several direction changes. In an unusual gesture, the fighters came 75 miles (120 km) out over the North Sea to greet us, and immediately started scoring. Once over the continent we would proceed on a south-east course, first appearing to threaten Hannover, then Brunswick, Magdeburg or Leipzig, elaborate tactics which had some effect in trying to convince the German controllers that our target was other than that planned. The real bomber force would then turn north-east and WINDOW-dropping Mosquitos would lay down dummy route markers along the projection of the old line of advance. How the controllers reacted could mean the difference between life and death to many aircrews.

A running battle with the fighters ensued to and through the target. Several large explosions occurred on the ground, the glow of which remained visible for 150 miles (240 km) after leaving the target. Bombing on sky-marking was spread over a wide area. There was a very strong headwind on the homeward legs and it seemed to take forever to reach England, but the chewing gum, then coffee had been enjoyed from halfway across the North Sea. The raid was classified as a mediocre success. 33 a/c FTR, or 6.4% of the Lancasters involved. About 231 aircrew did not come home.

It was known that the Germans readied their defence echelons before the crews in England even boarded their aircraft. Past experience enabled them to tell whether Bomber Command would fly on a certain night, because they could pick up the increased testing of H2S in aircraft on English airfields. After the contacts increased in tempo, they knew that preparations for a raid were in progress and began their own response drills.

We were briefed for an operation to Berlin on the night of January 25/26, but it was cancelled; however, we went there again January 28/29 in Nan for Trip No.8 as part of a maximum effort by 677 aircraft. At briefing we were given a route which passed over the Baltic Sea and Denmark, both outward and back, and were to be supported by a full range of diversion raids, including the bombing of night fighter bases by Mosquitos, and a Mosquito raid on Berlin about 5 hours before our target time, set for 0313 hrs (3:13 am) with a 20 minute bombing period. Including diversions, a total of 775 aircraft, would be involved. Going from briefing to reality, takeoff was twice delayed for weather reasons and we did not get airborne until midnight. Someone mentioned that it seemed we were alternating nights between visits to the local pub, and the sky over Berlin.

Enroute, there was severe icing up to 20,000 ft (6,096 m), but conditions improved in the target area. Fires from the earlier Mosquito raid were visible when we reached the Baltic coast and several fighter attacks were seen in that area We picked up a couple of fighters on MONICA, a device which provided crews with early warning of fighters approaching at speed but we never saw them, and managed to slip through quietly to the target, where all hell broke loose!

Bomber Command had experienced increasing success, but now the enemy night fighter force was gaining ascendancy with its Tame Boar tactics and its SN2 radars. Both the Wild Boar and Tame Boar fighters were at the target waiting for us, and there were lots of fighter flares, with the result that 27 aircraft were shot down before we got out of the target area.

The long route home was exacerbated by cold and tiredness, along with thick cloud and icing. The extremes of buffeting in cloud made navigation even more difficult than usual. One minute the pencil would be stabbing the desk from an updraft, the next a sharp downdraft would suspend your arm high in the air, it certainly was no fun fighting a pencil. After a 7:35 hr trip it was daylight, but the raid had only been moderately successful. We were glad to be back on *terra firma*. 46 aircraft FTR, 6.8% of the force, involving about 322 aircrew.

Our Nan was now fitted with an Air Position Indicator, an instrument that combined the DR compass and the pitot head. It was a welcome addition to our line-up of aids. It made things easier for both pilot and navigator. The pilot was able to deviate slightly from course from time to time and the navigator was able to navigate more precisely because he could rest assured that any deviation in direction had been recorded for future use; however, without the right wind and no fixes it could be relatively useless.

We were involved in whirlwind periods of action. In war you're not asked to approve your superior's decisions, only to execute them, and that is what we had to do. Our daily cycle went, 'Do a test flight, go to briefing, eat, go to Germany to bomb, come back, debrief and have eggs for breakfast, hit the sack.' When the busy periods were over it did not take long to become bored. We were usually exposed to constant and almost unbearable strain. Every time we departed on an operation we knew that a significant percentage of our compatriot crews would not return, and that the possibility of our being one of those remained great.

On January 30, we were back in the briefing room to hear about another visit to Berlin on January 30/31 (Trip No.9) in Nan. The unveiling of the map was accompanied by gasps and groans from the assembled crews. Imagine *three* sorties to Berlin in *four* nights! 534 aircraft were scheduled to go back, with a time on target of 2013 hours, and an intended time window for bombing of 14 minutes. There had been one night of rest and here we were .... still weary. Now we were on another 'maximum-effort' raid. There would be one diversion, 5 Mosquitos to Brunswick, and it was not unusual at this time for the Germans to have as many as 400 fighters available for the defence of routes and targets.

There was an afternoon takeoff in clear conditions, which were also to exist when we returned. Over Germany there would be thick cloud and icing to hamper the fighter force. Our route to the target was along a northern line just inside the German border. There was low cloud up to about 8,000 ft (2,438 m). Searchlights played on the clouds and, aided by a partial moon (the early part of the monthly moon phase) they provided subdued light that made us feel uncomfortable.

After our turn south we saw several bombers afire, 20 aircraft were shot down on the way into and through the target. After bombing through cloud on sky marking, we returned on a generally straight line for home base. It was the shortest trip home in many sorties and it had been a successful raid. We were airborne 6:35 hrs. About 231 persons FTR in 33 a/c, 6.2 % of the force.

The January 1944 losses had reached the crisis point of 6% .... higher on some raids. With such losses, the planners were doing their best to find innovative tactics that would lessen risk. Some were successful, and others actually created more problems. There were also the continuing problems that nothing could be done about, that of flame from engine exhausts and signals from radar transmissions. These sometimes helped fighters find bombers and, when found, the bombers could only react with peashooters against cannon.

At about this time there was an order from Air Ministry for navigators to remove the Observer wing, and wear the new Navigator wing. There was such an uproar that the order was withdrawn but, realizing that my training was as a navigator and not as an observer, the change was made.

February 2, we flew in Nan for day air-to-air gunnery practice in which the gunners practised on drogues towed by a Miles Martinet, then it was also my turn to fly the aircraft dual for a half-hour in our continuing effort to make sure that several crew members could keep the aircraft straight and level in the event the pilot became a casualty. After our flight, we spent some time heckling the pilots in their ready room. We reminded them that they weren't glamourous fighter pilots with sleek fighters, they were truck drivers delivering bombs.

During the down periods, weather, moon .... crews always wondered when the next Ops Order would show up on the bulletin boards and what might be the target? Even when we knew an operation was on, it could still be scrubbed by bad weather, no wonder we became interested in weather patterns. On February 3/4 we spent 3 hours in Nan on a Bullseye exercise. February 4 it was back on leave in London, again mostly in the area of Euston Square. On return we were up again February 12 for 1:30 hrs in Nan on a bombing exercise and local flying.

By this time our crew had settled down pretty well to our own tactics within those provided at briefing, for instance we always tried to be among the last of the aircraft to depart. This was done to conserve fuel. Those that were eager to leave early had to waste time somewhere to be on the allotted timing, and thus use up fuel that might be used to gain height if necessary, or ensure sufficient reserve on return to base. By February 15, there had not been a single major operation for thirteen nights, and there was a satisfying easing of tension among the crews. There had been a heavy snowfall with all aircrew on base joining in the shovelling. We were pleased to have been on leave and missed that action!

There had been briefings and cancellations on February 13 and 14. We were back and listed for a raid on February 15/16. As it turned out it was for Berlin (Trip No.10), with an early evening takeoff and a target time of 2113 hrs (9:13 pm) for a 12-minute raid duration, and this would turn out to be our last trip to the Big City. The route was inbound over Denmark again, and almost direct home. A new tactic would see the raid split into two streams flying about 40 miles (64 km) apart on the outbound legs. There would be a diversion raid at Frankfurt-on-Oder by 24 Lancasters, and Mosquitos would be bombing the night fighter airfields in Holland. We would be in the last wave, and would fly in Nan for 7:13 hrs in a raid by 891 aircraft. F/S Stark went with us as 'second dickey' (his ultimate fate is not known), the first time Suds had been called upon to be an operational mentor.

In the meantime, the first TIs went down, but they were back on the rear starboard quarter, and we were still going east. When Norm queried, there was no reply from me. On investigation Hobbs found me to be unconscious from lack of oxygen. My oxygen tube had become disconnected by rubbing on the navigation table. Hobbs attached me to a portable bottle and I regained consciousness, only to find Hobbs on the floor. He had panicked, was himself without a portable bottle, and was now unconscious. All I could do was tell Norm to turn to the target, and to remember the time and heading, while I got Hobbs up and about. He was laying there on the floor with a distinct smile on his face, and recovered quickly.

Slated for the last wave of the raid so, by the time we turned and flew back, we were now all alone at the target. Everyone else had finished and left, and we ended up bombing 17 minutes late. Then, because we would feel safer at a higher elevation, we climbed out of the target and headed for home. Fuel shortage occurred, no doubt due to having overshot the target, and we had to find someplace closer than our own base to land, so we diverted to the USAAF Bomber Base at Horham, saving about 30 minutes flying. 43 a/c FTR from this raid, 4.8% of the force and about 300 aircrew.

You always thought you knew the individuals in your crew, but in the tension of operations everything was different than in training. Roy's actions confirmed that he was a bit of a panic merchant, as had been anticipated. He and the rest of the crew all acted out exactly as had been expected: they were solid guys.

Our tour had begun in a baptism of fire, visiting Berlin six times in our first ten operational trips. Three of those Berlin trips were done in a span of four nights .... and we were alive! Our experience up until now had been varied and confirmed to us that, although flying is always portrayed as glamourous, we had to face reality, this was anything but a glamorous activity!

There were briefings for Berlin on February 16, 17, and 18 but these were cancelled for weather reasons. At the last of these Suds was informed that he had been commissioned, and was now a P/O. Now, with improved weather, we were briefed to fly in Nan for a 'maximum effort' raid of 823 aircraft February 19/20 (Trip No.11) with Leipzig as the target.

On most occasions an Ops Order called on a squadron to provide a certain number of aircraft; however, when it specified a 'maximum effort', every aircraft that could be made available was required. Usually this happened when an Ops Order was issued immediately after a very recent major operation. The route for this trip would be straight in toward Berlin, where there would be a diversionary raid by Mosquitos, with a right angle turn to Leipzig. The wind was found to be slight from the north, rather than as forecast to be a steady head wind. I did not feel safe with using it until it had been confirmed from good star shots, with the result that we turned north to do a dog leg, instead of south at our designated turn, in order to waste 20 minutes. So much for the 'broadcast winds' which had tried to tell us there was no change from those initially forecast.

The broadcast wind system relied on selected senior navigators in the Pathfinder squadrons reporting the winds they experienced to Bomber Command HQ. The HQ averaged them and rebroadcast them to the participating aircraft. In my experience those navigators could be just as wrong in their navigation as anyone else, and the winds which were broadcast were seldom used.

Fighters had infiltrated the stream early, the enemy controllers thought we were going to Berlin and an avenue of fighter flares was dropped along a continuing line at the place where we turned. It was nice to know that they would not be with us until they could catch up after the turn.

There was chaos at the target because many navigators had not succeeded in getting the correct wind. There were collisions and the Tame Boar fighters were having a field day. We were airborne 7:30 hrs. There were distressing losses, 78 a/c FTR, 9.5% of the force and about 546 members of aircrew. Again, it was the heaviest loss so far in the Bomber Command offensive.

About this time the tactic of using an adjustable zero hour (time on target) was introduced to overcome the risk of collisions, but none of our crew recalled being on a raid where one was used.

The raid on February 20/21 was Trip No.12 with Stuttgart as the target. We flew in Nan in a raid comprising 598 aircraft. Our time in the air was 7:00 hrs and, surprise, surprise, we were fired upon by a Lanc enroute to the target, which was cloud-covered and the cookie hung up, but it was jettisoned electrically in the target area. 9 aircraft FTR, 1.8% of those despatched.

February 24/25 was our next incursion (Trip No.13) in Nan to Schweinfurt in a raid by 734 aircraft with a flying time of 7:10 hrs. The raid was split into two separate parts separated by a 2-hour time space. It was a relatively quiet experience and our crew got an aiming point picture. Losses were 21, or 3.6%.

The next night, February 25/26 we took off in B-Baker for a raid on Augsburg, our Trip No.14, in a stream of 594 aircraft and flight time was 7:30 hrs. On the way to the target, routed south through Selsey Bill on the English Channel coast, we got caught in an enemy raid on London. Our route took us 30 miles (48 km) to the west of London and the antiaircraft gunners should have been able to identify that an outgoing raid was on its way south along that line. However, as we were going by, we seemed to be right in the middle of everything.

It is suspected that, un-known to us, German aircraft were passing through below our gaggle. We were going South and they were prob-ably going East to West or vice versa. Nevertheless, logic does not always win in war-time, and the defences started firing at us. It was greatly ap-preciated that their aim was off. Here we were trying to

Bombing-up, preparing to load a cookie for the Augsburg raid of February 25/26, 1944

bomb Germany on their behalf and they were treating us as an enemy! Otherwise it was a quiet trip. 33 aircraft FTR, or 4.5%. In those days we lived each day as it came and did not think much about any tomorrows. Our constant companions were the Holy Trinity .... wallet, calendar and address book, but we had to leave all these behind whenever we went on operations. We were fully aware that we were living dangerously .... we also had a most healthy respect for our opponents.

In early March and granted leave, wandering took me to Crowborough, Sussex to visit Don Rogers, Roland MacPhee and Frank Ayer, hometown friends in the VIII Canadian Hussars (Princess Louise's). They taught me to drive a Ram tank and we went on an exercise, where I managed to run over a pair of pigs. The cooks in the officer's and sergeants messes were not at all displeased to get them, even though they were road-kill, and the farmer was compensated. While there my friends informed me that Doris had deposited my son, Rod (nearing one year old) with Mom and had taken a job in the aircraft factory in Amherst. It would be three months before anyone in the family discussed this situation in their letters.

So, leave over and back to flying, on March 12 I was briefed with another crew to go on a raid to Essen because its navigator, my room mate Gord, was sick with the flu. The crew was known to have personality and coordination difficulties and was infamous for its large number of early returns. I can truthfully say I was never more scared! Thankfully, there was an engine problem and the crew did an early return .... again!! There was certainly no desire to fly with a crew other than my own, and certainly not that one.

We went 14/15 Mar on a Bullseye exercise in A-Able, flying 3:45 hrs. Then we spent 2:30 hrs on March 17 in J-Johnnie........first delivering a crew to RAF Burn to pick up an aircraft that had diverted there, and then on fighter affiliation with a

Hurricane of the Air Fighting Defence Unit (AFDU). The day was completed doing a bombing exercise.

March 15/16 we flew for 7:35 hrs in Nan on a foray by 863 aircraft to Stuttgart (Trip No.15). 37 a/c FTR, or 4.3%, involving about 259 people. F/S W. Cooke flew with us as 'second dickey' (he survived, but details are unknown). The target was late in opening, but bombing was in clear weather. We were fired upon in the target area by the upper gunner of a Halifax and there was hectic fighter activity, although it was slow to develop in the initial stages of the trip.

No matter how vigilant a crew, 'Schrage Musik' aircraft could sneak in easily in conditions of poor visibility. To counter this threat we had an aid called FISHPOND, which scanned below the aircraft, and 6 Gp added another air gunner to each crew, along with the installation of a ventral 0.5" cannon. It surprised a few enemy pilots and lessened their desire to press an attack. In our crew this eighth position was filled by Sgt A. 'Dusty' Claus, 19, a Canadian aboriginal with a ready smile, who came from a reserve near Oshawa, ON.

Because there were so many casualties in the recent period, surviving aircrew described themselves, with good cause, as 'fugitives from the law of averages'. We also found ourselves taking more interest in the locations of crash landing sites for damaged bombers which had been built at several locations along the East coast, particularly at Carnaby, Yorkshire, Woodbridge, Suffolk and Manston, Kent. These fields were equipped with a fog dispersal system called FIDO and were credited with saving many aircraft and crews that might otherwise have become casualties.

The night of March 22/23 found us in Nan on an uneventful but very successful raid (Trip No.16) to Frankfurt in an operation by 816 aircraft. Flying time was 5:40 hrs. 33 aircraft FTR, 4.0% of those despatched. Flight Lieutenant (F/L) McIvor flew with us as 'second dickey' (he would be killed along with his crew on a post-D-Day raid at Cambrai, France June 12/13, 1944).

A certain loneliness was felt on long flights over enemy territory because we had to drastically minimize intercom traffic to achieve good crew discipline. There was essentially no contact throughout, the only words spoken other than crew checks being those required to do the job effectively. We now also qualified for the France-Germany Star but, because we had the Aircrew Europe Star, had to wear a Clasp on that medal ribbon to represent it.

We spent some spare time at the craft shop on various projects, and did a lot of cycling in the local area, to towns and villages in the lower Yorkshire Vales such as Little Ouseburn, Newton-on-Ouse, Nun Monckton, Green Hammerton and Tollerton, spent some time in York, and also at the local pub in Green Hammerton, establishing a tradition of having a weekly visit there with our ground crew. We all looked forward to it, and it helped ensure good rapport with them.

We were really living two lives simultaneously, one in which we were committed to our flying jobs, the other in which we joined wholeheartedly in village activities. The ability to abandon thoughts of work while at the pub was of great assistance in maintaining our sanity. Our local experiences showed us that many crews could be frivolous, drunken, apparently childish in their antics on the ground, but acted as dedicated and coordinated professionals in the air.

Trip No.17 took us to Essen March 26/27 for 4:35 hrs flying in Nan. The raid involved 705 aircraft. It was our first exposure to Happy Valley, as the Ruhr was called by aircrews. It had been the nemesis of many crews over the years. 9 aircraft FTR from this rather short and easy trip.

F/S Ted Vaughan was with us as 'second dickey'. He said on return that all that FLAK had caused him to be nervous, and he wondered if we would get back. He was greatly relieved when told that all those bumps were the prop wash from aircraft ahead of us, and that we had been happy to know that we were tucked tidily into the bomber stream. Too bad we hadn't briefed him, or that he hadn't asked! It was about this time that we realized that we had all become fatalists.

9

NUREMBERG AND HEAVY LOSSES
March 30/31, 1944

in which Bomber Operation No.18 is covered

On March 30 we responded to a posted Ops Order, reporting to briefing for a raid, coded *Grayling*, to Nuremburg March 30/31. This would be Trip No.18. There would be a total of 795 aircraft despatched and the trip would be done in Nan.

There would be moonlight, without fading to darkness at Nuremberg until 0148 hrs (1:48 am). The last aircraft on target was planned for 0122 hrs. The wave we were slotted in could expect darkness through most of the return journey but it would take forever to get home. Theoretically, the Pathfinders were to open the target at 0105 hrs. The main force was in five waves from 0110 to 0122 hrs, all of which were intended to pass through the target in that 12 minutes, at a rate of 57 aircraft per minute, almost one per second!

All crews were surprised and dismayed that we would be operating, because it was now in the monthly moon period. The only solace the briefing officers could offer was the possibility of some high cloud forming along the route to the target. There were gasps, then utter silence when the target was divulged. Our feeling was, what the hell are they doing now? Do they have some new gimmick to protect us with, that sort of thing? Ted Vaughan was with us again as 'second dickey'. This time any concerns he had about danger would be warranted; however, Ted would go on to finish a tour, and our next meeting would be at a squadron reunion in Edmonton in 2001.

We left the briefing and had our operational meal of bacon and eggs with the feeling that a difficult journey was ahead of us, one fraught with more danger than usual, and we would later find that our premonition of problems was fulfilled. The route passed close to Beacon Ida, where risks were great ..... and we had the uncomfortable feeling that the Ides of March were upon us. With a load of almost 4 tons of bombs, normal for the distance involved, we were airborne 7 hours, 45 minutes.

Over the water on the way out, you could not help but notice the beauty of moon and clouds with the North Sea far below shimmering in the moonlight as we passed overhead. After crossing the Belgian coast, Clive fused the bombs and tension increased. After using star shots to plot a fix, the wind effect was found to have changed and came from a much different direction. Instead of winds at 80 knots which had been expected, speeds of 120-130 knots were being experienced. Whether to believe them was the problem, especially when the broadcast winds were much less. We were moving toward the target faster than expected, and we were not experiencing buffeting from the slipstreams of other bombers. It made the crew feel terribly exposed to realize that other aircraft were not in close proximity. Was the last wind you used wrong?

Lanc IIs at Linton

Many navigators probably did not believe their findings, and stayed with the winds which were forecast at briefing, or those broadcast to them. Their aircraft travelled where they were blown, contributing to a longer spread out, and probably more losses. In the event, I did not allow enough variance and we found ourselves straying off course.

Vapour trails formed in bright moonlight, then the fighters joined in and there were aircraft going down all around us. We had not seen that much fighter activity over Germany before but it was reported that only about 200 were involved. To add insult to injury, the lower cloud cover was white below us because of the searchlights focussed on it. The effect was approaching that of daylight. Bombers were easily seen and the fighters were having a heyday. All they had to do was direct their attention to us. We were sitting ducks. There were many attacks and several aircraft, including a German fighter, went down around us in a very short period of time.

Our Nan was not attacked but we had to alter course and gain height to miss parachutes and get into drier air. Fear was inevitable, death was near. Most of the aircraft lost had gone down before the target was reached. At 23,500 ft (7,162 m) we felt much safer and were above the German aircraft that were dropping the flares. Then Suds asked me to go forward to identify markers that he thought might be German decoys because their brightness did not seem to show sufficient contrast. He thought that, coming out from my lighted area, the colours might be assessed better. I confirmed that it appeared they were not ours, and stayed forward to watch the sights. After turning on the last leg toward Nuremberg there was a lot less enemy action so we went down closer to our briefed bombing height and levelled out at 21,500 ft (6,553 m); however, we were still approaching the target more quickly than the initial estimated time of arrival in my log.

Then we felt and heard the staccato patter of shrapnel hitting the aircraft. Going back to my seat it was found, to my surprise, that the cushion was missing. There was a gaping hole in the seat which had to be forced back into alignment with a flying boot. The cushion was laying, minimally damaged, on the floor near the seat so I put it back and resumed my navigation duties, although I felt quite shaken. Missed only by a minute or two! Rather than guts sprayed all over the nav compartment I was fine, but had a very nonplussed feeling, and must have been in mild shock. My usual composure was not regained for several days. Roy would say later that if I had been in my seat, his wireless set would still be serviceable. Our bombs were dropped onto TIs, and we surged upward.

On most routes the maximum height for FLAK was 19-21,000 ft (5,791-6,401 m) although it could go higher. We felt safer above that height, and Suds and Les were usually able to get Nan well above the common level, but the defenses could adjust to a ceiling of 36,000 ft (10,973 m) if desired. Thankfully, they usually concentrated at the level where most of the aircraft were flying.

Then, after we turned west for England Suds told me that there appeared to be another set of markers on the port side about 30 miles (48 km) away. Did we bomb Nuremberg or somewhere else. Schweinfurt? Was the altimeter correct? Was the speed reading right? What else could be wrong? It was decided that nothing could be done about the variables, and my concentration had better be on getting home.

It took hours to get back to base. The headwind was gale force. As we progressed, a fix from star shots told me the wind was getting stronger and we kept falling back. Doubt crept in. Would we ever get there? The slow progression gave me lots of time to think. Assuming that we had been north of track, it was almost certain we had bombed Schweinfurt, and that the markers we saw after we bombed were at the real target, but .... there had been Pathfinder markers where we dropped our bombs! I had serious doubts about our height and wondered if something was wrong with the altimeter; however, there were many variables and our only problem may have been the wind. If we had bombed Schweinfurt we were some 50 miles (80 km) north of where we should have been.

We felt that the coast was getting further away, rather than closer as time went by. It took over 4 hours to go from the target to the English Channel near Dieppe, where the disastrous raid and severe Canadian Army casualties had taken place in August 1942, but except for the time involved nothing untoward happened on that leg. Finally the GEE box lost its clutter and proved we were at the coast, then tension abated somewhat. After all we had been through, we expected that we might also have intruders to contend with at base (there was a JU88 at an airfield in Norfolk that night) but no, we had bad weather instead; however, we were able to land safely in deteriorating conditions at home base. My feeling as we approached for landing was, 'Are there going to be any squadron crews, other than ourselves, when we get to debriefing?'

At interrogation we learned that there had been 52, or 6.9%, early returns which was about average for those times. This represented 52 crews who did not go through the trauma, but neither did they get credit for a trip. We were still uncertain about precisely where we had been. Normally we described everything as we saw it, this time we withheld information other than to say that the winds had been a problem, and that a lot of aircraft had been lost. Goodness knows there were lots of other activities to describe, such as aircraft taking a direct hit in the bomb bay, exploding into balls of white and orange, falling quickly to earth without the appearance of parachutes. And it is not surprising that this night became known as 'the night when everything went wrong'.

We were all in the mess that evening to hear the BBC news reader, Alvar Liddell, say in his stentorian but nicely modulated voice:

Last night our bombers attacked Nuremberg. 96 of our aircraft failed to return.

The 'voice of doom' (our name for Liddell) had spoken. Dead silence prevailed for several seconds after this announcement (there still is a difference of opinion about the actual number of aircraft despatched and the number lost). It was difficult to fathom the number even though we expected losses would be very heavy. All present agreed that, unless the choice of targets and the tactics used were changed, our chances of survival were almost negligible.

At noon, we visited Nan to see how much FLAK damage had been suffered. Truth was the shrapnel that hit the wireless set was not the one that went through my seat. There had been five hits, two through the left bomb bay door and three through the fuselage next to the bomb bay. Two pieces were found, one of about 2 lbs (1 kg) in the wireless set and another of 3 lbs (1.36 kg) near the nav desk. The other pieces may have been in the bomb bay and gone back onto land when the bombs were dropped. How they had missed the bomb load on the way up remains a mystery.

The Germans had won at Nuremberg, and the raid was Bomber Command's *biggest loss of the war*. In addition to the 96 aircraft that FTR, 11.9% of the force despatched, which were lost over the continent, 13 bombers crashed attempting to land in England, making a total loss of 108 aircraft, over 13%. Total crews lost represented some 750 men all lost within a few short hours, *many more than were lost in the entire Battle of*

Britain, and victims of, in Harris's words, the 'very nasty, tough, uncomfortable and frightening game' of being a crew member in Bomber Command. A loss rate over 5% was considered unacceptable by Bomber Command HQ. It was obvious something had to change! The factories could not replace aircraft fast enough to keep the offensive sustainable at such a loss rate.

My roommate, navigator Gord Schacter went missing on this raid, shot down by a night-fighter. He and four others in his crew became prisoners of war but the remaining three crew members were killed. I would next meet Gord in 1966, and again at the 2001 reunion.

On occasion aircrew officers were called upon to assist in cataloguing personal effects of FTRs, preparing casualty telegrams for the adjutant and assisting the service police in identifying which items in a room belonged to the casualty, a duty which I was tasked to perform. I also put in a note for Gord, 'In case you get back!' He was able to read it on his return home in 1945.

Also lost was Bill Dixon, a navigator with 578 Sqn, and an acquaintance born in Aulac, another village near home. The loss of friends was always hard to take. Every crew became hardened to seeing others go down, and felt that surge of guilty gratitude that it was someone else's turn.

When losses in both aircraft and personnel occurred it started a comprehensive movement of replacement. New aircraft were fed up the pipeline from the factories, and everyone in the personnel pipeline effectively took one move forward. We did not think about it at the time but this pipeline went right back to the air force schools, and even farther into the homes in which the volunteers had resided. Fathers, mothers and siblings were sitting there wondering how their kin were making out. All they knew was that they were in England, and in the front line under fire. Each announcement on the radio reminded them, and rekindled deep concerns.

The extent of our inurement was evident when Gord went missing. The third occupant in our room was Captain Charlie Duke, a recently arrived Canadian dentist. Not having gone through the long process toward accepting death as we had, he was so upset that he requested a move to a training station away from the bomber losses. He was moved somewhere else the same day and was never seen again.

Of the bombers involved in the raid, 64% had bombed and returned successfully to England *without* encountering a fighter or even being hit by FLAK. For them it had been just another raid. This underlines the fact that you could go merrily on your way, do your job and return without incident while others were going through hell!

Nuremberg has been described as the greatest air battle of all time, and not likely to ever be overtaken. It should have been a routine 'maximum effort', it wasn't! ....

it was a major disaster, the target being only lightly damaged and all those bombers missing. I call it 'the night I was almost robbed of my 23rd birthday'. Is it any wonder that, following the war, a full moon bothered and distressed me for several years.

In retrospect we *had* suffered the Ides of March. 178 four-engined bombers had been lost in the last seven days. From November 1943 to April 1944 there were in excess of 1,000 bombers lost. Front line strength could not be sustained indefinitely in the face of such losses. The loss of 1,000 bombers represented a loss of aircrew compatriots approaching 7,000 personnel. It was during times like this that a person was thankful for having his crew. We did most everything together .... fly and fight, party, and grieve!

Although there would still be a few trips into Germany, the remainder of our tour would largely be involved in Bomber Command's tactical support for the Normandy invasion, the 'softening up' described by Winston Churchill as 'creating a railway desert' in the Normandy area. This involved night raids on transportation facilities, communications, German defences in France, and logistics centres.

To tell the truth, this simple change away from the more dangerous targets probably, at least in the opinion of our crew, saved our lives. It ushered in a dramatic change in the fortunes of the bomber crews who had so recently emerged from the nightmare of the Battle of Berlin.

Both England and Europe had been plagued by atrocious winter weather. This made target marking by the Pathfinders, whether ground or sky marking, very chancy because many German cities, and in particular Berlin, oftentimes had a cloud cover in place in Winter. If incorrect winds are used for the bombsight setting, both ground or sky markers won't be in the correct positions, sometimes accounting for significant bombing error.

The approximately 1,920-km (1,200-mile) return trips were largely over enemy territory and there were times when we were not sure we were away from night-fighters, even as we approached base and prepared to land. Most of the bomber losses were incurred by fighters, a lesser number by FLAK and not so few by collisions in the concentrated bomber stream.

10

THE TENSION EASES
April 1944-June 1945

which covers operations Nos.19-29 and the post-operations period in the RCAF

In Nan, April 10/11 saw us included in an operation by 148 aircraft to the rail yards at Laon, France (Trip No.19), bombing the yards in moonlight. There was some fighter activity but, as a distinct change for us there was only one aircraft lost, and we had the pleasure of getting an aiming point picture, but were

Ron up in the air during a take-off delay, Suds in the cockpit

disappointed that results of the raid showed only marginal success. We were airborne for 4:47 hrs. Then we went in Nan for our Trip No.20, to bomb the rail yards at Noisy-le-Sec on the northern outskirts of Paris on the night of April 18/19 in a gaggle of 181 aircraft, and got an aiming point picture. We were airborne 4:38 hrs and there were 4 aircraft losses. The target was severely damaged but there was a high death rate among French civilians.

Accuracy was vital on railway targets in heavily populated areas, but we could not always achieve it. In 1985 I visited friends in the area of this target and was shown a piece of shrapnel still lodged in a picture frame in their living room. They had been at home during the raid, and they still marvelled that more of their neighbours had not been killed.

April 22/23 we went on a raid to Düsseldorf (Trip No.21) in Nan. It involved 596 aircraft. At the briefing we were told that our target would be a factory slightly away from the main target, and that we would be doing precision bombing using G-H, a virtual bombsight. The overall raid achieved widespread damage, the markers were concentrated and the bombing was successful. We hit our separate objective;

however, there was a lot of night-fighter activity. Flying time was 5:25 hrs. Fighters and FLAK caused 29 losses or 4.9% of the aircraft, about 200 personnel.

During our conversion to Lancasters we had done extensive training on G-H using Lincoln and Ely Cathedrals as practise targets. Intended as an aid to do precision blind bombing, it was first used October 7/8, 1943 at Aachen by 139 Sqn, on an operational trial basis. After we used it at Düsseldorf, it was removed from the aircraft; however, it did surface later and was used to good advantage during the Normandy landings. It would have a profound effect on the method and extent of bombing operations from then forward because, as the Army front lines moved eastward, the range of the device was extended by moving the mobile ground stations into Europe.

Again in Nan, our foray (Trip No.22) over enemy territory took us to Karlsruhe April 24/25 in a raid by 637 aircraft. Icing, static electricity, freezing rain and St Elmo's fire were experienced on the way to the target, which was poorly marked, and the raid was not very successful. After flying through those treacherous skies, we were very glad to land after a 6:20 hr flight. The force suffered losses of 19 aircraft, or 3.0%.

On April 26/27 we were briefed for another raid of 493 aircraft on Essen but we had an early return because an engine became unserviceable. We logged 2:36 hrs but it did not count toward tour accomplishment because we did not get to the target. This was the only early return we experienced.

Among the missing on that raid was a fellow squadron navigator, American Lieutenant Shep Shove, from Connecticut, USA who was known from my time at West Freugh and Atherstone. 6,129 Americans had volunteered to join the RCAF before the United States was plunged into war by the Japanese raid on Pearl Harbour December 7, 1941. And they could be found in all trades. There was usually one or two of them at our squadron.

The American Government wished to transfer these men to their national strength, and invited them to do so from about October 1943. The procedure was for the officer or airman involved to join the USAAF, and wear its uniform. Many then went to serve with the 8th Air Force; however, others requested a return to previous employment, and Shep and others at Linton were granted that request.

April 27/28 found us in A-Able going to bomb Freidrichshafen on Trip No.23 in a raid of 322 aircraft. This was our longest operational flight at 8:10 hrs and a round trip of 1,500 miles (2,400 km). No fighters were seen leading up to the target, because of successful diversions, and there was considerable damage done to the target. The enemy fighters caught up with the bombers at the end of the target period, and managed to shoot down several aircraft. We could still see the fires from 200 miles

(320 km) away on our return flight. 18 a/c FTR or 5.6%, involving about 126 aircrew. On May 1, leave was commenced, this time North by train to Edinburgh, where I saw the sights and did tourist things, had a very good rest and enjoyed several superb pub meals.

Leave finished, our next foray (Trip No.24) in Nan took us to bomb the channel gun battery at Merville-Franceville on the Normandy coast May 19/20. This 4:05 hr flight involved 63 aircraft and there were *no* losses. Although there was a lot of haze in the area, we got an unexpectedly good aiming point picture.

Lancaster Mk II, LL722, N-Nan 'Lady be Good'

We suspected now that we were bombing coastal batteries to lessen the opposition to a future invasion fleet, which we thought should be setting sail before too long. We now began to get the feeling that, with luck and the change to French targets, *we might get out of this alive*. Unfortunately, this and later raids were unsuccessful in neutralizing the Merville battery, probably because of the type of concrete construction, and the thick cover over the guns. Merville would get very special treatment on the morning of D-Day when it was attacked by airborne troops, some of whom actually landed, Kamikaze-style, on the roof of the battery itself.

Our Sqn CO, W/C Jacobs, was KIA on a raid to Dortmund on May 22/23, and buried at the Reichwald War Cemetry. He was replaced as CO by W/C A. R. McLernon.

Our Trip No.25 took us to Aachen West, May 24/25 in Nan for a raid by 442 aircraft. During the 4:27 hrs we were airborne on what was a generally quiet trip, we saw many dummy markers as far as 30 miles (50 km) west of the target and were pleased on return, to see that our aiming point picture showed the precise centre of the target. 25 aircraft FTR or 5.7%, including about 175 crew members.

After doing fighter affiliation on May 28, we went on operations for Trip No.26, a raid May 31/June 1 by 129 aircraft against radio installations and masts at Au Fevre on the Normandy coast. There were *no* losses but our aircraft was hit by lightning over England during the return journey, and most of the exterior paint and all the aerials were burnt off. Again we were able to get an excellent aiming point picture and arrived back at base after being airborne for 3:50 hrs. In our minds, it was now certain that the invasion would be soon.

June 2 we flew 1:15 hrs in Nan to do fighter affiliation and landed back at base to learn that Suds had been promoted to F/L, a case of filling a dead man's shoes. He had missed being a F/O, and now outranked me! He and Les had a reputation as the squadron's best engine performance and fuel managers. This was most important because there was not a lot of surplus fuel available, fuel loadings allowed very little leeway. Enviably, aircraft we flew in were able to achieve the greatest altitude among squadron aircraft, and we arrived home first on many occasions but, unlike some crews, not having cut any corners.

Then came D-Day (*Operation Overlord*) and our Trip No.27. We participated in *Flashlamp* on June 6, a predawn multiple-target raid in which 100 bombers attacked each of ten heavy gun batteries along the coast of Normandy. Our target in Nan was the battery at Longues-Caen. We were still busy on the lookout for fighters. Little did we know that the majority of the fighters in Northern France had been moved back into Germany the day before in response to the bombing raids. On the return leg of the trip, all of a sudden, a cry went up, and everyone was talking at once.

To hell with crew discipline, a view of the invasion armada had just appeared through a break in the cloud. Then the cloud thinned out and we saw ships, flying their blimp protection, almost from horizon to horizon, a significant number of the 8,000 ships used on D-Day. It made one wonder how many persons might have seen that marvellous and historic sight from the air? And what they had missed if they weren't there.

Down below, the channel appeared from our height to be calm and blue, but at sea level it was anything but that. It was rough and the Army boys were going through the most difficult and dangerous experience they had yet encountered .... but we were almost at the end of our tour, having gone through very fiery times for six months over Germany, now flying above them in relative comfort, little resistance, reasonable weather and short trips compared to what we had gone through earlier. Otherwise, the raid was uneventful and our crew departed for home. This very quiet trip took 4:40 hrs and there were only three losses in the ten raids involved.

It has been said that if you had to bail out in the English Channel area between England and France, you would land within 300 yards of a ship. You could also, as a result, become involved in what the Army calls a 'shooting war'. I always thought ours had enough shooting in it!

On arrival back at base we hovered around the radio to get the BBC news of how the landings were progressing. Meanwhile, 4,000 landing craft were disgorging troops on the beaches. It had been the greatest assembly of ships for any purpose, and the largest seaborne invasion in the history of mankind. And it was surprisingly successful!

In the evening of D-Day we went back to France on another multiple-target effort, Trip No.28 in Nan to our assigned target, a road junction and aqueduct, south of the invasion front and behind the German lines, at Coutances. There was a total of 1,065 aircraft raiding similar targets. 11 a/c FTR representing 4.5% of the force that flew against that night's varied targets.

After 4:20 hrs flying on another quiet trip, we landed at RAF Long Marston because of an engine and hydraulics failure, then flew back to base the next day. There were 18,000 air force sorties on D-Day. Nan, with us aboard, did two of them.

There are certain days or tumultuous events imbedded indelibly on one's mind, days of great expectations, great joy or heavy sorrow. Declaration of war in 1939, 'VE' Day in 1945 and more recently September 11, 2001 are imprinted on the minds of all who lived through them. Graduations, marriage, a birth or the death of a loved one, are also events that are never forgotten. Such a day was June 6, 1944!!

Three days later, June 9/10 we did our last operational trip (No.29), to Le Mans airfield, behind the German Normandy front, among 401 aircraft on similar targets spread across the area behind the coastal landings. We bombed a row of hangers from 900 ft (274 m). The trip lasted 5:42 hrs and there were two losses from the night's targets.

After all that time .... after dark cold nights in the skies to reach major German cities .... after a tour of operations over Germany and France .... we were going to be cast aside. We band of brothers were informed June 11 that our tour of operations comprising 30 trips for Suds (he had done his 'second dickey' trip at the beginning), and 29 for the rest of us was completed and we would be posted individually to instructional duties. A great sense of relief was felt, but we also knew that the comradeship we had experienced would be deeply missed. We had survived the best the Germans could offer and the drastic losses in Bomber Command over the previous winter. The experience was something you couldn't buy for a million bucks, and you couldn't expect to be offered a penny for it!

Since our arrival at the squadron, very few crews had finished an operational tour; however, several crews now had more than 25 trips completed and would finish shortly. During our tour the crew had experienced all kinds of situations but, fortunately, only slight damage to our aircraft on any one operation. We had participated busily in the Battle of Berlin, the raid on Nuremberg when 96 heavy aircraft were lost, and we were part of the Normandy invasion. Not bad for nine months at Linton-on-Ouse!

A little skill and a lot of luck had got us through. We had successfully spun the wheel of fortune many times and had completed our tour. Believe it or not, we would miss being on Ops, going almost daily from chaos over enemy territory and the mercurial weather, to the relative serenity of the English countryside with its marvellous scenery, the pub culture, the birds in the hedge rows and the companionship of the crew.

The crew at tour's end, left to right, rear: Butcher, Hampson, Claus, Bore and, front: Hobbs, DeMille, Sutherland and Boulton (Hamilton Studio, York)

Some of the memories of the time are: asking how many gallons of petrol were being loaded, in an effort to fathom where the night's trip would take us, saying good-bye to crews as we got off the crew truck to ready for departure, hearing the Master Bomber broadcasting directions at a target, and the emotion we felt when we heard a Canadian voice, even though we would not know whether it was Johnny Fauqier or Reg Lane, both of whom undertook that unenviable job, or someone else.

Upon being screened from operations the crew was granted leave, and took an afternoon train to London .... into V-1s (flying bombs). That night, June 12 the initial buzz bombs arrived. One fell in front of the hotel where I was staying and part of the front wall of my room disappeared. We were not aware that they were anything other than ordinary bombs, but outside early the next morning one went by, under fire from the ground. After observing its unswerving flight for several seconds, I remarked that there didn't appear to be a pilot in it, to which several people in the immediate area looked at me as if I had lost it. One man stated, "You're barmy, myte!"; however, that evening on the BBC it was reported that the bombs were, in fact, pilotless aircraft, V-1s. The enemy hadn't succeeded in killing me on Ops, now it appeared there was an attempt with buzz bombs.

Our crew represented stability, friendship and security in a most uncertain world, and I would miss them deeply. We had the usual mandatory crew picture taken, and took our ground crew boys out to a pub dinner, as a gesture of our extreme thanks for their commitment to our well-being. These were the men who kept Nan serviceable through rain and shine, heat and cold, and carried out repairs when she came back damaged. They were always on hand when we needed them, and spent a lot of time in the cold waiting for us to return. After a rip-roaring time at the pub we bade them farewell, and never saw them again.

At the time we finished operations our aircraft had been on 47 bombing trips, having been used by other crews when we were not on the Battle Order. We were finished, but 'Lady Be Good' flew on with other crews, one of which was that of F/L Bob Clothier, DFC who flew the squadron's 3,000th operational sortie to Stuttgart in Nan July 24/25 while he was on his second tour at 408 Sqn. He went on after the war to become an actor, and played the character 'Relic' in the long-running Canadian Broadcasting Corporation (CBC) TV program, The Beachcombers. Our aircraft was still in existence at the end of the squadron's Lancaster II phase. Her fate is unknown, but ultimately she was scrapped, along with most of the aircraft that had been involved in the war.

Bomber Command losses were heavy, among wartime commands on both sides, U-boat crews were the only ones to suffer higher loss rates. During the war period, 55,573 aircrew were lost (9,919 of them Canadian), in aircraft of all types.

Of those aircrew who formed into crews at OTUs and subsequently went to Bomber Command, 51% were killed on operations, 12% became casualties in the UK, either killed or seriously injured in crashes, 12% became prisoners of war (many of whom were injured), 1% were shot down and evaded capture, and 24% survived the war unharmed, at least unharmed physically.

Interesting stats: 3,431 Lancasters were lost during the war, almost half of those built. The top three German aces who flew against Bomber Command shot down 250 bombers, or about 1,750 personnel, or 12 squadrons. One of them had 123 credits. 408 Sqn flew the most sorties and suffered the most losses (tied with 419 Sqn) in Canadian squadrons. It also suffered most losses and the highest percentage losses in 6 Group Lancaster squadrons. Casualties were so high that, during the six months we were on operations, the squadron lost 34 crews, 170% of its established number of 20 aircraft, replaced with reinforcements almost twice over.

Although we had several rather traumatic events, none of them was of sufficient, or significant, importance to become entries in the Squadron Daily Operations Book. Our tour would have to be described as *routine for the times*. The scary parts would remain in our memories, best described as hours and hours of boredom, broken only by moments of sheer terror.

My total wartime operational flying time was 170 hrs, all night operations in Lancaster IIs. Since joining the RCAF from a flightless youth, I had been airborne only 574 hours.

With our tour of operations completed, the crew was dispersed to various instructor duties except for Clive, the bomb-aimer, who did not want to be an instructor, and clamoured to stay on operations. After some arm-twisting, he was posted to 405 Canadian Pathfinder Sqn. As a senior bomb-aimer, he would be killed, along with his crew, on a night raid against the Deurag refinery at Misberg, Germany March 15/16, 1945. The aircraft and its bomb load were reportedly blown apart as it approached to mark the target. Clive is buried at the Limmer British Cemetry in Hannover, Germany.

My instructor posting was to 1664 Conversion Unit at Dishforth, another permanent station a little further north in the Yorkshire Vales, as a Navigation Ground School instructor and I continued to fly as a navigator in Avro Ansons, Oxfords, Wellington 1Cs, Lancaster 1s, Halifax IIIs and Halifax Vs on non-instructional duties. Activities ranged from trips to London with 6 Gp Communications Flight and aircraft ferrying, to short five minute hops around the Gp from station to station on deliveries of various files and rush packages.

In this new geographic area the pattern of bicycle tours changed again to include Easingwold, Stillington, Boroughbridge, Bishop Monckton and Ripon, all popular places with both staff and students.

Next, Linton-on-Ouse would be host in early August to His Majesty King George VI for an Investiture for RCAF personnel, with Queen Elizabeth and Princess Elizabeth in attendance. DFCs to 408's W/C McLernon and one of the flight commanders, S/L Bill Hale were included in the presentations.

As our Nan would be the aircraft that provided the backdrop for the ceremony, we thought it appropriate that we attend as a crew in conjunction with a period of leave in York. We all stayed at our favourite hotel, the White Horse, and it would be our final assembly as a crew. In 2004 it was pleasing to see Nan as the backdrop in a picture of the investiture ceremony, on the front end paper in Larry Milberry's *Canada's*

Air Force at War and Peace, Volume II.

Suds and I had just been informed that we had been awarded the Distinguished Flying Cross[4]. No reason could be guessed for why we got them, perhaps because we had survived. Investitures would have to wait until they could be arranged later. Mine had been recommended May 16, 1944 after completion of 23 sorties. Suds was recommended at the end of our tour. The only plausible reason for the difference in timing seems to be that the Navigation Leader acted more promptly in sending mine in than Suds' Flight Commander did in sending the papers for his award.

At the entrance to the 408 Sqn Nav Section after the investiture in August 1944, left to right: A/C Slemon, His Majesty King George VI, Her Majesty Queen Elizabeth, A/V/M McEwen, Princess Elizabeth, G/C Annis, A/C Fauquier, the Aide to the King, and A/M Breadner

When I went to London on Christmas leave after promotion to F/L, I learned that most of my friends in the Euston area were killed in the disastrous V-2 missile offensive which had begun in September, and was taking its toll.

Naturally, as instructors preparing navigators for operational duty, our instructional cadre took a deep interest in comings and goings, in target selections, successes and failures. Navigation aids and weather forecasting were much improved as the armies advanced.

During this period, the contentious Bomber Command raid on Dresden was carried out February 13/14, 1945 when the Russians were within 100 miles (160 km) of the city. One faction says the raid was aimed at assisting the Russians, who had clamoured for years for some help in their efforts, by destroying a major transportation centre arrayed against them, and this prevented the Germans from using the city for a last-ditch stand in the area, moving reinforcements to face the successful Russian advance.

The other view, and the one favoured by some politicians, was that it was not needed even though it was well known that Dresden was a manufacturing centre for gun and aircraft components and an important junction, belying that it should have had 'open city' status.

---

4   Particulars of RCAF Honours & Awards may be seen on the Internet at <u>www.airforce.ca</u>

The geography of the area shows that Dresden is in a unique position, the only built up area facing that part of the Russian front. Where else would the Germans have gone to set up a last-ditch operation to attempt to hold the Russians? And, in a last ditch operation, what would have happened to Dresden? Probably the same thing as happened in fact. In total war Commanders are faced with taking action that will forward the cause to a successful conclusion. It appears the raids on Dresden were aimed at pushing the envelope and getting the war over without hordes of Allied casualties.

The official history describes how Churchill took a direct hand in the final planning for *Operation Thunderclap*, a multi-target operation which would include attacks on Dresden. There was political support from other sources but, once the raid took place, Churchill and the others made determined moves to distance themselves from the destruction of Dresden. Whether the city should have been spared can never be proven, but it became a turning point in how history looked at Bomber Command.

There was some, but little, public outcry about area bombing during the war. In other words the politicians, the Cabinet and most of the population saw area bombing as an essential part of winning the war, until it had served its purpose and victory was in sight, then those same individuals acted as though they weren't acquainted with the Chief and crews of Bomber Command. The Command was allowed to become the pariah among the fighting formations of the Allies. It would appear that the government foresaw the possibility of embarrassment, and abandoned those who had worked so hard for it. Thousands of young lads had sacrificed their lives in the Bombing Offensive!

Harris was promoted to Marshal of the Royal Air Force and elevated to Knight Grand Cross of the Order of the Bath as the result of a recommendation by Churchill. He was not granted a peerage; however, that omission was placed at the feet of the incoming government under Clement Atlee. Back as Prime Minister in 1953, Churchill was instrumental in having Harris awarded a baronetcy, *his choice* of taking an award that was lower than the peerage that was offered. Even this was not going to silence those who wished to demonize and degrade him.

Many, including fighter pilots, felt that a special campaign medal should have gone to Bomber Command aircrew. Many of them completed tours and went undecorated other than the medals, such as the Aircrew Europe Star, given automatically to all who did just one operational trip. Such recognition could have been expected, but was not to be!

With both my tenure at Dishforth and another leave in London finished, a move was made March 19 a little further north to RCAF Station Topcliffe, another permanent station, where my posting would be as officer-in-charge of the Navigation

Ground School at 1659 HCU, which flew Halifax IIIs. Instructors with me at the time were F/Ls Art Crain, DFC and Ray Haworth, DFC, F/Os Eugene (Corky) Bannoff, DFC and Ed Gargett, DFC, and F/O Don MacLean, DFM, who had been a navigator with 617 Sqn on the Mohne and Eder Dams raid.

This new area allowed me to add Thirsk, Skipton and a few smaller villages to my bicycle tours, completing a good general knowledge of the Vales area, one which has been remembered nostalgically over the years.

Then came a most welcome day, the day the guns were silenced in Europe, VE-day May 8, 1945. This ended Hitler's War, but left the war in the Far East to be resolved. Street parties soon developed that day throughout England, including the one in York in which I participated, where it seemed everyone in Yorkshire was in attendance. Citizens and service personnel alike rejoiced in having the lights on, no more blackout! It also signified that a bathtub could now be filled above the black line at the 5-inch (12.7-cm) level.

After several years of rationing and austerity, there might soon be oranges, bananas and street maps in the stores, and street signs would be returned to their usual place. When the party ended, there were not many sober people around. There were many hangovers, but most folks viewed them *as the result of their patriotic duty* on the occasion of war's end!

In his last communication to his 'troops', Harris issued a Special Order of the Day on May 10, 1945. It read in part:

> Through those desperate years, undismayed by any odds, undeterred by many casualties, night succeeding night, you fought. The Phalanx of the United Nations.
>
> You fought alone, as the one force then assailing German soil, you fought alone as individuals - isolated in your crew stations by the darkness and the murk, and from all other aircraft in company.
>
> Not for you the hot emulations of high endeavour in the glare and panoply of martial array. Each crew, each one in each crew, fought alone through black nights rent only, mile after continuing mile, by the fiercest barrages ever raised and the instant sally of the searchlights. In each dark minute of those long miles lurked menace. Fog, ice, snow and tempest found you undeterred.
>
> In that loneliness in action lay the final test, the ultimate stretch of staunchness and determination .... (detailed reference to personnel) .... etc.
>
> To all of you I would say how proud I am to have served in Bomber Command for four and a half years and to have been your Commander-in-Chief through more than three years of your Saga.

As time passed and Bomber Command was winding down in England, aircrews were sought for Tiger Force, to fly Lancaster VII then Avro 694 Lincolns in an expanded bombing offensive in the Far East. Having volunteered, I then went to Bournemouth May 18 on my last leave in England, and expected a posting to Tiger Force soon after my return to Topcliffe.

A posting did come through but someone forgot to relay it to me. I should have proceeded to RCAF Station Middleton St. George to fly back to Canada with 419 Sqn June 1. Upon receiving a hurried call from the Station Administration Officer, and being told of the omission, it was too late to fly home. As an alternative the folks in the Movements Section rushed me to Greenock, Scotland by staff car June 5, to catch the *Ile de France* because, as the story went, I was scheduled to be one of the Squadron Navigation Officers in Tiger Force, the reason for rushing me to Greenock, arriving there with little time to spare before sailing down the Firth of Clyde and out into the Atlantic, Canada beckoned.

The passage home was much different than on the way over in 1942, here I was on a troop ship among 10,000 returning veterans, each with limited space; however, the three days at sea was much better than the seventeen days of the previous trip .... and no U-boats! Without a doubt, it was smooth sailing. Fortunate in winning a bottle of rye on board, I was even more fortunate to get a chance to smell the cork. That was my share, a bottle has never been drained faster! Then, almost before we knew it, the time had passed and we were entering Halifax Harbour with a great deal of emotion and fanfare.

I went home for a 30-day debarkation leave. My first activity was directed toward an attempt to resurrect my marriage, but that was unsuccessful, Doris had other ideas and we parted. I agreed to take Rod, and my mother continued to look after him. I was able to renew friendships but, like the son at LeBlanc's store in Memramcook who had joined the Army, many had not yet returned from overseas.

With leave over, I reported for duty at No.664 (RCAF) Wing, RCAF Station Greenwood where Group Captain (G/C) (later LGen) E.M. Reyno, was the station CO. That station would be my home base until October 12.

With the cessation of hostilities in the Far East August 14, and the unconditional surrender of Japan September 2, the guns were silent and the war was over.

An exercise was then undertaken to ferry the 165 Lancaster X aircraft that had returned from England in June, from the Repair Depot at Scoudouc, NB to prairie airfield storage sites in Alberta. Crews were made up of a pilot, flight engineer, navigator and wireless operator. I crewed up with F/L Bob Brodie, DFC, a pilot who had been decorated after his *very first* bomber operation with his crew at 426 Sqn.

September 5 our crew, along with others, was flown from Greenwood in Dakota 969, for the short flight to Scoudouc, and left the next day in Lancaster X, Serial KB978 in a group of 25 aircraft, for Pierce, Alberta via St. Hubert, Quebec and Winnipeg, Manitoba. The trip was done in flights spread over 7 days and 12:50 hrs of flying. From Pierce

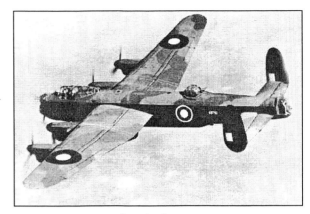

Canadian-built Lancaster X

we were flown to Calgary, Alberta in an overloaded Dakota 571, which hardly got off the ground for the whole flight, then we all went back to Moncton by train, and were flown to Greenwood. Back at Greenwood, it was learned that 408 Sqn[5] had been disbanded, and that there had been a fire in the barrack block in which I lived. My log book was water-damaged and scorched, but it remained salvageable. The contents had to be rewritten to a new book, and both books taken to the station CO for verification. It was not easy to reconstruct some of the pages, but there was sufficient legibility to do it successfully.

September 21 we left Greenwood, again in Dakota 965, picked up Serial KB871 at Scoudouc and departed the next day for Claresholm, Alberta via St. Hubert, Armstrong, Ontario and Gimli, Manitoba; however, we had to lay over in St. Hubert until September 26 due to bad weather. That morning the 25 crews were briefed, 'It has been requested that you reroute over Parliament Hill'. I was designated lead navigator of the gaggle, which was acclaimed by the press at the time for its excellent formation (?) flying (we hadn't even tried anything other than a gaggle).

We showed the roaring strength of the RCAF at the capital city, then went to Armstrong, an abandoned site that had been a Ferry Command refuelling station in a brush clearing beside the CNR tracks in Northern Ontario. There we over-nighted in sleeping bags under the aircraft. First we had experienced the emotion of doing a flying demonstration over the Nation's capital, and then the grim reality of a cool night out in late September.

September 27 we went to Gimli, where we found that Intelligence had been unintelligent, the station had closed the previous week. With all the commotion created

---

5   408 Sqn would rise again post-war in other roles: photo mapping of the North and Northern reconnaissance in Lancaster Xs, Cansos and other aircraft types; Army support in Dakotas, T-33s, C-119 Boxcars and C-130 Hercules, and is now stationed in Edmonton, Alberta, with tactical operations as its current role, using CH-146 helicopters.

by 25 Lancasters in the area, the NCO-in-charge of the site was soon located. He made arrangements for us to eat at downtown restaurants, and found enough beds and bedding for us to stay overnight. September 28 it was back to town for breakfast, then we departed for Claresholm, and delivery of the aircraft. The total time from Scoudouc to Claresholm had been 11:50 hours in four stages over 6 days. Again we were flown to Calgary, this time in Dakota 961, and were granted leave to visit Banff, Alberta.

Conveniently that visit started September 30 and we found that we could get both the September and October liquor rations in one purchase. With plenty of liquor, and beer cooled in the bathtub and the toilet tank, there was quite a party. We also managed to see Banff as tourists, making it a memorable occasion.

Our visit over, we boarded the train for the second trip back East. The first days on board were quiet, but after leaving Winnipeg it was discovered that a passenger car of RCAF Women's Division (WD) personnel had been added to the train, and all hell broke lose. The conductor couldn't keep folks in their proper cars, so the car with the WD contingent was removed overnight at a lonely siding somewhere near the Manitoba-Ontario border. Some arrests were made by the service police, only to be rescinded on arrival at Greenwood.

My wartime flying ended October 12 as it had started .... in an Anson. I was taken in Anson V 12082 to be processed at the RCAF Release Centre at Moncton, NB. On October 13, I was transferred to Class E Reserve effective October 27, 1945 and returned to life as a civilian.

Checking through my log book to write about the operations we were involved in, two great reasons to rejoice came to mind. It was a miracle that we survived our operational tour, and have to credit the changeover in April 1944 from distant German targets to a bombing campaign in France in support of plans for the invasion of Normandy. That enterprise was much less risky because of the shorter distances involved, and the less intense defences. Crews lost during that period would not agree: if a crew went down, their particular risk had been all-embracing. The other miracle is that my log book survived the fire at Greenwood.

Our Ground Crew

Here's to the men with greasy hand
Who fuel our planes when we come in to land
Who fix the canopies, stop the leaks
Change the tires and oil the squeaks
Tend to the rigging to make them fly straight
Wait for the planes when the pilots are late
Who smooth the scratches, rivet the panels
Check "Loud and Clear" on the radio channels
Who read all the write-ups and make the repairs
Check lines and wires for chafing and tears
Who pull the chocks and work the wings
And do a million other things
That make an aircraft safe to fly.
So here's a salute to the hard-working guys
From a group of fliers who too seldom ponder
The men who keep us up in the wild blue yonder.

- Anonymous

11

SUMMARY AND CONTROVERSY

the aftermath of war and 'The Valour & the Horror' furor

A lot of returning veterans had trouble adapting to civilian life but, other than realizing that reality had to be faced and it was necessary to go back to work, there was little difficulty for me. I had the advantage of having worked before going to war where many had not, and knew what to expect. The old home town seemed the same, its inhabitants had not changed much either. The universe was unfolding as it should. So, it was back to pounding nails as a carpenter! There were days though, when, with everything similar to what it was before the war .... it was difficult to believe what was known to be true, *that my part in the war had really happened!*

After the Battle of Britain in September 1940, Winston Churchill had said:

> *The Navy can lose us the war, but only the RAF can win it. Therefore our supreme effort must be to gain overwhelming mastery of the air. The fighters are our salvation but the bombers alone provide the means of victory.*

There is little doubt that air power was an overwhelming factor in the outcome of the war, and that Bomber Command was a major participant in creating the situation that would allow the war to be won, but its power grew from a slow start and its growth of strength had many ups and downs.

With a truly focussed bomber offensive and Lancaster manufacturing given the highest priority throughout, Churchill's statement might have been achievable, but other things were also important, and had to be dealt with. With less diversions of effort and better navigation aids, it might have come true, ... but it didn't!

Night bombing as practised by Bomber Command in WWII had never been used before, independent of army and naval forces, to conduct a prolonged and concerted campaign. It was inevitable that problems would arise because the campaign was without precedent, tactics were being developed as the need arose, without adequate navigation systems, and with inadequate weather information. The long and expensive bombing campaign started with an ineffective force at war's beginning, but grew steadily toward maturity leading up to the time our crew was involved.

As Winston Churchill wrote to Air Chief Marshal Harris at the end of the war:

All your operations were planned with great care and skill. They were executed in the face of desperate opposition and appalling hazards, they made a decisive contribution to Germany's final defeat. The conduct of the operations demonstrated the fiery gallant spirit which animated your aircrews, and the high sense of duty of all ranks under your command. I believe that the massive achievements of Bomber Command will long be remembered as an example of duty nobly done.

The official history of the Bomber Offensive describing the battle status with regard to hazards involved, stated:

Outpaced, out-manoeuvred and outgunned by the German fighters and in a generally highly inflammable and explosive condition, these black monsters presented an ideal target.

It was apparent that the existing technology of navigation was out-stripped by the need for precise positioning, and this would keep Bomber Command from being as effective as it should have been throughout most of the campaign, something that was never satisfactorily overcome, even though additional aids were arriving in the latter part of the war.

By the standards at that time cities where armaments were manufactured and the citizens who worked in the plants became targets subject to 'area' or 'carpet' bombing, legitimate or otherwise, because navigation aids had not yet been developed to adequately pinpoint targets that existed within them, and military goals could not be achieved otherwise. On the French targets generally, Bomber Harris was surprised that the Pathfinders could mark with pinpoint accuracy, and that the main force could get such concentration of effect. This was where the bulk of navigation aids could be effectively used ...... on short trips within range.

As historian Professor Terry Copp wrote in general terms about the war, in Legion magazine of February 2004:

WWII engulfed the world in violence on an unprecedented scale. There has never been another conflict which has involved so many different parts of the world or brought so much suffering and death. The people who went to war against Hitler's Germany were involved in a crusade to destroy a force of such great evil that there was no solution other than total victory. They went to war with a sense of indignation and resignation. It was a decision taken reluctantly and with a feeling of horror, but a decision which most people felt necessary. Hitler gave them no choice.

So the European part of WWII was over! It was a lengthy series of strategies and campaigns, and it was the age of the largest of air armadas. In the final analysis, several factors appear as milestones that allowed the Allies to win in Europe:

a) The outcome of the Battle of Britain in favour of Fighter Command, and the destruction of the assembled invasion barges along the enemy coast by Bomber Command, enabled Britain to survive and become the springboard for the invasion and liberation of Europe.

b) The enemy was unsuccessful in closing the sea lanes between America and Britain because of the interdiction of enemy U-boats and surface vessels at sea by Navy and Air Force resources. Other actions included Bomber Command attacking U-boat lairs and manufacturing sites, and mining coastal traffic and U-boat transit routes. Bomber Command also sank 7 out of 15 major German warships.

c) The ability of industry, in large part American, to manufacture and provide abounding amounts of munitions and supplies.

d) A unique role was played by Bomber Command in undermining the enemy's ability to continue pursuing total war, the only Allied force able to take concerted action to the heart of Germany. It tied down almost a million German personnel in manpower for air defence and firefighting, and over a million for bomb damage repairs, denying these assets of 2 million personnel for use in other endeavours, including munitions manufacture and the Russian campaigns. It was the forerunner to overcoming the Axis domination of Europe.

e) Bomber Command provided 'on-call' support for ground troops when difficult obstacles were encountered. These are examples of the way in which the Armies were moved forward with greatly reduced casualties from what would otherwise have been expected:

i) Bombing in the area of Caen during the prolonged stalemate helped clear it as an obstacle earlier than would otherwise have been possible;

ii) By countering stubborn resistance in front of Le Havre, bombing enabled access to the first channel port through which to move supplies with far less casualties on the ground than expected;

iii) Bombing cut all supply lines to bring German armour to a halt in the Ardennes Battle of the Bulge;

iv) The bombing at the Rhine crossing enabled passage into Germany with just 36 casualties; and

v) at one time in September 1944, with greatly extended supply lines, and less and less supplies, the ground forces were reinforced in their advance with the delivery by Bomber Command of 325,000 gallons (1,230,260 litres) of gasoline in jerry cans, even though the aircraft delivering it consumed almost that much in making the delivery.

When the Allied armies were established in Normandy after D-Day, German Field Marshal Rommel said, "Stop the bombers or we can't win!" Without the persistent attacks of the bombing offensive, and the resultant sapping of German strength, could D-Day have ever taken place, or been successful? In other words, could Germany have been beaten? Few people nowadays have any idea of the work done by Bomber Command, other than the well-advertised bombing of German cities.

There have always been those who would rewrite history. In our case it was the McKenna Brothers and the CBC. The accuracy and intent of the Nuremberg Raid segment *Death by Moonlight* in the highly controversial TV series *The Valour and the Horror,* first shown in 1992, was a subject which many Bomber Command veterans were incensed about. I entered the resulting uproar through an invitation to speak at Heritage Renfrew January 26, 1993. That group in Renfrew, Ontario, mostly non-veterans, recognized the problems with the so-called documentary very early on, and wished to counteract the misrepresentations.

The production purported to be a factual demonstration of the horrors of war, and a tribute to aircrews. It certainly turned out to be a horror in itself, revisionist history by individuals who have suffered little hardship. Although their difficulty in looking at the realities of war is understood, ... it is more difficult to condone their twisted assessment of what they encountered. It is not possible, even being most generous, to see other than deliberate misstatement of the facts available from their own research, and the result was a polemic of their choosing, using a lot of half-truths and innuendo which ignored that we had been involved in 'total war' at a time which was not that of today!

Generally speaking my comments in the presentation attempted to show why the production was flawed for the following reasons:

a) The main character, A/C/M Harris, was portrayed by an actor with no likeness to him whatsoever, in demeanour, personality or manner.

b) The bombing policies were described as attributable to Harris. He did not set bombing policy. It was established by the War Cabinet, although he did interpret his orders somewhat liberally on occasion. The lead-up to area bombing as a policy was gradual. Germany was under the Nazi party in a totalitarian police state. In everyday living, and then when it started out on conquest, it used codes of practice which were brutal and inhumane. It did not recognize International principles of war, dive bombing civilians in Poland from the beginning. Any country which was targeted, including England, could not afford to use conventional strategies, or it would vanish into the area of German control. The British Government was slow to recognize the danger of playing entirely by the old rules, but it eventually approved the area bombing policy, after prolonged hesitance and much reluctance. Inevitably though, there were those who opposed the policy, no matter what the outcome might have been.

c) To accuse that losses were hidden it had to be assumed aircrew were either stupid or ignorant, or both. It was well-known that losses were broadcast on the BBC nightly, and crews themselves could gauge what was going on from their front row seats. They could figure the odds of survival, and discussed the subject often.

d) The statement that civilians were purposely being killed is off the mark. Today we would wonder why, but to judge the situation in WWII, you have to think in a WWII context, and understand the factors leading to decisions in those times. Civilians have been killed in all wars, a case of being in the wrong place at the wrong time. The charge should have been against the Germans for starting a war without plans to evacuate young mothers and children to safety. Evacuation from the cities had been voluntary, and it was not until August 1943, after the Hamburg raids, that young mothers and children in Berlin were directed by Goebbels to evacuate to the country. By mid-September 1.5 million of the population of Berlin had departed. And we have to remember, of course, we are not talking about wars of the 18th and 19th centuries where men only were involved. Men and women working in industrial factories supporting a war effort became legitimate targets, and

e) There were factual errors throughout the film, even the name of our bomber base was given incorrectly.

The production did not reflect the relevant available research, such as that of British author Martin Middlebrook in his 1973 book, *The Nuremberg Raid*, which is considered to be the definitive and detailed work on the subject. His research in both

British and German archives was extensive and meticulous. He interviewed or corresponded with many of the senior officers who planned the raid, as well as many who were personally involved and 379 other RAF and RCAF aircrew (including me) on the British side and, on the German side, Luftwaffe aircrew and German civilians from the area.

The film also made much ado about the 'Lack of Moral Fibre' (LMF) designation. Most of the aircrew personnel were in a suspended state of 'controlled fear' throughout their operational tours. The LMF phenomenon appears mainly to have occurred in crews that did not have a good sense of togetherness, and was very hard on the individuals involved. It goes without saying that these crews were also dangerously susceptible to joining the list of losses.

The thin line between the quick and the dead was never so slim. Crew members knew it! Most could take it, a few others were unable to see a future and went to pieces. Inevitably, some of them found it impossible to continue and gave up, then were classified LMF.

The LMF condition appears to be hauntingly similar to the Post Traumatic Stress Disorder (PTSD) suffered by today's military, a condition brought on by severe stresses in a person's life, just the sort of thing our boys who went LMF suffered. Some persons have more resistance to dangerous stresses than others, but when it is all used up it is gone! They are the ones who find they cannot continue to face repetitious events of a dangerous nature. A critical survival mechanism, it is just as real as any accident. Those who suffer it take time to heal, and would seem to be better off referred to a specialist in 'severe chronic pain' rather than a psychologist or psychiatrist. Both LMF and PTSD can be likened to the 'shell shock' of WWI and 'combat fatigue' in WWII.

Now look at this situation with regard to all bomber crews .... with a little analogy. There were some crews made up entirely of teenagers. Others were not much older. So picture seven teenagers in the family car going for a joyride, but picture those same guys in a bomber on serious business .... more than 500 miles (800 km) from home. Will they act responsibly? ...... while being shot at? .... will they press on to the target? .... will they drop their bombs and turn tail? .... will they alter course to port and go to a neutral country? Sweden .... or go starboard to Switzerland, only a few minutes from Friedrichshafen, one of our targets.

Aircrews were on much longer leashes than Army and Navy personnel, in fact, no leashes at all, other than their conscience and the threat of the LMF designation, which would have seen them dishonourably discharged in many cases. *Honour* and *Dishonour* struck strong feelings in those whose convictions had led them to volunteer.

So, consciously or not, is it possible that the concept was used to keep us on the straight and narrow .... to strengthen the leash, no matter how ancient and barbaric the concept.

Our superiors appear to have thought that a 'dishonourable' situation, stronger than some of the realities we faced on operations, was needed so that we would not be as prone to giving up. Hardly a modern psychological approach .... but one that had been used for centuries in the management of soldiers and sailors. What was done in Bomber Command appeared to me to be a much enlightened approach in comparison to what is reputed to have happened in some Army units and Navy ships during World War II.

Our commanders were following tradition, and probably improved on it somewhat. Hardly justification for condemning them, they were not operating in today's conditions as the *Death by Moonlight* producers were. Lacking modern medical practices, what other course of action was available to them?

These days anyone who experiences the slightest trauma receives counselling, even high school students who get drunk at a party have been included. We had to get back into the air when directed, although some would take the opportunity to speak with a padre. Otherwise, counselling was not widely available in WWII, we either overcame any problems we had, or became LMF. In view of the stresses involved it appears a real miracle that only *zero point four percent (0.4%)* or less of aircrew at Bomber Command units (OTUs, HCUs and Sqns) broke under the strain.

Newspaper reports of the presentation at Renfrew brought a deluge of support from people in all walks of life throughout Eastern Ontario, mostly supporting my contention that the CBC should be sued for abdicating its responsibility to monitor production, and offering donations for that cause.

After the support shown, my position had to be reviewed. My location in a small village, Clayton, Ontario far from the mainstream was a problem, and my other activities precluded time to do the subject justice. A group in Toronto included capable ex-aircrew men with access to much more administrative and legal support than I could muster. Accordingly, it was decided to support rather than lead. The Toronto group formed the Bomber Harris Trust and commenced a class action suit.

Meanwhile hearings in the Senate of Canada corroborated that the production was flawed, as did the CBC Ombudsman in a highly critical report. Testimony came out that the CBC includes a standard 'boilerplate' clause in its contracts giving it 'right of approval' at every step in production. Therefore, the CBC was responsible for the content as released and screened. In other words the CBC's own regulations showed that the buck stopped there! It is clear that the CBC's responsibilities were not met, and its officers have shown an arrogant and cavalier attitude in the aftermath of the complaints.

Then there is the clamour by the McKenna's, the producers, that the film is true and definitive history. It seems ridiculous to even think of the film in that light, they complain too strongly in view of the evidence.

It was advanced that veterans wanted to censor the film, but that was not the case, and the Senate hearings verified that it had not been our intent. What we asked for and wanted, was merely that there should be more truth and *some semblance of balance* in the presentation.

Eventually, the courts did not allow the class action to proceed. This meant that the courts had not deliberated on the situation, not that the veterans had lost! In a letter to Barney Danson who had been a Minister of National Defence, Patrick Watson, CBC Chairman stated:

> *Should substantial historical inaccuracies be revealed by any of these processes, we have undertaken to take substantial corrective measures on air.*

Substantial inaccuracies were revealed by the Senate committee, by veterans who had been on the raid, and by the CBC's own ombudsman. So what was the CBC reaction .... to show it again. And where did the inspiration for that come from? In the opinion of many, it was a 'stick-it-up-your' approach which was even more insulting to veterans than the film itself. It would appear that the CBC learned nothing from the experience.

Ultimately, the only satisfaction for veterans is that those who hold opinions contrary to what really happened are free to broadcast them. And the war having been won, they are able to do it in English.

They don't seem to realize that our contemporaries *lost their lives to make this possible,* and that better interpretation of historical events is required. Heirs should be able to receive historically correct and unbiased information on what their forebears experienced in war, not someone's search for a sensational statement. Dazzling re-writing of history is not excusable!

Nevertheless, in spite of all the naysayers, RAF Bomber Command was a crucial part of victory in WWII, and I am distinctly proud to have been one of its RCAF members.

12

OUR CONSTRUCTION COMPANY
1945-51

in which construction and other activities are outlined

While Charles and I were overseas, Dad had built a carpenter shop in Sackville and there was sufficient acreage for expansion. While this was going on, he was also in the early stages of building a house nearby, and selling the family home in Middle Sackville. When that was sold in 1944, the purchaser insisted on early occupancy, so several blankets were suspended at the shop to make rooms in one corner and the family moved in for a short period, during which sister Evelyn, then aged 14, says she didn't advertise where she lived. They soon moved into the partly-completed house, which was finished while occupied.

When we returned from overseas, brother Charles and I entered into partnership with Dad, as *A. F. Butcher & Sons, Contractors and Builders.* Perhaps university should have been considered then but, having made the decision, I was doomed 'to know a little bit about a lot of things, not much about anything', a real alumnus of the School of Hard Knocks.

My RCAF reestablishment credit was used to purchase a six-inch jointer for the firm, since then it has trimmed one side of my left thumb and the face of my right one. Even though it went through the fire in Sackville, Charles would bring it to Ontario with him on a visit in 1978, and I would still be using it until moving to BC in 2001!!

My working contribution to the partnership was supposed to be as the General Manager/Administrator, with a second commitment to provide the architectural, drafting and estimating input. To this end an International Correspondence School course in Architecture was pursued for three years. It was also recognized that I would work as a carpenter on occasion, if necessary.

We equipped the shop with a modern moulding machine, powered by a Cummins marine diesel engine. The engine also ran all the smaller items on an axle-and-pulley system: vertical band re-saw, jointer, cut-off saws, sanders, band saw, and a blower to eject sawdust and shavings into an exterior elevated tower, where trucks drove underneath to be loaded by gravity, for disposal of the accumulation.

On the general contracting side, we operated in Sackville and the surrounding area, doing contracts for the Enterprise Foundry Company, Enamel & Heating Products Ltd, the CBC Sackville Overseas Service, the Tribune Publishing Company Ltd, Mt A, the Town of Sackville, and others. We also did house building in Sackville and in the area as far east as Cape Tormentine, NB.

We sold most items in the lumber and building supply specialties, buying what we could not manufacture from supply warehouses in either Moncton, NB, Amherst, NS, or Montreal, Quebec. Equipped to finish rough dimension lumber and make mouldings, we bought the green newly-sawn lumber, mainly spruce, fir and pine, from local sawmills and stacked it to air-dry for a year or more before using it to make the finished products.

The earlier connection with Pittsburgh Glass & Paint Company Inc, was expanded, and our company became its Maritime provinces representative. I attended an introductory course at the Montreal branch office to acquaint with price and measurement estimating for work in their specialties, which for us was mainly glass store and theatre fronts in the Maritimes: Sackville, Moncton, Saint John, Newcastle and Campbellton, NB; Charlottetown and Summerside, PEI; and Sydney, Halifax, Amherst and Truro, NS. All cut, polished and edge-ground glass ready for installation had to be prepared and shipped in from Montreal. This made it essential that installation drawings be precise, Montreal was distant in those days for the correction of any errors.

Another facet of glass work was the replacement of plate glass windows anywhere in the Maritimes. A typical job would see a tradesman go by truck to a location, pick up a crew, and do the installation. On one occasion it was my turn, when a relatively large window had to be replaced in a hardware store in Lunenburg, NS. The glass, based on measurements provided by the store, had been shipped from Montreal boxed and upright on a railway flat car. As usual, a crew was rounded up and there was surprise to find that a team of oxen would be the motive power to take the glass to the store.

Then it was found to be 3 ins (7.6 cm) too wide for the opening. It had to be cut, and the lay of land was not suitable for cutting it on the ground. The temporary crew was so afraid of handling glass that it took some time to convince them it was safe. The upshot was that I had to be very rough with the glass to convince them that it would not shatter in their hands, and it was then cut while standing vertically.

On another occasion I was faced with replacing a curved plate glass in the entranceway at one of the Eastern Electric Company's sales offices. It was to fit a 90-degree arc. Again the size was wrong. The piece to be cut off was less than one half inch (1.2

cm), and it obviously had to be cut in the upright position because it was curved. The attempt was successful, but I never wanted to work with another curved glass panel, it was much too nerve-wracking.

As time progressed it was found necessary in 1947 to build a 2-storey addition across the front of the shop, the first storey for finished lumber, plywood and moulding storage, the second storey a new carpenter shop. Then, in 1948 an office and draughting room extension was built on one side of the still so-called *shop*, even though it had outgrown that term many months before. These additions made it much easier to work with our building supply customers, which included professors at Mt A. The advice they needed for their do-it-yourself projects was varied and interesting.

There was an extreme shortage of cement in the Maritimes in 1948-49. It became necessary to import from the USA, for our own use and for sale. It was bought in Calais, Maine for about what the normal wholesale price would be landed in Sackville, so it was an expensive commodity by the time it arrived at home. To transfer to us one level of profit in the cost, we decided to haul it ourselves in the 1948 Chevy 3-ton hybrid dump/platform truck. Usually a trip was made each week, leaving before dawn on the 200 mile (320 km) outgoing trip, picking up the load at about noon, and returning home to arrive sometime in the late evening. Three of us took our turns on what was a tiring day.

Doris and I had separated in 1945. The divorce, which had been applied for later, became final in 1948. That year the Royal Canadian Air Force Association (RCAFA) was formed, and an application submitted for membership resulted in me becoming one of its original life members.

Then life improved considerably with my marriage August 11,1949, to Bernice (Bunny) Gould, the daughter of Thaddeus (Taddy) and Angela Gould, from an Acadian French family. Both she and her sister, Doreen, had been at school with me in earlier years. I was now able to establish a home of my own. We each brought a son, Don and Rod, into the family from our previous marriages.

Our new home was the first three-bedroom house, priced at $4,000, that was ready for sale in a subdivision our company was building in Sackville. Then our family increased to three children with the birth of our daughter Brenda, December 28, 1950. She was a little late as a Christmas present, *but a most welcome gift nonetheless*, as she rounded out our intended family, one of Bunny's, one of mine and one of ours.

An interesting sideline in our business was wood and coal sales. This was still the era of wood stoves in kitchens, and furnaces using coal or hardwood for space heating. We established contacts in the Joggins/River Hebert/Minudie area of Nova Scotia as the source of dried hardwood cut to furnace length, and obtained coal from bootleg coal mines in the same area. These products were picked up and delivered direct to customers, precluding any holding of inventory.

We had a crew working on small 'labour and materials' jobs at the Enterprise Foundry and Enamel & Heating most of the time, and there was occasionally larger contract work underway at one or the other. At Enterprise we built a stove assembly plant, while at Enamel & Heating there were many, one associated with a major expansion and the use of fork lifts in the plant. All covered alleyway connections between buildings had to be enlarged to accommodate the fork lifts, an issue stores and a forklift recharging garage was constructed, also two warehouses, one for finished products and the other for raw materials.

At Mt A, our major project was to build basement class rooms under the Owens Art Gallery, which had originally opened in 1895. A one-storey stone building, it had a 3-ft (1-m) crawlspace, and there was no surrounding acreage on which to expand. An innovative process was needed to create the 9-foot high additional space. After excavating a small cube of earth by hand, a gas-powered conveyor belt was built to reach from the newly excavated space to load trucks. The remaining earth was also excavated manually using picks, shovels and wheelbarrows, and moved to the belt, then to trucks for disposal. As each 12-ft (3.66-m) length of excavation along the wall was completed a wooden form was moved progressively, section by section, and filled with concrete to form the basement wall and stabilize the existing building foundation. A concrete floor and finished walls to create rooms completed the project.

The water supply for Sackville was located at the height of land at the Walker Road on Beech Hill. Its shallow wells provided questionable continuity. The system was changed to artesian wells and we contracted to build access roads to the wells, and well-houses. Because the fill for the roads was to come from excavated material removed to level the building sites around the wells, it was necessary to tow the trucks into the location with a bulldozer and work our way out, building the road as we went, until the existing road network was reached.

We did not have front-end loaders for loading, so had to push the excavated soil over a sluiceway tied with mooring cables and covered with soil. A bulldozer would not dislodge such a sluiceway, and could push excavated soil out onto a truck below, while another bulldozer replenished the pile at right angles.

There were problems with trucks getting stuck in soft soil as the roadways were built, but the overall project was completed in the required time. That then-isolated spot is now within shouting distance of the Trans Canada Highway, built several years later.

For a short period each Spring, as frost was coming out of the ground, we could not do in-ground construction and all large trucks were off the road due to weight restrictions. Owners with 1-ton trucks used them to haul commodities for others, on runs from Saint John, NB and Halifax, NS. Ours joined them in this annual venture. I did one of the trips to Saint John and the load was cartons of molasses in quart containers from the Crosby Molasses Co, an ironic harking back to my two previous experiences with puncheons of the stuff.

Snow was another late spring problem. One late April morning, we arrived at work to find that six units of 1-ton 'cab and chassis' trucks from Lounsbury's, the local Chevy dealer, which were at the shop for installation of wood-stake truck bodies, had disappeared. They were soon found under a deep cover of snow deposited overnight by a late-spring blizzard.

With all of our extra activities, space was again at a premium at the shop site so, in 1949, a head-office cum hardware store was established in rented quarters at the Cole Block on Main Street, enabling service to walk-in hardware and paint customers. Other orders were also taken there for later delivery.

I had been working a lot of overtime when I was called to Moncton in 1949, to be invested with the DFC (awarded in 1944) by the Hon D.L. Mac Laren, Lieutenant-Governor of New Brunswick. When I got the picture of the investiture, I was alarmed at my appearance, looking like something the cat dragged in. I must have been almost down to my weight as a teenager. It wasn't New Years, but I made a resolution to look after myself, including 'no over-time'. This decision did not sit well with Dad, but I stuck to it, and immediately saw an improvement in weight and energy.

In the fall of 1950, I was deeply disenchanted and considering a move to something that would enable me to be more my own boss. My partners viewed management of the business as something you did after normal working hours, not as a job in itself. With the size to which the company had grown, not only was a full-time general manager required, but also an office manager, who would also tend the building supply customers. We had been getting by using the stenographer in that capacity, but that position was also overloaded. After many arguments I asked if they really expected the partnership to support four families if we did not ensure more growth and good management (brother Albert was now planning to join us). Overall, it was obvious that something had to be done, the full potential of the company would not be realized unless the management requirements were met.

Having failed in my effort to get the management problem solved, the next step was to investigate businesses available for purchase in similar endeavours in other areas.

The first attractive prospect was a lumber and building supply firm in London, Ontario. I knew the owner from my time in the craft shop while at AOS. Its location was perfect, and its market was under-served. The owner said he wished to retire, while retaining 50% ownership. This suited me, because I would have to finance a substantial part of my investment. All the arrangements were made, financial backing obtained, and I travelled to London to sign the documents, only to find that the owner had made a last minute decision not to retire, and the deal fell through.

The Airmen's Prayer

Pilot divine, and Lord of all on high,
Thine are the starry squadrons of the sky.
Lead us whose wings for freedom's sake now soar,
Into our hearts thy faith and courage pour- -
Oh hear our prayer.
Set thou our course, whose trust is laid on thee,
Oh thou who chartest all eternity.
Through cloud and sunshine, through the darkest night,
Guide thou our wings who battle for the right —
Oh hear our prayer.
Father and friend, in whose almighty name
We dedicate our lives to freedom's flame,
Bless now our wings as on through space we wend,
Bless us who thy call commend - -
Oh hear our prayer.

-Wing Commander G. L. Creed
Royal Canadian Air Force

13

BACK IN THE AIR FORCE
1951-1952

which covers employment at RCAF Summerside and Air Force Headquarters, Ottawa

During the war the RCAF contained 78 squadrons; however, with the end of hostilities it very shortly withered to just five squadrons. It wasn't long before events in Korea, and other factors, made it necessary to greatly enlarge RCAF operational resources. By 1951, there was an immense program involving many projects to upgrade the infrastructure, to enable the force to meet its expanded roles.

Our firm had done building upgrading and extension contracts for Fred Johns, OBE, ED, BSc, in his position as President and General Manager of the Tribune Publishing Company in Sackville. A member of the RCAF construction branch during WWII, he was now back in the air force as Chief of Construction Engineering (CCE) with the rank of Air Commodore (A/C). His branch was in charge of the infrastructure expansion program and, because of the extraordinary workload, had a very limiting shortage of construction engineering (CE) officers. When he phoned in January 1951 to invite me to rejoin the RCAF in the CE Branch I agreed but, because I did not have an engineering degree, it was recognised I could not join the branch as a 'direct entry' officer. Having been a navigator, it was possible to rejoin in that classification, and Johns would make arrangements for the transfer between branches.

Accordingly, it was necessary to go through the enlistment process as had been done in 1942. Accepted as an air navigator with the rank of F/O and a new number ...... 36171, I was posted to the Air Navigation School (ANS) at RCAF Station, Summerside, PEI March 1, 1951 for attendance at a refresher course for 'retread' navigators preparing for enrolment in the one-year Staff Navigation Instructor Navigator (SNIN) Course. Ground school was attended and 16 hours were flown in DC3 Dakotas on air navigation exercises and a sea search until May 10, when my reassignment to the CE branch became effective.

With the branch transfer, a posting to Air Force Headquarters (AFHQ) in Ottawa was received, effective June 1, 1951. In the meantime, there was a move to the station CE Section for employment as an Assistant to the Station Construction Engineering Officer (SCEO).

In that position I was involved, among other duties, in supervising renovation of the station recreation building, a well-built wartime structure, which would be used as the new Station Theatre. Faced with the need for a sloping floor, a chain saw was used to cut around three sides of the floor, and it was jacked into place and stabilized. This resulted in a significantly lower cost than if the floor had been removed and replaced.

On arrival in Ottawa in June it was learned that, although the Headquarters (HQ) of the CE Branch was located in Temporary Building B in cental Ottawa, it would soon be moving to an H-shaped complex of Armco Steelox buildings under construction on Victoria Island in the Ottawa River. Accordingly, arrangements were made for living accommodation for my family on Mountain Road (Chemin de Montagne) in Hull, Quebec within easy commuting distance of the new work location.

At the officer level, the branch included a few personnel who were remnants of the wartime CE strength, but the majority were recent graduates who had gone to university using their reestablishment credits at the end of WWII. There was a lack of experience at the lower officer levels, and the recruitment of several persons from industry was intended to improve that situation.

The role of the branch was the purchase, management and sale of real property; the construction, maintenance, reconstruction, alterations, rehabilitation and administration of buildings and facilities on RCAF property, and fire prevention and firefighting. Field officers in the branch were often faced with problems that required solutions not usually found in day-to-day realty management.

The enormous effort underway at HQ utilized civilian architectural firms, but most of the copying of plans and specifications for tender calls was done in Ottawa, and they were bundled there for distribution. The plan room ran shifts on a 24/7 basis and it was not surprising on weekends to find everyone, including the Chief and other senior officers, sitting around a giant turntable assembling specifications.

Ozalid drawings were being printed in the same large room and there was inadequate ventilation. Of course, the room reeked of chemicals, and the smell was almost unbearable, but we all survived.

Generally my initial employment encompassed writing amendments to general specifications to adapt standard building plans to specific sites. Amendment directions such as, 'Notwithstanding the instructions in the specifications, this amendment shall govern the cladding to be used' were established.

It was during this period that laughable surprises showed up in texts which had not been fully edited (words in italics have been added in each instance):

★ From a draft Organization Order -The RCAF will be responsible for maintenance as follows (a) All airfield pavements and airfield lighting. (b) The RCAF will provide specialist supervision of maintenance works, design and other related garbage (*matters*),......etc.

★ From an AFHQ Specification - All electrical apparatus shall be grounded to (*in accordance with*) the latest edition of the Canadian Electrical Code.

★ From RCAF General Specification #1 1951 Sec 1 (b) para 2, Interpretation - The drawings and specifications are complementary to each other and what is called for by either shall be as blinding (*binding*) as if called for by both'.

Next was involvement in the Armco Steelox Building program. These prefabricated buildings were being used in large numbers for all sorts of purposes. After a short introduction at the Armco Canada plant in Guelph, Ontario, I was treated as somewhat of an expert on their construction and use, but without much justification.

To augment income, a moonlighting job was taken selling Frost residential fences, utilizing referrals provided by the Frost Fence area office. Robert Campeau, Ottawa's predominant house builder, was talked into including a Frost leaflet in my name in each of his 'new owner' packages and this produced several customers. This left as my only duty the layout and measuring of fences, submission of orders to the area office, and collecting commissions. Over the years since then I have had military people think they recognize me from somewhere, we go through all the possible military locations and end up agreeing that they bought a Frost fence from me in the Ottawa/ Hull area, without realizing they were dealing with a member of the RCAF.

It was a very interesting period, but it was going to become even more so. With the buildup of fighter squadrons in 1 Canadian Air Division (Air Div) in Europe, an Air Materiel Base (AMB) in a nearby location was essential. A/C Harle Long took over as CCE and A/C Johns, was appointed as a special consultant, to supervise the development of a Base in England, and the four RCAF stations in France and Germany, already under construction (he would later be seconded to the Deputy Minister's Office, Department of National Defence (DND) as Assistant Deputy Minister, Construction and Properties, and promoted to A/V/M).

Arrangements were under way to have a wartime RAF station at Langar airfield transferred to the RCAF to be the site for 30 AMB. It was located between the villages of Langar and Harby, on the border between Leicestershire and Nottinghamshire, England, near the town of Melton Mowbray.

In the process of preparing the site for its new role, which was expected to commence as early as 1952, I was tasked by Johns in July 1951 to go there on short notice to walk the site, and determine which existing buildings could be used. Alterations and renovations needed for the selected buildings were to be assessed. Plans would be developed for additional new domestic accommodation, and for the wide-span prefabricated steel buildings which would be needed as supply warehouses.

A briefing was given to me by Supply Branch officers concerning their requirements for the site, and it was intended that my stay in England would be of three weeks duration; however, the CL-2 North Star which was taking me over as a passenger suffered a three-day weather delay at Reykjavik, Iceland. Already the time available had been cut by 15% and I hadn't even arrived. It was obvious that overtime would be required, and shortcuts would be necessary. Once in London, it was found that some of the papers which had been given me at the last moment were classified *Secret*, and I had not been 'security-cleared', someone had overlooked that little consideration.

Upon arrival in Melton Mowbray, a hotel was selected as my headquarters. I commuted daily to the site by taxi, after buying a pair of high rubber boots. Prepared lunches were taken with me daily, each containing a famous Melton Mowbray pot pie, a slab of Stilton cheese and a bottle of milk.

The RAF Langar site had been abandoned when WWII ended in 1945. Little is known about its past, but 207 Sqn was there with Lancasters in 1942, and an Avro plant located there refurbished 322 Lancasters during 1942-54. The only activity when I visited in 1951 was the Avro plant on the far side of the field from the old RAF station area.

There were premonitions about what might be found behind some of the doors being opened as I tramped around in the long grass. The buildings were found to be in reasonable condition, certainly much better at that time than a 1980 picture of the Langar wartime aircraft hangar seen in a recent RAF Association newsletter.

First, an interview with Mr. Octavius Atkinson, owner of Atkinson Buildings LLC in Nottingham, provided the measurements and pricing necessary for the wide-span buildings. Armco Steelox buildings would be used for the forklift recharging garage and for domestic needs. Atkinson also provided excellent advice on construction business practices in England.

Secondly, relevant measurements were taken, and decisions made regarding what renovations and additions would be required for existing buildings, and what new buildings would have to be obtained. The site plan was marked up to include all these decisions and to locate the new buildings.

Thirdly, a review with providers for the required utilities indicated that electrical capacity could be achieved by increasing the size of transformers, and the water supply capacity was sufficient. A rail spur line would have to be built into the site from a cement plant at nearby Barnstone village. Lacking sufficient time for a ground survey, the chief test pilot at the Avro plant was engaged to fly me along the route in his Auster aircraft, while the lineage to be used along the valley was sketched on a map .

The last step was to prepare the drawings in London. There was no drafting capability at the Canadian High Commission so a drafting table was bought and the drawing done. An office supplier was able to produce a table and instruments on 24-hour notice, but paying for the rubber boots, Auster flight and the drawing resources was not so easy. Carte blanche purchasing authority had been delegated before leaving Canada, but the information had apparently not reached those in England. It would take almost a year for some of the accounts to be settled by the supply officer in London. He lived up to what we jokingly called the supply branch motto, 'We have and we hold'.

During the drafting phase, A/C Johns arrived for a meeting with Air Ministry regarding the final transfer action on the site. It was soon apparent that the RAF A/V/M, with whom we were meeting, considered more negotiations to be required. Johns considered them finished. To complicate things, both these senior officers stuttered. Familiar with feeding words to Johns, I now did so for both of them. Once they reached their stride, and forgot to stutter, they proved to be very effective negotiators. The A/V/M was expecting the RCAF to give the RAF a number of Sabre aircraft in settlement (the word *squadron* was mentioned at one point), but it ended up with an agreement that the decision to provide Langar gratis to the RCAF had been made at their last meeting some weeks before. This meeting was only to confirm it. Meanwhile, there were concerns that the work done thus far might be for naught!

By working long hours it was possible to complete the drawings on time for the return flight, and home was reached on schedule. Everyone was happy that the job had been completed in the allotted time; however, it was soon found that some of the briefing material given me before departure had not considered several important factors. It was true that Supply had planned on using forklifts but, as policy, they had fencing systems in their Depots and Station Supply Sections which would restrict forklift movement, and because of my short time back in the air force I had never seen

119

the inside of a post-war supply depot. After much agonizing they decided it was right to design for forklifts, and that fencing would be a hindrance. As one of the results, contracts were eventually awarded to remove all of the isolating screening from depots and supply sections in Canada.

Feeling that my work was being performed satisfactorily but also realizing I knew very little about air force field work, Bunny's health was also a restriction. Although I was slated to be the Base Construction Engineering Officer (BCEO) at the new AMB, the family doctor thought it best that the family remain in Canada. Accordingly, a compassionate posting was requested to one of the Canadian stations being rebuilt for the enlarged RCAF. S/L Jim Easson went to Langar to prepare the site, and would continue there. The base would serve the RCAF until closed in 1968, when it would again revert to a civilian industrial site.

My requested posting arrived in December, and my new job effective February 18, 1952 would be as SCEO, RCAF Station Saskatoon, Saskatchewan. My stay at AFHQ had only been nine months, but it was a very busy time, and a lot was learned about the workings of the HQ. This knowledge would stand me in good stead in my future work in the field.

AN AIRMAN'S GRACE

Lord of thunderhead and sky,
Who placed in man the will to fly,
Who taught his hand speed, skill and grace
To soar beyond man's dwelling place

You shared with him the eagles' view,
The right to fly as eagles do;
The right to call the clouds his home
And grateful, through Your heavens roam.

May we assembled here tonight,
And all who love the thrill of flight,
Recall with twofold gratitude
Your gift of Wings, Your gift of Food.

-F/L John MacGillivray, RCAF padre

14

A MOVE TO THE WEST
1952-55

*which outlines employment at RCAF Station Saskatoon
and 14 Training Group Headquarters, Winnipeg*

We sold our car, and my family and I travelled to Saskatoon by air. On arrival we bought a 1949 Chevrolet sedan which had previously been a taxi, and booked into a motel on Eighth Street. We stayed at the motel for an extended period until a house was found on Avenue S in the southwest corner of the city, where we would live awaiting completion of the PMQs at the station. The housing situation in Saskatoon was desperate, even grain bins in the country were offered, if we would renovate them for use, and everything available was drastically overpriced.

We were fortunate to get a reasonable house at an affordable price, mainly because an offer was made to do necessary maintenance while we were there. Sewers were being laid in the area at the time and it was not uncommon to see ads in the paper for the sale of outdoor toilets. Because of the competition, some of the ads extolled the virtues of the product almost to the point where you would think manor houses were involved (two hole, recently painted, comfortable padded seats, etc).

Saskatoon was a typical prairie city in mostly level plains. As one English immigrant on his way across the prairie had said, 'the biggest expanse of bugger all I've ever seen'; however, it didn't take long for me to discover virtues not recognized by that man, and fond memories of the area remain.

The CE section at a RCAF Station was established generally with a capability to accomplish:

a) operation and basic maintenance of buildings and facilities of a nature for which it is difficult to arrange contracts,

b) the supervision of building and facility contracts awarded to industry, and

c) the supervision and execution, using civilian day labour, of a limited number of projects which can best be handled in-house.

Examples of the latter are: when the work cannot be defined accurately enough to develop a tight specification; that the requirement cannot be adequately determined prior to dismantling; or the project has arisen in a manner which will allow insufficient time to prepare plans and specifications, call tenders and award a contract; where suitable contractors are either not available or are not interested; or it is more economical to do tho work by civilian day labour after all overhead costs have been considered.

The RCAF Station, located at Saskatoon airport north of the city, was the first place where responsibility was undertaken for field work of this nature. The airfield site was operated and maintained by the Department of Transport (DOT). The RCAF was responsible for its own operations and domestic sites, co-habiting the airfield with DOT.

Construction Engineering Section, Saskatoon 1953

The station was commanded by G/C R. S. (Bob) Turnbull, DFC & bar, AFC, DFM, MiD, Croix de Guerre with Silver Star (France). It was home to No.2 Advanced Flying School (AFS), commanded by W/C Don Skene, which flew North American Mitchell twin-engined aircraft on advanced pilot training. It was initially intended that my pay would be augmented with $30 a month from practice flying; but, after logging time in the Mitchells, a Norduyn Norseman on floats, and C45-Expeditor aircraft, W/C Skene informed me that his school did not need navigators, they were doing pilot training. He ignored the cross-country and communications flights his pupils did, where valuable navigation practise would be available.

Although his decision defied air force policy, which encouraged qualified aircrew to stay current, it had to be accepted because Skene was Acting Station CO any time Turnbull was away. By coincidence, Skene and I would sit at coffee together in Ottawa 15 years later, both then at the same rank, and he at last unable to give me a hard time!

The station had been part of the BCATP, but was turned over to civilian use in 1945. In 1952 it was being renovated and new buildings were being constructed: steel arch hangar, ground school, construction engineering section, barrack blocks and two chapels, along with a new central heating plant and underground heating distribution system, and a new water treatment facility. Concurrently, DOT was rebuilding the runways and civilian airport passenger facilities.

The major new construction at the station was being supervised by Defence Construction Limited (DCL). Single and duplex houses, and row-housing were being built as PMQs by Central Housing & Mortgage Corporation (CHMC). The SCEO and his staff were required to maintain a continuing oversight of all new construction because he would be inspecting, taking over, and assuming ownership of each facility on behalf of DND when it was completed.

All-ranks personnel who had recently moved to Saskatoon with the enlargement of the station were suffering because of the high accommodation costs in the area. With grossly inflated rents, even the delivery of Chinese food was resorted to by me for a short period. Others were likewise affected, taking part-time jobs wherever they could find them.

One morning it was revealed that Wells Construction Ltd, the main contractor for the new structures, was having difficulty getting local people involved in window cleaning and other minor services. A breakthrough! At a suddenly organized meeting of Foreman of Works, Warrant Officer Second Class (WO2) BA (Andy) Andrews, myself and the senior civilian carpenter, Ron Chaput, we decided that we could provide a service while assisting the airmen. We immediately formed the ABC Construction Company (taken from the surnames) and made arrangements with Wells to enter into contracts.

14 Training Group (14 Gp) in Winnipeg (the immediate Headquarters to which Station Saskatoon reported) was informed about what we were doing, but there was never an official reply. We felt that we had obviated a potential conflict of interest when a personal call came from A/C J. G. Bryans, CBE, CD, Commander 14

Bunny, Brenda and Ron on the doorstep at PMQ

Gp, thanking us for being concerned about the airmen. Later our company branched out, still employing airmen, to do an office renovation for Husky Fuels, an acoustic ceiling in the Yale Hotel bar, various jobs for city householders, and undertook other work as far afield as Meadow Lake and North Battleford. With the opening of the new PMQs, the situation was largely alleviated. As airmen moved into housing they ceased to be interested in employment with ABC. Eventually, by Fall 1953, it was possible to close the company.

It was RCAF policy that a SCEO was required to live in PMQs to be immediately available in case of emergency, if such accommodation existed at the location. My family moved in late Spring 1952 into one of the first two PMQs available, and others followed as houses were finished. It was almost a pioneering exercise. Roads had not yet been built, there was an emergency phone on a utility pole outside my house for all PMQ occupants to use, and there was prairie gumbo everywhere. It was so bad that wooden walkways were built, and mothers were cautioned to keep their children under tight control. We got through this phase with a lot of mud-covered children and some discouraged and angry occupants! We had to remind them that we had opened the housing without finished roads and landscaping only because of concern for their financial welfare. As a Town Councillor in 1952-53, there were certainly many complaints to field, but everyone was much better off. Rents for PMQs were set at an average price, which precluded the gouging practised 'on the economy' when an influx of renters showed up.

A break in usual activity occurred when I was sent to the General Electric plant in Oakville, Ontario for a 2-week course in fluorescent lighting maintenance. It was an excellent course, and the principles involved would apply later in many maintenance activities.

The beginnings of a chapel, Saskatoon, 1952

The 49 Chevy, was leaking oil in late 1952, a condition not unexpected considering its previous use. Because of financial constraints it was necessary to do the over-haul as a 'self-help' project. An unused wartime building was scouted out, an A-frame built, and the job proceeded with tools and intermittent advice from the NCO mechanics in the Mobile Support Equipment Section (MSE). Surprisingly, the engine worked well when rebuilt and the car served on loyally.

In early 1953 fresh news from home brought information that the paint and hardware store had been closed, the family business consolidated in the original building, and there were a lot less employees. Shortly thereafter, the original building burned, severing power to NS and PEI for several days (power lines passed within 6 ft, or 2 m of the building); however, the business would be reestablished and remain active in an existing building at another location.

A/C Bryans took photos on the visits he made from 14 Gp. Two weeks later pictures and relevant questions arrived .... what are you doing about this? .... or that? Answers and solutions were supplied in return and, if they were not adequate, back to the drawing board.

The redevelopment of the Saskatoon site had complicated the traffic pattern. Vehicles travelled through the RCAF domestic site to reach the civilian airport so, with a new terminal under construction, an access road was built by DOT from Avenue A along the line of 45th Street West across the Hudson Bay Slough, to serve both the airport terminal and the PMQ area.

With the opening of PMQs there was now a circuitous route from that area to Avenue A, and North to the old station entrance. Accordingly, the simple solution was proposed to build a new entrance to access the station from the new Airport Road, saving an average of 4 miles (6.4 km) in the daily round trips of PMQ occupants. SCEOs at other stations had been having difficulty getting approval for centre-road check points. Our submission was successful, and we installed the first modern station entrance among 14 Gp stations.

In the summer of 1953 mobilization surveys were being done at most wartime RCAF airfields to determine their value in case of need. Andy Andrews and I did the one at Medicine Hat, Alberta. We started out using one of our pickups, then found ourselves in the middle of the prairie with a flat tire, and an unserviceable spare. While pondering our predicament, a Saskatchewan provincial survey crew came along in a similar pickup, and the first person who jumped out was Ken Stenbraaten, who had been a fellow navigator at 408 Sqn, now a land surveyor. He happily loaned us his spare with our promise it would be returned when we got back to Saskatoon. We did the survey, the only strange finds being that one hangar housed turkeys, and another pigs. Otherwise the wartime station was in a similar condition to others that had been abandoned at the end of WWII.

The wartime recreation building at Saskatoon would become the new station theatre. Renovation was accomplished utilizing the method used at Summerside earlier. We managed to get public funds for the whole project whereas the project at Summerside was done using public funds for the repairs, and non-public funds (NPF) to make the building a theatre.

NPF were accumulated in a Station Fund from bar sales in Officer's, NCO's and Other Ranks Messes, from admission sales at facilities such as theatres and recreation centres, and other regulated NPF activities.

They were spent for amenities not provided by the Government, such as sports and recreation equipment, prizes, and other costs. Although the acquisition of NPF real property, and approval for the construction of NPF infrastructure, such as curling rinks and golf courses was reserved for AFHQ, there were instances when recreational structures such as putting greens, swimming pool change rooms and mess patios, and some even much more expensive items were built without going beyond the CO for approval.

The separation between public and non-public funds was always a bugbear for CE officers because many COs, unable to justify the construction of amenities using public funds, would finance them through Station Fund and try to involve a SCEO in an attempt to scrounge part of the cost from assets provided by the public. In many cases these amenities were for the benefit of the station population-at-large; however, others benefited only a few. Reputedly eccentric English noblemen built follies, and so did some COs. Most projects were built with a genuine desire to improve life for the airmen, but there were others that were ill-considered, frivolous, and ego-driven.

SCEOs always thought that NPF facilities should be more rigorously controlled, particularly with regard to their effect on station operating costs as a whole. On one hand, air force operational activities were prescribed and became routine, so NPF activities were one of the few areas where a CO could show some initiative. As more and more things were built, some COs eventually tried to outdo each other in providing additional amenities.

On the other hand, an SCEO put under pressure by a CO to contribute public resources to NPF projects, had to figure out his response by himself. He had to consider the hazards involved in diverting labour, materials or service, and look to his conscience. There was really no one to whom he could complain. If he went to higher Command and was agreed with, he still was at the station and remained under pressure from the person he had complained about and, in some cases, careers were ruined, notwithstanding that the SCEO was acting with logic and within established regulations. There was at least one case of a SCEO refusing to commit on a questionable project, and he was put in the position of having to resign .... but he had the last laugh! After leaving the RCAF, he became Vice-president Real Estate at a major Canadian bank.

The first combination Public Funds/NPF project I became involved in arose from discussion at a COs weekly meeting, shortly after G/C E. H. Evans took over as CO upon Turnbull's move overseas to RCAF Baden-Solingen. The Group Commander had recently visited and expressed a view that stations under his command could stand greatly improved landscaping. Our prairie location limited the summer period that plants could be in the ground. Everyone agreed that we needed a greenhouse if we were to compete for the annual landscaping award that the commander intended to provide. We had a gardener but no greenhouse. Of course there was little money available in Station Fund, and everyone looked at me as though it had just become my problem, and it may have done.

Later it was pointed out to the CO privately that my getting involved at the level suggested was stretching the limits of what could be done. Evans agreed that regulations should not be circumvented, and said he would ensure that undue demands were not passed along. I prepared a memo concerning the distribution of responsibility between the Station Administration Officer, who was responsible for the Station Fund, and the SCEO. And Evans signed it.

The plans for the greenhouse were prepared by the CE design team and allotted a building number from a recently removed wartime storage building. The new structure contained a root basement and potting room, with a green-house extending from that structure at mid-level. Items other than glass came from a stock of materials abandoned by No.2 Construction & Maintenance Unit (2CMU) when it departed after completing the rehabilitation of wartime barracks.

The greenhouse, Saskatoon

Wells Construction had received glass in the wrong sizes for a building at the University of Saskatchewan, so Station Fund bought the glass and a few accessory items which were required. Labour was provided by a work detail of young airmen from the hangar line, and volunteer work by tradesmen and others, with supervision by the CE section.

The building was included on a marked-up plan that went to AFHQ for the design of heating distribution changes which had not been included when the original contract was awarded. So the expected inevitable happened, a phone call from the heating specialist at AFHQ asking, 'What is the function of building #40'. The response, 'It's a storage building', ... 'What is stored in it?', ... 'We store our plants there over the winter until we can put them outdoors .... we are in a very cold area, you know, etc, etc.' The discussion over, the change order was awaited. On its arrival, Building 40 was included in the heating plans and we were set up to receive first prize for our landscaping efforts the next year.

Very cold winter weather was one of the features at Saskatoon. Minus 40 was not unusual on winter nights. On one occasion, such a cold spell lasted for almost two weeks. Most vehicle engines would not have started, so they were left running overnight, and a small crawler tractor with rubber treads was used to do my rounds of supervision. In Summer 1953, that knowledge bore heavily on our minds and led to a watchful weather eye. The old above-ground heating distribution pipes, on wooden posts, had been removed to enable connection of buildings to the new underground system, but the new central heating plant contract was in trouble because of the late delivery of mechanical parts. Completion in time for the heating season was nigh impossible. We had to search for a solution, but found that 14 Gp Staff Officer Construction Engineering (SOCE) was not at all concerned. Help would not be forthcoming from that quarter .... we were on our own, and possibly in the cold without heat! The first attempt was to ask the Canadian National Railway to loan us a steam locomotive, but none was available.

The Central Heating Plant, with the new road from Avenue A at the right, and rail spur construction in the foreground

Next, because our two heating supervisors had experience on traction boilers used for prairie harvests we went, hat in hand, to the Western Development Museum in Saskatoon. Three traction boilers that required some rebuild were available in a display and were acquired on loan with the proviso that our heating staff would upgrade them, use them for the winter, then overhaul and return them. Our intention was to have two in use and one as standby, so the three boilers were towed north to the station. The upgrading completed and a wooden shelter built over them, these boilers went online in August and our temporary heating problems were alleviated. We were only left to wonder if the makeshift arrangements would stand up to prolonged use.

The central heating plant was finally at the stage where trial use could be attempted in December 1953, but our problems were not over. The plant was designed to use the lignite coal available in Saskatchewan, some of which remained stored outdoors from the previous heating system. Contractor's excavation to install the new underground distribution system had mixed trace amounts of clay into parts of the coal piles, but enough to set up conditions for spontaneous combustion.

The heating staff was reluctant to store this old coal in the overhead hoppers in the new plant, but there was no alternative. Even though the least possible amount was put into the bins above each of the four boilers, the bins all caught fire at about the same time, midnight on a Sunday. There was no point in putting the fires out in the concrete bins, there might be damage to the bins themselves, so Andy Andrews and I each got a dump truck, backed into the heating plant, used the automatic servers to load the coal into the trucks and, with flames falling out the back, made several trips to a safe dumping area. Fresh coal was obtained and the old piles were burned where they stood. At last Saskatoon had its long-awaited new heating arrangements.

The traction boilers were held in reserve until the end of the heating season, then overhauled and driven back to the museum under their own steam. Heating supervisors F/S J. (Scotty) Logan and Sgt T. E. (Butch) Sabraw were instrumental in repairing and operating the boilers. They also proudly led the parade on return to the museum. Some of the other CE personnel involved with me in various roles in this project were foreman of works F/S J. L. Curran, and supervisors Cpls G. W. Dempsey and W. H. Vine.

With my promotion to F/L January 1954 our family was in a much better financial situation. So much so that I hitched a ride by air in April to the General Motors factory at Oshawa, Ontario and drove back in a new 1954 Chevrolet Belair sedan, singing my way across the prairies to stay awake.

Our time at Saskatoon over, we moved to Winnipeg in May 1954 where we took up residence on Kenaston Boulevard near Fort Osborne Barracks and I went to work at 14 Gp HQ, Stevenson Field, as assistant to the SOCE, S/L Paddy Nevin. The Fore-

man of Works was Sgt (later F/O) Gord MacKay. The team was responsible for staff work involving CE matters at eight Stations: Winnipeg, Gimli, Portage la Prairie and MacDonald, Manitoba; Saskatoon and Moose Jaw, Saskatchewan; and Penhold and Claresholm, Alberta.

Officer's Mess nearing completion

Problems requiring solutions ran the whole gamut, some much more serious than others. Sometimes SCEOs had to take extraordinary measures to convince higher echelons that certain projects were required. One resulted from the high takeoff and landing speeds of the new jet aircraft used for training. F/L Tom Steele, the SCEO at Portage la Prairie had this problem, the runway was not sufficiently smooth and required a new surface, but he was not able to convince the SOCE that the existing situation was not acceptable. His solution was to invite Nevin to visit and see the situation for himself. The evidence was presented by driving him in a Chevy pickup truck at the landing speed of the aircraft, about 110 mph (177 kph), along the runway involved. We were not aware until then that the pickups would go that fast. Tom proved the point, the project was approved on an urgent basis, ... and Paddy was somewhat more than shaken. Yes, times have changed, now a ripple in the asphalt can cause a real problem, unlike the old days, as this extract from the 1915 Training Manual of the RAF indicates :

A permanent landing ground should be at least 300 yards by 300 yards in size. Landing grounds with telephone posts on their boundaries should be avoided. Acetylene lamps may be used to light up the landing ground .... the most suitable form of flare is a bucket with a half gallon of petrol in it. This will burn for half an hour.

There were several temporary duty trips to help solve problems at stations, and attendance at the University of Alberta for a 2-week course related to Construction in Permafrost. It was also an active practice flying period involving duties as a check navigator at ANS (which had moved from Summerside), in C45 Expeditor and Dakota aircraft.

In Summer 1955 a new Commander arrived at 14 Gp, A/C H. H. C. Rutledge, OBE, MiD. On meeting, his first comment was that I should get a new hat. He was seen outside later that day and it was observed that his hat was in much worse condition than mine. Accordingly, ... the purchase was delayed.

At Assiniboine Park, Winnipeg. Rear, Don, Bunny and Rod. Brenda in front..

My mother-in-law's health was very poor, and her family doctor asked that Bunny be moved closer to her, so a posting to the Maritimes was requested on compassionate grounds. In due course, a posting to Greenwood, NS was announced, but it would occur in Winter with a date of December 12, 1955. So we would depart what one acquaintance fondly remembered as Winterpeg, Manisnowba.

The real milestone in this posting had been the acquisition of a first TV set, black and white and snow all over. Reception in those days was not the best but we did appreciate using this modern convenience.

15

AND BACK TO THE EAST
1955-59

which outlines employment at RCAF Station Greenwood, Nova Scotia

Upon leaving Winnipeg, we suspected that the drive ahead of us might be difficult. After a somewhat snowy experience, but no crises, we arrived in Greenwood on schedule and were allotted a PMQ on Third Street. We were very glad to arrive there safely, but our furniture was not as fortunate. It ran into trouble near Kenora, Ontario when the moving van ditched on icy roads, resulting in most of the furniture being received as match sticks, and requiring almost total replacement. But, now we would not have to go cross country to visit parents, what had been a very long trip would be just a short jaunt into the next province.

The new cantilever hangar at Greenwood

Shortly after arrival at Greenwood a Corporal (Cpl) plumber was met in the CE Section. He had been stationed at Linton-on-Ouse as a Sgt air gunner. Then later, when I met his wife, we were both surprised. She had been the WAAF bat-woman who looked after the section of barrack rooms which included the one in which my room was located when I was on 408 Sqn.

Soon, in late January, 1956 I was hospitalized for a week and diagnosed with colitis. It would persist for many years, flaring up from time to time but largely kept under control by judicious use of diet and medication. There appeared to be some justification that this might be the 'twitchy rear end' that first came to the fore after the Nuremberg raid in 1944. Even today my rear admiral (the specialist) insists that a colonoscopy be undergone periodically.

Greenwood was a DND airfield with almost no civil flying, except by two small training aircraft belonging to the Greenwood Flying Club. The Station CO was G/C C. G. W. (Bill) Chapman, DSO. Initially reporting to the SCEO, S/L K. A. McLeod (now G/C retired), my responsibility was for the CE design cell of eight personnel, engaged in project preparation and contract inspection. When McLeod moved on to be SOCE at Maritime Air Command (MAC) in May 1956, I replaced him as SCEO and then reported to the Chief Technical Services Officer (CTSO), W/C G. P. Bradley.

The CE section had responsibilities similar to those outlined earlier for Saskatoon, but was much, much larger. Along with the usual activities, the station was being prepared for the debut of the new Argus maritime patrol aircraft. A new operations site opposite the old wartime hangar line was being built. Included were a cantilever hangar, a steel arch hangar, specially-designed Maritime operations hangars, a second central heating plant and other buildings. Soon the CE section was using day labour on three major construction and alterations projects, because of the short lead times available. One of these included the complicated electro/mechanical installations for 9 Field Technical Training Unit (FTTU), for Argus technical training, in one of the wartime hangars.

It was one of the most technically challenging projects undertaken by a CE Section, and it was a pleasant feeling to confirm that our electricians were capable of the intricate wiring involved. Superiors had wanted to import electricians, but they had agreed with me that it was not necessary to do so.

Canadair Argus (RCAF photo)

The arrival of the Argus aircraft saw the flying operations areas of the station split by the newly-extended main runway. Railway crossing gates operated from the control tower were the preferred solution to stop vehicle traffic when the runway was in use. Insufficient information was available, so two of us flew to Pittsburgh, Pennsylvania in an Expeditor, to get information and detailed specifications of the available gates and control panels, and then ordered an appropriate set of gates and controls for pickup by a Dakota. Duly installed, these worked very well indeed; however, A/C M. Costello, CBE, the MAC Commander continued to worry that vehicles might go around the closed gates.

We kept adding fencing to the point that it almost became an airfield hazard in itself. After a period of forcing traffic to drive around the end of the runway, he relented; however, he insisted that an air force policeman be kept at the location when the gates were used. And the gates alone had been a sufficient guarantee of safety!

Greenwood had three separate groupings of PMQs. Unfortunately, there was repetition in numbering which could cause problems locating a particular house in an emergency. The Fire Chief reported that the fire hall had been complaining about the situation for years to no avail. The solution was simple: 1-2-3 Streets were given the names of flowers, and 1-2-3 Streets North were given the names of trees. Numbering in the third area remained unchanged, and we then had a happy Fire Chief.

Housing became very scarce in the local area with the buildup of personnel for the Argus debut. There was little that could be done to increase availability in the local economy. Approval was requested for a publicly-funded mobile home park with thirty spaces. It was built next to the north PMQs with good

The Mobile Home Park, Greenwood

roads, concrete pads and individual service hubs containing water, sewage, power and telephone.

Most of the aggregates used at the station to make concrete were trucked in from the Bay of Fundy shore, about 5 mile (8 km) distant. On one occasion two dump trucks and a small loader had been sent to bring back sand. One of the trucks got stuck and the second driver, although briefed earlier not to do so in such a situation, tried to extricate it. The result was that both trucks were stuck, and the tide was coming in. Nothing could be done. Fundy has very high tides, often approaching 40 ft (12 m), and the salt they bear is corrosive.

After the tide went out the trucks were rescued and, because the paint was pitted from exposure to the salt water, their exteriors repainted. Rather than do the painstaking work of painting the interiors, they were covered with the rubberized undercoating normally used as rust protection for vehicle chassis. Although not a pretty sight inside, they were used normally for the rest of their service life.

Earlier, while stationed at 14 Gp, I had been involved in screening proposals from stations for construction projects, and had been both surprised and alarmed that there was little justification included with many of them. The originators appeared not to realize that they would be screened on the merits of what was stated. If a project was worth submitting it deserved to be well-written. Accordingly, everyone at Greenwood who had an interest in having something built at the site was made responsible for a full-blown justification text, and the CE design team attempted to improve on what was provided. Each project was the subject of a meeting which investigated all the reasons for *not approving* it, and attempted to find ways to overcome them. After all, if the merit of something is difficult to describe, make it sound convincing!

There is no point in spending time preparing and submitting a project only to have it rejected. Applying this approach proved fruitful. Most of the projects submitted from Greenwood in 1957 resulted in early approval.

The CCE staff at AFHQ had recognized that the administrative methods of the CE branch were outdated, and a formal study was undertaken to determine the direction to be taken. The result was known as the Hindle Report. It recommended sweeping changes, and the course to be taken to upgrade and improve procedures. These were all implemented, including a Preventive Maintenance program based on crews working from trailers, moving from area to area as work progressed.

G/C Chuck Ingalls, Director of CE Maintenance (DCEM) at AFHQ, while on an inspection visit, went to a trailer in the PMQ area and was alarmed when he saw lettering on it which read, 'Preventive maintenance - the way to better living!' My response to his obvious dismay was, 'You can advance a theory in practice among the clients only if you show that you believe in it. If we believe in preventive maintenance, we have to sell it'. A hurried survey among about ten PMQ occupants clarified that our CE section was on the right PR track, and Ingalls went away happy.

Meanwhile, it had been obvious that the PMQ interior painting program was producing labour costs which exceeded the normal percentage in relation to material costs. Investigation showed that delay was incurred by occupants not being able to decide the colours they wanted, and then changing their minds. Savings were immediately apparent when a change was made to six standard colour schemes for the occupants to choose, and no second thoughts.

George Sampson was the predominant local painting contractor at the time. My son, Don, who had trained as a paratrooper in the Princess Patricia's Canadian Light Infantry (PPCLI), broke both ankles in a training drop and had to leave the regiment. He opted to leave the Army, and was working for George. He confided that he could tell on Friday if George planned to go to church on Sunday, he painted his shoes black to cover the week's accumulated colours. Nevertheless, he was the best paint contractor we had, his work was excellent.

WO1 Dave Levasseur, the newly arrived Fire Chief, who was nearing retirement, lamented that he had tried for years at various stations to win an award for fire prevention programs he had developed. It was known the fire hall would work hard at it, so he was told that, if he did the work to support Fire Prevention Week, I would write it up. He followed through, and he and I prepared a 50-page fully-documented submission in album form, made up of photos interspersed with text. We were successful, and the 1958 Canadian Grand Fire Protection Award of the National Fire Prevention Association came to Greenwood, the first RCAF station to win in the large-station category.

Ron, right of centre, with #2 crew at the fire hall,
backed by fire engines and a crash tender

Snow clearance was always something that had to be close to perfect, especially at an operational station. At times crews had to work around the clock, particularly in winters of heavy snowfall as experienced in 1958/59. The snow kept coming and coming, temperatures remained constant, and it accumulated to the point where one wondered where the next lot could be stored. The arrival of spring temperatures was most welcome after it had become necessary to truck and dump snow into the Annapolis River.

In 1958 G/C J. C. Scott and F/O Beau Howe arrived to be the new Station CO and my new Design Officer respectively. Shortly thereafter, the station was allotted $200,000 for a Winter Works construction project to build 200 garages at PMQs in 1958/59.

This created four problems. A garage in the Maritimes could be built for $500, half the $1,000 allotted (Ontario pricing); there was no dry lumber available in the area; concrete floor slabs could not be laid there in winter and, for the first time, political interference was experienced.

It was obvious that changes in routine would have to be made to accommodate the desire of the Federal Government to spend the labour costs involved on social welfare, and we were told unofficially that spending half the money was not an option, after all it was 'winter works'.

A P2V and a Lanc X at Greenwood

Calculations showed that all the funds could be spent if the first 100 garages were prefabricated into finished wall and roof panels in one of the unused wartime hangars, using plywood, and if onsite construction and finishing took place in early Spring as soon as the ground could be worked. Some of the plywood for the second 100 garages would be used as forms for an Olympic-sized swimming pool which the Station Fund intended to build, then used for garage panels. The pool would be completed in parallel with the garages, and both projects finished by late-Spring. In the process, a large stock of overbought supplies from previous years was significantly reduced.

There had been sparring off and on over the years with George Nowlan, the local Member of Parliament. He grabbed the winter works project as his own, and was going to ensure he got all the political bonuses possible from it, working it for all possible brownie points, but he had not yet learned that cooperation was supposed to work both ways.

Now, we were in receipt of a Ministerial Inquiry (Minquire), instigated by Nowlan, about the purchase of plywood for the garages. He had reported that the SCEO at Greenwood had purchased British Columbia (BC) Douglas Fir plywood for the project, instead of buying locally. He knew as well as the rest of us that the only lumber available in the amounts required would have to be cut in the woods, sawn, kiln-dried and milled, and there were no kilns in the local area, local lumber being allowed to air-dry with the passage of time.

The reply to the Minquire said, "Yes, plywood had been used but had not been specified as stated, the purchase order had read 'Douglas Fir plywood' and we didn't care which province it came from". There was no further correspondence on the subject, even with BC the only province producing Douglas Fir.

When the project was completed there was a big surprise. We counted 201 garages!! It was also obvious that lay-offs would occur. On a Saturday morning, three carpenters showed up on my doorstep in an early state of inebriation, to complain about being laid off. I told them that it was beyond my control, which it was, but perhaps they should see George Nowlan, he might be able to help, and visiting a boot-legger on the way might not be a bad idea. Employment was also beyond Nowlan's control. On a visit to the station shortly thereafter, he acknowledged he was fully prepared for a period of truce.

In early May 1959 my posting to AFHQ was announced, to be effective in June. Then, one day the newly arrived CTSO, W/C Art Branscombe came to my office, to say that the CO was outside in the staff car, and wanted me to go for a ride. We set out with the CO driving on a 30-mile (48-km) trip to Lake Pleasant, near Spring-field, NS. Briefed on the way, it was learned that the homestead where G/C Buck McNair, DSO, DFC and 2 bars, Chevalier of the Legion of Honour (France), Croix de Guerre avec Palm (France), was born was for sale at a price that was too good to be true.

Abandoned since the 1930s when the family moved to Saskatchewan because of the Depression, it was proposed that the site be obtained for a summer resort to be developed there by Station Fund for the families at Greenwood. I wondered why it was necessary to locate it halfway to Bridgewater, because there were good sites available throughout the Annapolis Valley and this was only creating value for land which was otherwise worthless. The message was also loud and clear that the public purse was expected to cover some of the cost.

I would have to resist! Not only did it appear that the legalities of using public resources would be overlooked, it was thought that building a resort because a serving officer wanted to sell some land in a less than attractive location was not strategic planning, at best poorly researched.

When we arrived at the summit of the spine of hills that runs northeast to southwest through the centre of Nova Scotia, we had to leave the car and walk a considerable distance, because there was still rotting snow in place on the road, and it was impassable by car because of that and the mud. As we walked, the excellent virtues of the site were extolled, and it became obvious that I was expected to become a believer. The CO could already see families lounging about under the trees, playing water games and swimming.

What was impressing me was the dry moss hanging from the trees, and that the wind blowing up off the Atlantic Ocean was very, very cold. It was obvious to me that the low price was indeed much more than the true value.

There was a lake with an old saw mill site and a decaying sawdust pile. The location for the proposed clubhouse and other buildings was near lake-edge, which was studded with hummocks that clearly indicated a swamp. No problem. The hill, although it was pointed out that it was sharp granular material that would wear off bulldozer tracks very quickly, would be bulldozed into the swamp, and sand could be brought in for a beach. Many dollars could be seen wafting away in the wind.

As I pointed out all the problems that could be seen ahead, and the deficiencies of the site, the CO was countering them, to the point that he stomped his foot on a hummock and said, 'Look, Ron, this is rock solid!'

The Group Captain dropped into the bog up to his armpits. He had said earlier that he was going to have a resort come hell or high water. For him, the high water had come first! Art and I cast knowing glances to one another over his head, and had difficulty keeping straight faces as we lifted him out. Fortunately the hummocks that we stood on held, and we were successful in retrieving Scott from the icy depths.

Then we walked back to the car, the CO in obvious distress from the wet and cold. On arrival at the car, he removed his pants and jacket, opened the windows and turned the heater up to full blast. He drove home in shirt and shorts with little conversation, and it has been wondered since how he might have managed to enter his home without being seen by somewhat surprised neighbours.

Lake Pleasant was not mentioned again during my time at Greenwood, but my replacement, S/L Roy Greenhalgh was up to his ears in the project within weeks of arrival. Camps were established there for helicopter training and for upgrading bulldozer drivers. The legitimacy of the helicopter training is not known, but I do know the bulldozer operators were skilled, and did not need a course to push earth down hill.

In any event, a helicopter was dropped into the lake and had to be airlifted out by a heavier one, and the bulldozer tracks had to be replaced more than once. The project was finished in due course, and the summer resort was open.

Personnel who have spent vacations there say it was enjoyable but a cool (in temperature) place. And it all started because a retired group captain let it be known that he wished to sell the family homestead. The same effort at a site with fewer drawbacks would have been much more effective .... and with more enjoyable results.

Greg Chisholm arrived to be Design Officer when Beau Howe was posted to a newly established radar station, CFS Chibougamau, as SCEO. Beau recruited my son Don to go with him as Paint Foreman, and both were there for several years. Don had two volunteer jobs: as local president of the Union of National Defence Employees (UNDE) and as chairman of the Eastern Quebec Regional Protestant School Board.

My two Foremen of Works, WO2 Roy Ballieull and F/S Lou Rivard, participated with me in several social projects, one of which was boat building. Our intention was to build three skiffs, one each, built one at a time; however, only one was finished when I left Greenwood, so I told them to toss a coin to see which of them would own it. Another of our endeavours was building furniture, and a third was shad fishing in the Annapolis River each Spring, accompanied by home brew which had been made through the Winter.

While at Greenwood an active program of practice flying was followed, flying as a navigator with 404 and 405 Sqns in P2V Neptunes and CP107-Argus aircraft to Norfolk, Virginia and Bermuda on maritime patrols, and local flying in C45 Expeditors.

Flights with 103 Rescue Unit were also undertaken. They provided the most excitement, with flights in Consolidated Cansos, Dakotas, Otters and an H21 Helicopter. There were sea searches, the rescue of a cut and bleeding hunter from an ice floe during the annual seal hunt, trips north to Knob Lake and Great Whale River, Quebec on one occasion taking Eskimos to hospital in Halifax, on another barbequing beef steaks in an open Canso blister with navigator F/O Gus Cloutier, who would become a Major-General, and later the Sergeant-at-Arms in the House of Commons.

On another occasion, en route to Summerside in a Canso, we found ourselves becalmed, so to speak, and because of a gale force head wind were actually standing still over my home town, which was in a roughly straight line with our departure and proposed arrival locations. It necessitated a return to Greenwood with the purpose of the trip incomplete.

I look back on my time at Greenwood as my best air force posting, a very comfortable station where everyone was effective and had a good time. My tenure there ended June 26, 1959 and the Canadian Forces Decoration was now worn. It is slangily credited as compensation for 'Twelve Years of Undetected Crime.'

16

MORE YEARS IN THE HEAD-SHED
1959-1963

which covers more employment at Air Force Headquarters

The family moved by car to Ottawa and took up residence in rented accommodation on Saunderson Drive, in a house owned by S/L Don Allison, a fellow CE
officer who was moving to the Air Div in Europe. So here we were, back in the city
called Pottawa by some, where potholes are reputed to be patched with Volkwagons
turned upside down, because they just fit nicely. Certainly that is an exaggeration,
but the conditions for creating potholes, several freeze/thaw cycles, certainly exist
and big potholes are in evidence each spring.

My posting was as a staff officer in G/C Ingalls' DCEM, first with W/C H. D.
Monteith, working on maintenance problems referred from the field then, after
promotion to S/L in July 1960, with W/C A. H. Fallis, DFC developing field management procedures and overseeing the preventive maintenance program.

This entailed responsibility for writing and publishing Canadian Air Publication
(CAP) 209, the RCAF Construction Engineering Administration Manual, the preparation of which was one of the important recommendations in the Hindle report,
itself treated as somewhat akin to the Bible. One of the objectives of the design and
text of the manual was that all procedures should be optimized for a seamless changeover when computers were introduced to CE sections. To assist in readying for this
requirement, an introductory computer course at IBM Ottawa and a Civil Service
course in Forms Design and Control were attended, and there was participation in
several symposia on writing.

It soon became obvious why my predecessor had a filing cabinet full of draft
manuscripts, some of which were revisions of previous revisions, and much undated
miscellaneous paper. It was easy to get acceptance and approval of new material at
the lower levels, but the higher it went in the staff the more static a draft would
encounter.

Some people in the higher echelons just could not believe that SCEOs in the field
had actually developed local procedures to meet their needs, and that those procedures matched closely the ones which were included in current policy, but not yet

published. Quite satisfactory proposals, which could be used with minimal change, were received from many SCEOs.

The problem was to get them into the manual. They had not been developed at AFHQ, so they were suspect. Ultimately, realizing that the book would never be finished in such a climate, drafts were processed and published without referral up the line. It could be called insubordination, but it worked! No complaints were heard from senior officers about the publishing methods or the content, even though authority to publish had not been delegated. During my time, CAP 209 grew from two covers and no content, to 28 chapters and a thickness of 2 ½ ins (6.35 cm), covering all subjects for which the branch was responsible, and including revisions which were required after minor anomalies appeared through use. As the only officer at AFHQ at the time who had practised the new preventive maintenance methods in the field, visits were required, from time to time to the CE Officer's School, RCAF Centralia as a guest lecturer on both administration and preventive maintenance.

In 1962 a CE inspection team went to Europe as passengers in a CC106-Yukon aircraft to visit RCAF stations Baden-Solingen, Zweibrucken, Gros-tenquin and Marville, the former two in Germany, the others in France. It was composed of S/L Donn Smith, who was primarily interested at that time in the problem of condensation in curling rinks, S/L George Cheyne who would look at various heating problems, and myself on CE maintenance and administrative procedures. The visits went well and we had an opportunity afterward to visit several locations in Germany before returning home.

Trier impressed me deeply, an eerie feeling came over me with the seeming recollection that I had been there before, even to knowing what the sight would be around the next corner .... reincarnation? .... or a past dream?

On the way home all went well until Donn awoke, startled, from a nap. He had just spent the last week discussing condensation .... and what was dribbling onto him from the aircraft ceiling? .... condensation!

From time to time there was involvement in assessment of proposed projects and other special assignments. There was also responsibility for writing columns in the quarterly newsletter, *CE News*. It was hilarious what could creep into what were intended to be serious writeups for the submission of projects for approval.

One, submitted for *CE News* January 1961, under Quotable Misquotes was headed, 'Somebody Goofed'. It stated, "An AforP justification contained the line, 'Based on the 42 living corporals & ACs.' Hopefully all corporals and airmen were alive. Only a few would be 'living-in' in barracks."

And another selection in the July 1961 issue under the heading 'All that Glitters':

Recently an AforP concerning landscaping at an unnamed RCAF station was being reviewed at AFHQ. The landscaping specialist, noting one item of $1,400 for grass seed, minuted the document back, along with the facetious remark 'Grass seed must be liquid gold at this station'. In due course a revised AforP was received showing 'Grass Seed (Species-Liquid Gold)' and with the price unchanged.

The preventive maintenance program also made it into *CE News*. A typical entry was placed in the July 1961 issue under the title 'Give Your Lawns a Beatle Haircut': 'Yes, SCEOs, it is true. Your lawns really would appreciate joining the teenage craze. Give them a Beatle haircut this week and see them smile later on, when the weather is dry. It may not look like a putting green when newly mowed, but the depth of grass will protect the roots and the density will retain moisture much longer. It may be hard to break the tradition of baldness created by those manning depot barbers - but over the long haul it will cost the Air Force less to maintain your lawns if you cut the grass at a 2-inch height. Remember - weeds grow best in brush-cut lawns - moisture disappears - and roots are less healthy, Yeh! Yeh! Yeh!'

Work on project approvals brought me into contact with G/C Cam Mussells, OBE, DSO, DFC, then CO at RCAF Uplands, south of Ottawa. Being an energetic and forceful CO with a penchant for one-upmanship he had a habit of visiting CCE staff, with the hope of getting a slight edge on other COs, and nudging his proposed projects forward on the road to approval. He was getting to be a nuisance, and a strategy to contain him was required. On his next visit, Harry Fallis referred him to me as prearranged.

My mission was to stop his unannounced visits. He was told that his visits really slowed down his projects because of the time used up in discussion, and that it had to be an 'arm's length' process. It was also announced to him that each of his projects would be allotted to one of several unnamed officers for action, we would process them with his hopes for approval in mind, but the names of the processors would not be available. He was assured that phone calls to me would result in information about the stage of processing a particular project was at, but no more. That was the last of his visits about projects, but we became friends with respect for each other's position. Later involvement in processing Minquires concerning the CE section at Uplands was made much easier by the fact that we knew each other and could converse with candour.

Involvement in a study related to amalgamation of the Navy, Army and Air Force fire services, and assistance in another related to the Construction and Maintenance branches of the three services engaged me in complex negotiations, and set the tone for those amalgamations later when the Forces were integrated.

While at AFHQ, navigation proficiency was maintained flying with the Practice Flight at RCAF Station Rockcliffe in DC3 Dakota and C45 Expeditor aircraft. Flying to Shearwater in Expeditors with Royal Canadian Navy pilots and lunching there was particularly inviting, but that meant having to put up with carrier-type landings at both ends of each trip.

The air force pilots flying out of Practice Flight were mostly squadron leaders, wing commanders and group captains who some day expected, and also hoped, to be out in the field again.

In July 1963 Harry Fallis informed me that a posting to RCAF Station Downsview was being prepared, with a return to AFHQ scheduled in eleven months. There had been a highly critical DM audit regarding the Downsview CE Section, and my mission there would be to bring the section back to an acceptable level of administrative efficiency .

17

FORCES INTEGRATION / UNIFICATION
1963-1971

which outlines employment at Toronto (Downsview), Ontario

The family travelled by car to Toronto, arriving August 1, and moved into PMQs. This process was not without some moaning and groaning. Now a teenager, Brenda had grown very fond of Ottawa and was not prepared to part with her friends. The knowledge that we would be back in a year did little to improve things but, in any event, that was not going to happen either.

RCAF Station Downsview reported to Air Transport Command (ATC). It included Downsview airfield, in an overall tract of 1,700 acres (680 hectares). Started in 1929 by the DeHavilland Aircraft Company of Canada (DHC), it was taken over by the Federal Government in WWII, then reverted to DHC at the end of the war. In 1947, DND began a major land assembly, and in 1952 reached an agreement with DHC under which DND acquired the airfield and buildings, assuming full control of the facilities in 1954. Construction during 1952/56 resulted in development of the site as it existed on my arrival in 1963.

G/C (later BGen) R. A. B. Ellis was the Station CO. My immediate superior was S/L J. O. H. (Jack) Neff, the CTSO. Units which received logistical support from the station were, under DNDHQ: Defence Research Medical Laboratories; under AFHQ: Institute of Aviation Medicine and Personnel Applied Research Unit; under ATC: 436 Transport Sqn (C119 Packet) and 14 Wg HQ RCAF Auxiliary, with its 400 and 411 Sqns; under Materiel Command: 1 Supply Depot and 1 MSE Maintenance Unit (heavy vehicle rehabilitation and manufacture); under Training Command: Air Force College, RCAF Staff College and RCAF Extension School; many minor units with various specialty functions, a lot of air cadet squadrons and several RCAFA Wings. Some support was also provided to DHC in accommodation leased from the RCAF. The RCAF and DHC both conducted their flying operations from the airfield under RCAF flying control.

The duties of the SCEO were similar to those at Saskatoon and Greenwood, but those stations were out in relatively uninhabited open spaces somewhat removed from cities and towns. Downsview, on the other hand, was cheek to jowl with the largest metropolitan area in the country and, growing quickly, the built-up area was beginning to surround it. This geography dictated that the most important CE issues would revolve around property control and community liaison. I would also be heavily involved with RCAFA Wings in the area, having transferred from membership-at-large to 442 (David Hornell VC) Wing.

An early problem involved the height of the Highway 401 interchange (spaghetti junction) at Yorkdale Shopping Centre. As designed it was 16 ft (4.88 m) too high for the airfield height clearance slope. Ontario Transport cooperated to redesign the various structures to save some height, the rest was gained when they lowered the whole assemblage, along with the main roadway, to conform.

It was different with the Toronto Police Board. Its staff designed a tall police communications tower for a site near the Highway 401/Avenue Road intersection, ... and they were going to build it! It was pointed out that if it was built it would have to be demolished, unless the airfield was moved, and I volunteered a doubt it would move. After they conducted prolonged correspondence with DOT and DND they admitted they would have to move elsewhere, even though the chosen site had shown the best reception characteristics available to them.

There were also proposed high-rise apartment buildings in close proximity, from time to time, where the height restrictions had to be enforced.

The recovery of the CE section from administrative chaos involved saying goodbye to some civilian employees. Not discovered in the audit was a situation in which two foremen were extracting favours from day labour tradesmen for them to remain off layoff lists, rather than last hired, first to go. After correcting this corrupt practice, the biggest problem was control of resources, and credible bookkeeping; however, within six months it was possible to have the audit cleared, and all remaining personnel absolved of any wrongdoing.

In 1964 the family planned to visit the states of Pennsylvania and New York, and the Washington, DC area on vacation. Plans included borrowing a house trailer from the MSE officer, F/L Al McMillan. Our planning for the journey was completed with a visit to Canadian Tire for the installation of a trailer hitch attachment which, incorrectly installed, fell apart as we proceeded east at highway speed on Hwy 401 near the Leslie Street overpass, still not even out of Toronto.

At that time the eastbound highway at Leslie was two lanes wide. When the trailer separated, held only by its safety chains, traffic in the area quickly shied away, while the car and trailer plunged first to one side of the road, then to the other. The whole road and its verges were being used; however, the situation was brought under control after difficult and trying manoeuvres. Having driven trucks under all kinds of road conditions, the knowledge gained was probably all that saved us from a major accident.

The touchy subject of public relations suffered a blow when a T33-Silver Star jet aircraft overshot the runway on landing and came to rest in the middle of Wilson Avenue. A hue and cry went up from the media, *DND is endangering the citizens of Toronto*; however, we started looking for an unused automatic-engagement aircraft arrester barrier and found an older model at RCAF Station Chatham, NB. After installing it, we held a press conference and displayed the apparatus. The media would be quiet for a while! When the barrier was engaged later by an aircraft, the knowledge did not get into the daily papers. Only *we* knew and *we* were not about to tell.

S/L Jerry Kit succeeded me as SCEO in June 1964, when I replaced Jack Neff as CTSO upon his retirement, and moved into what had been the office of the President of DHC in WWII, before its new plant was built. The move to this position made me responsible for all technical services, including telecommunications, ground training, ground defence, aircraft maintenance, mobile support equipment, logistics and supply, armament, and construction engineering. Fortunately, effective and efficient officers occupied each specialty position. I also represented the CO at many functions when he was otherwise committed, and this metropolitan area produced a lot of them, usually on short notice.

When G/C C. Allison replaced Ellis as CO later in 1964, he went through personnel channels, and asked that my appointment as CTSO continue, because of my experience at the site and the community relations contacts that I had established. His request was approved, and would nullify the prior determination of the CE branch to post me back to Ottawa. Allison occupied a house traditionally used by the CO, nicknamed *The Ponderosa*, which had been the home of James Franceschini, the founder of Dufferin Materials & Construction Ltd. It had been included in an expropriation for an airfield expansion and its assets included an extensive horse stable, used at the time by Station Fund to house horses belonging to officers and airmen. Allison, who had been a Sabre pilot, was known for his everyday early morning T33 practice flights, and his need for manure for hobby gardening. With limited sources on base, he augmented his supply by arrangement with the Toronto stockyards.

I held the appointment of RCAF liaison officer for the Toronto Region RCAFA and its eight Wings in the area from Oshawa to Oakville. Collaboration with Ontario Region RCAFA on items of mutual interest was also involved. As a life member of the association, this duty came naturally.

Integration of the Canadian Forces began when Hon. Paul Hellyer, the Minister of National Defence (MND) set in motion, through a White Paper on Defence, the integration of the Army, Navy and Air Force into 'a single unified defence force'. In June 1964, integration became reality when the relevant bill was passed by Parliament. Dark days, ... many personnel voluntarily left the three services prematurely; however, others took the approach that we could serve a worthwhile purpose, by keeping a lot of our old service traditions alive, if we stayed and fought for their retention. The main effect on me was reclassification to the new Military Engineering List and the use of social insurance (SI) numbers for personnel records identification. I also joined a newly-formed unified association, the Military Engineers of Canada.

Again in 1965, when Allison was promoted to BGen and moved to ATC, a new CO, G/C E. J. Boland, CD arrived and again, a request was made that I be retained in Toronto for the same reasons as before. Boland tasked me to prepare a comprehensive paper for the Planning Board of the Borough of North York, entitled *The Background, Functions and Impact of the RCAF Downsview Site, January 1966*. This document set the tone for future relations with the Borough, and was reprinted for wider distribution in July 1966.

Later in 1966, CFB Toronto was formed, with 1,200 personnel, to replace the RCAF station, with Boland as Base Commander (BComd) and me as Base Technical Services Officer (BTSO). We also became known from then on within the Canadian Forces (CF) rank structure as Colonel and Major respectively (see Table 4). With the formation of the Base, it was necessary to undertake consolidation within the Base for all Navy, Army and Air Force units in the Golden Triangle area from Oshawa to Fort Erie, the geography which the Base encompassed. A tri-service committee was formed to do the consolidation with me as the Chairman and RCAF representative.

My promotion to Lieutenant-Colonel was announced in December 1966. Unification, the next step in casting off the Navy, Army and Air Force, and achieving a unified force occurred in 1967, the year I gave up smoking, my project to celebrate Canada's Centennial.

At this time my home town was well represented in Base strength by six personnel, spread among several ranks and professions/trades, a WO2 Air-frame Tech, an Artillery Captain, a LCol and Maj Military Engineers, a Sgt Supply Tech and a Cpl Transport Driver.

CFB Toronto was one of the first Bases where detailed consolidation of all Forces units, under a single support umbrella, was completed. There were complex organizational issues to settle and the Toronto area contained many, especially when Brigadier-Generals, previously of the Army and Navy, perceived their units were going to be supported by an organization based on RCAF procedures, and not directly within their control. We fooled them by selecting the best procedures, gleaned from each of the three services.

Base consolidation resulted in us providing support for many additional units. When all the closings, amalgamations, and other changes were completed there were about 150 units remaining, both large and small, comprising about 20,000 full and part-time personnel. These included about 3,000 regular force personnel and DND civilian employees, representing 25 separate formations; about 6,000 sea, land and air reserves .... mainly militia from 55 separate units, and some 10-11 thousand cadets in 70 some individual units. The annual cost of payroll and support services was about $25 million.

Table 4- Comparative Rank, RCAF and CF

Royal Canadian Air Force	Canadian Forces
General Officers	
Air Chief Marshal (A/C/M)	General (Gen)
Air Marshal (A/M)	Lieutenant-General (LGen)
Air Vice Marshal (A/V/M)	Major-General (MGen)
Air Commodore (A/C)	Brigadier-General (BGen)
Senior Officers	
Group Captain (G/C)	Colonel (Col)
Wing Commander (W/C)	Lieutenant-Colonel (LCol)
Squadron Leader (S/L)	Major (Maj)
Junior Officers	
Flight Lieutenant (F/L)	Captain (Capt)
Flying Officer (F/O)	Lieutenant (Lt)
Pilot Officer (P/O)	Second Lieutenant (2nd Lt)
Subordinate Officers	
Officer Cadet (O/C)	Officer Cadet (O/C)
Non-commissioned Ranks	
Warrant Officer, First Class (WO1)	Chief Warrant Officer (CWO)
Warrant Officer, Second Class (WO2)	Master Warrant Officer (MWO)
Flight Sergeant (F/S)	Warrant Officer (WO)
Sergeant (Sgt)	Sergeant (Sgt)
Master Corporal (MCpl)	Master Corporal (MCpl)
Corporal (Cpl)	Corporal (Cpl)
Leading Aircraftman/woman (LAC/LACW)	Private (Pte)
Aircraftman/woman (AC/ACW)	Private (Pte)
Aircraftman/woman, Second Class (AC2/ACW2)	Private Recruit (Pte)

The merger was immediately effective, the payroll was reduced by 150 personnel, properties released for sale, and up to $500,000 annual operation and maintenance savings had been realized, with almost no capital expenditure and without reduction in commitment.

Boland and I worked well together, but we had our problems, in what must have been a very difficult situation for him, stemming mainly from his diagnosed condition of narcolepsy. Weekly conferences became discussions between the branch heads as he slept, and decisions had to be taken without his participation. His midnight phone calls on items lacking urgency, when he could not sleep, were galling and led to many arguments. In effect, the other branch heads and I had been running the Base from a period not long after his arrival. We tried to keep him informed, but it was difficult.

Increasingly aggressive, he called me to his office when Canadian Centennial Medals were being distributed in 1967 and said, 'I have one of these medals left, have you any recommendations about who should get it?' One left. No one in technical services had received one, and the branch comprised more than 75% of Base personnel. I also thought he would argue about *any* name that might be put forward. My carefully calculated response was, 'I suppose you considered all the effort exerted by me on behalf of you and the Base, and have discarded that notion.' His reply, 'Here, take the Goddam thing!' So, that is how I managed to give *myself* a medal, although it is suspected that might have been his intention from the beginning.

I had continued to maintain proficiency as an air navigator on communications and cross-country flights with Station Flight in DC3 Dakotas, C45 Expeditors, and Otters. Included was one flight in a T33 Silver Star, the only service flight in a jet aircraft that involved me as a crew member. Particularly enjoyed were flights in a Float Otter north to Haliburton, Ontario to visit Sir Sam's Inn and to the Madawaska River, when the maples were showing their full fall colours. The decision was now made to give up proficiency flying because of continuing heavy demands on my time, and my last flight in the RCAF was in Otter 9415 June 27, 1967, with a flight of 1:20 hrs described as 'Confederation Day, Form PCTCE', the purpose of which is not recalled. My total service flying time was now 1,741 hours.

The Borough of North York continued to have many concerns about the airfield, the most important one in 1968 being the bottleneck created by the cutting-off of the Sheppard Avenue east-west route when the airfield was expanded in the 1940s. Boland delegated me to participate in joint studies with the Borough, which named its Director of Transportation Services, ex-F/O Sid Cole, DFM as its representative. Sid had been a crew member with F/L David Hornell in the event that resulted in a posthumous VC for Hornell.

Initially the Borough proposed a tunnel under the airfield along the old Sheppard Avenue alignment, but that would have been a very expensive proposition. The result was a road around the airport to the North which had been drawn as a red line on the wall map in my office at the first meeting with Sid, when he had brought up the idea of a tunnel. Road construction broke the east-west traffic bottle neck. It also had the added advantage of creating a new and more efficient Base entrance at Borough expense and the opening up of acreage to the North, which was added to the Borough's industrial site inventory.

Son Don had met Jacqueline (Jackie), resident in Chibougamau, Quebec, the daughter of a lady I had known as a youngster in Port Elgin, NB, only 18 miles (29 km) from Sackville. Although we remembered Don being adopted by me when Bunny and I married, it was found when they were preparing for marriage, that it was a myth. Investigation revealed the relevant application, unactioned but still ready to go, in the files of the Sackville lawyer whose predecessor had commenced preparing it 20 years earlier. Don and Jackie were married April 6, 1968 and Bunny, Brenda and I drove to Chibougamau to attend the wedding.

In June 1968 Boland retired suddenly. An intended new BComd, Colonel (later LGen) J. I. (Jim) Davies, CD, had been slated to arrive in August, but he was attending a course and could not be made available earlier. Accordingly, the Commander ATC, MGen A. C. Hull, CMM, DFC, CD, appointed me in temporary command of the Base for the interim period.

Over the years, the number of horses owned by RCAF personnel and kept in the stables, had declined sharply. Progressively, horses owned by civilians had replaced them, and they were being heavily subsidized. This, and other changes, had degraded base activities in the view of the branch heads so, at my first meeting with them, it was directed that the stables be closed, and the statement was made, 'You remember how we ran things before Boland's arrival. Lets get back to that condition as soon as we can'. They were more than pleased to comply.

Col Abe Leiff, CO 1 Supply Depot, who was probably the most senior G/C in the former RCAF, was coming up for retirement during my tenure. Recognizing that my seniority was eons below his, it was felt that someone much more senior should be presiding at his retirement party. I contacted Materiel Command, under which the depot operated, to ask if they would send someone, but little interest was shown and no one attended. When Leiff's party was held all went well until Bunny was presenting Mrs. Leiff with a bouquet. Upon presentation, water squirted out and sprayed the recipient, the end of what had been a very pleasant but overall, a very embarrassing situation.

One of the pleasant duties for the BComd was meeting dignitaries arriving in Downsview by air for business in downtown Toronto. There were many occasions of meeting Governor-General Roland Michener and Mrs Michener, and others.

Meeting the Governor General, the Hon Roland Michener and Mrs Michener at Downsview airfield (also on back cover) (CF photo)

While meeting MND at the flight line one day, he told me that he had received from Basil Hall, the Mayor of North York, a letter desiring my promotion to Colonel and appointment as BComd because of the vastly improved relations which had resulted from my efforts. He said that it was a surprise to receive such a letter from a civil authority but, in any case it was not possible. He said, 'I have enough people down my throat now, and there would be complaints from a lot of officers who are much more senior' (seniority at the time was less than two years), but said he wanted me to know the esteem in which North York Council held me.

In August 1968, Col Davies arrived and control of the Base was relinquished to him in a handing-over parade. Being Acting BComd was a great experience! Surprisingly, much satisfaction was felt from having the RCAF Ensign with my rank stripes flying on the flag pole and on the staff car, but now I would revert to my usual position as BTSO. One of the first things Davies told me when he arrived was that ATC had arranged for me to remain at CFB Toronto for a further period. Working with Davies was an enjoyable experience and we both felt that we were achieving something, but there were continuing challenges, which resulted in both successes and failures.

In 1969 an attempt was made to build NPF Self-help Housing alongside the North PMQ site to alleviate the high cost exposure by airmen to housing stocks in the area. At my instigation, several major developers entered a competition for the design and construction of the project, and DND allotted the land required; however, when the proposal was submitted to CHMC, the energetic work done by a lot of us resulted in failure because DND was not prepared to provide the initial capital that CHMC insisted be supplied in advance, and we had no other source.

Early 1970 brought more media activity regarding the possible closing of the Base and disposal of the land. There were new people on North York Council and there was a dream to build a $37-million domed stadium on airfield property. Airfield height clearances immediately came to mind. Because of the critical aspects regarding the airfield, we were right back to fighting again for the existence of the site. Our continuing aim was to thwart a concerted public outcry that it be closed because of aircraft hazards.

Again, participation with North York resulted in the Borough requesting DND to transfer operation of the airfield to Borough control as an Industrial Air Park, thus ensuring continued availability for both civil and military use; however, a decision was deferred regarding under which sponsorship it would continue, and the furor subsided.

It was felt that the new Base organization had now been in existence long enough to brief interested organizations on its status, so it became the subject when organizations asked BComd to speak to them. I prepared presentations on integration/unification which he gave to several audiences, and I represented him in talks to the local RCAF Association and the Business Club of Metropolitan Toronto. I also spoke to the Royal Canadian Army Service Corps Officer's Association about CF involvement in the Front de Libération du Québec (FLQ) crisis in Quebec.

Several offers had been received to leave the Forces and take employment related to construction, one of which came from a representative of the Ford Motor Company, to supervise the construction of a plant in Brazil, and to maintain it after it went into production. That, and other offers were declined, I was not quite ready to leave.

My volunteer service in the local community included Mayor of the Downsview PMQ's 2,000 citizens on two ocassions, and Chairman of the Teen Town Council 1965-68, when daughter Brenda was the secretary.

Brenda was employed in the office at DHC. She had met LAC Berny Demers, a young technician in the Station Supply Section, from Chicoutimi, Quebec. Married at the Base Chapel August 8, 1970, they had the pleasure of being driven by the Chief Administrative Officer, LCol Tom Webster in his classic 1940 Buick sedan.

In September Toronto Region RCAFA divulged to the BComd its plans to hold an event to be advertised as Canada's First International Antique Airplane Fly-in and Air Show, at a location to be determined later. The (American) Antique Aircraft Association would be the cosponsor, and the proposed dates were June 25-27, 1971.

Davies involved me as an adviser in this rather ambitious project, and to arrange with DND for the use of an airfield, obtain a volunteer ex-RCAF public relations consultant, and organize a committee structure for the extensive undertaking. Its objectives were to make a donation to the Hall of Aviation History (RCAF Memorial) fundraising campaign, the purchase of an additional glider for Air Cadet training and a DeHavilland Chipmunk aircraft for presentation to the Antique Aircraft Association, in recognition of its involvement in the event.

Permission was obtained from DND to use Mountain View airfield near Picton, Ontario for the event. Representation to Crown Assets Disposal Corporation resulted in the purchase of the Chipmunk. All of the planning was completed for what was expected to be a popular event. Howard Elliott of 442 Wing was named by Toronto Region to be my opposite in our part of the planning and implementation of the event, representing the planning committee of Toronto Region. He and I made many trips to Mountain View; however, my colitis had flared up in the meantime, and Howard insisted that the location of every toilet from Downsview to Mountain View was known to me.

In October 1970, while Acting BComd during Davies' absence on leave, the furor about the airfield arose again in the media for no apparent new reason, likely because there was little news that day. After several interviews on TV and meetings with reporters, which inevitably were misquoted, it settled down once again.

Early 1971 saw another 8 RCAFA Wings which had been supported by CFB Clinton before its closure, in the area from Kitchener to Windsor, added to my liaison duties. There were now 16 Wings in the package, ranging in location from Oshawa to Windsor. Little did I know at the time that this Association participation would be a factor in my future employment.

Then, June 25, 1971 rolled around. Everything was ready for the antique air show with the workers in place; however, *it never happened*. Notwithstanding all the planning, and even though intensive research had been included regarding weather patterns and the likelihood of good weather for the event, the weather did not look kindly upon us. The only aircraft that arrived was a Ford TriMotor from the US. All of the light aircraft that intended to fly in were storm-staid in New York State, their pilots afraid, with good reason, to cross Lake Ontario because of a violent summer storm that engulfed a broad area of the US and Canada. The Canadian participants read the weather, and stayed home. The storm persisted with furor until the advertised dates of the event had passed. All that effort had been lost, a most desirable event gone wrong, and it hasn't been tried again.

CFB Toronto inherited from RCAF Station Downsview the responsibility for supporting all military aviation participants, both national and foreign, in the annual Toronto International Air Show. Support for static displays at the Canadian National

Exhibition were also included and, with the formation of the Base, Navy and Army ground displays were added to that responsibility. There was a lot of work involved leading up to and during these events each year. There were also many social events after the closing ceremonies.

Safety was always a critical factor in moving aircraft and equipment to the CNE site for static display. Most aircraft involved arrived at our airfield, but the high-performance aircraft had to use the International airport, because of insufficient runway length at Downsview. With increasing traffic over the years, transfers were becoming more and more difficult, particularly from International. After near misses over the years, aircraft moves were always carried out in the early-morning hours when least traffic would be encountered. In 1970 a series of meetings were held about the increasing risks involved, and it was decided that an impenetrable moving screen of police cars would be provided to attend the movement of a CF104 Starfighter from International.

Nearing retirement in 1971 (also on back cover) (CF photo)

The early stages of the move went well, there were many cars in attendance with flashing lights; however, when we got onto the Queensway going east with only the outer westbound lane open, one inebriated driver going west attempted to change lanes, bounced off two police cars and broke through the screen before meeting the aircraft, with his vehicle still at high speed.

The top of the car was sheared off by the left aircraft wing, and the driver decapitated. The worst fears of the Toronto Police and the RCMP had been realized. That was the end of high-performance aircraft on static display at the CNE. The inquest agreed that all possible precautions had been taken, but questioned the wisdom of slow-moving convoys on city streets except for authentic emergencies.

Back to more positive things, with so many air cadet squadrons to support it was inevitable that we would be busy attending annual parades as reviewing officers. This activity was shared among the BComd and the four branch heads. My participation took me on several occasions to parades in Toronto, Richmond Hill, Weston,

Hamilton and Oakville. The sponsoring committee in the Richmond Hill Legion branch presented me with my initial one-year membership in the Royal Canadian Legion, as a token for a review done there.

A new CANEX store for Forces customers, operated by Base Fund (formerly Station Fund), had been developed. It was opened in a ceremony attended by BGen Cam Mussells, by then promoted and the Director of CANEX.

A new Base HQ building was also built. It had the appearance of a fortress and, although one of its justifications had been to gather the staff into one building, I managed to remain in my palatial office up on the hill. Davies accepted that my retirement would be coming up soon, and agreed a move was unnecessary.

The relative population of regular, reserve and retired Military Engineers of the three services in the Toronto area was demonstrated starkly by attendance at a Military Engineers Association mess dinner in honour of LGen Lindsay, Chief of Technical Services at CFHQ, and an ex-Royal Canadian Engineer (RCE) officer. The other attendees were 31 ex-RCE officers and myself, the dot of light blue in the picture which was taken, and the lone ex-RCAF attendee.

Certainly the post-retirement job which was gravitated to by me was out of the mainstream for an ex-military engineer. Upon seeing an ad that the RCAF Association was looking for a General Manager (GM), a decision was made to write a customized and focussed resumé aimed at getting the job. My submission was successful, and steps were taken to leave the Forces on September 17, 1971. Accumulated and retirement leave would make my official retirement date March 19, 1972. What was to have been a very short posting to Downsview had ended up eight years later with retirement. There were certainly lots of people who had come and gone during my time there.

I made one last request of the Forces, to be retired as a Wing Commander rather than as a Lieutenant-Colonel .... *and it was approved*, possibly the last so granted.

Now having retired, it was possible to look back on the irony of the situation. Having been recruited to help improve the experience level in the CE branch, I was now ending up after being employed outside the branch for almost half my postwar RCAF and CF career.

18

FROM ORDERING TO REQUESTING
1971-76

which describes employment at the RCAF Association Headquarters, Ottawa, Ontario

My retirement was very short, finishing work at Downsview on Friday, arriving in Ottawa on Sunday, and reporting for work on Monday, September 20. The National HQ, Royal Canadian Air Force Association (now Air Force Association of Canada), was at Beaver Barracks, on Metcalfe Street in central Ottawa, were I would be employed as General Manager (now called Executive Director). The job entailed operation of the HQ as the staff officer to the National Executive Council (NEC). I was also responsible for coordination assistance to six regional groups and 75 branches across Canada, and in California.

There was certainly a transition to be made. Having just left a military organization where 'orders' were given and (usually) obeyed, and now working in a volunteer association where actions were 'requested', you hoped they might take place. Sometimes they did, many times they didn't. Quiet coercion was the name of the game!

The previous incumbent, A/V/M Frank Ball, DFC, CD was leaving the job, I would be his replacement. Upon arrival it was found there had been 101 applicants. The focussed resumé did it! I recall thinking, 'With that vote of confidence I had better do a good job'.

My briefing from the National President, Al Goodwin of Moncton, NB, showed that there was certainly a lot to be done. It seemed apparent to me that the Association was in a precarious financial situation, with little reserves. Also, and unexpectedly, it was found that the Deputy General Manager was running a competing local parallel organization, the RCAF Prewar Club, out of our National Headquarters and there was little crossover in membership. The decision that we did not need a Deputy General Manager was not a difficult one. Ways to find other savings were initially less obvious, but investigation revealed many opportunities.

Generally the Association provides unity of purpose among serving and former participants in military aviation and their contemporaries in civil aviation, sponsors aeronautics in all its branches, participates in community programs, and works with the RCAF Benevolent Fund. It promotes and encourages an adequate and effective aviation component to meet the needs of National defence, and promotes and encourages responsible citizenship among Canadians.

The HQ was renting accommodation from DND at a very cheap rate compared to normal city rents, but it was paying for far more space than was necessary. One of the early cost-saving moves was to build a wall to divide what had been a very large General Manager's office *cum* NEC conference room into a smaller office for the GM and an office for the secretary. It had been used for the NEC function on only two occasions each year, and other such rooms were available in the building by arrangement when required.

Reaction was swift! With the renovations just begun, A/M Hugh Campbell, CBE, Order of the White Lion (Czechoslovakia), War Cross (Czechoslovakia), Commander Legion of Merit (US), CD, former Chief of the Air Staff, RCAF and a Past National President of the Association, visited to tell me it was wrong to get rid of the conference room. It should be left as it was. He was informed that we were broke, a lot of thought had been given and that, if the conference room stayed an additional $8,000 in annual income would be required. If he knew of a source for that sort of money on a continuing basis, without increases in outlay, it was possible for the room to stay.

After further discussion, he was reminded that he had sent me a letter of congratulations, when he was Chief of the Air Staff, on the excellent way my duties had been accomplished in the CE Section at Greenwood. I had been allowed to manage then, and suggested the same courtesy should be extended now. To be an effective GM, I had to be allowed to make decisions within my duties. As he had no answer from where the extra money would come, we finished our meeting with lunch at the Gloucester Street RCAF Officers Mess, and he became a supporter in the quest for improved management of the Association. But I had *thought* about the possibility of departing!

Generally in volunteer organizations the few do all the work, carry a silent majority and suffer the complaints of the remainder, who are certain they know best but get only minimally involved. The challenge is to create a strong image with which more people can identify. In the Association, many Wings had created a good local image as a community organization, but generally the atmosphere of a social club prevailed in isolation. It was just too easy to sit back and socialize. Many Wings gave lip service to the higher aims and objects of the Association to promote military and civil aviation, but they got full marks for their unstinting support of air cadets .... and there was always someone ready to start a castle revolution. There were several instances in Wings where cliques, with ambitions and an agenda of their own, challenged a Wing Executive. In some cases they had won to the detriment of the Association, in others over the long haul, they only succeeded in embarrassing themselves.

The only purely air force organization for all ranks, the Association suffered perennially from a fragmentation of ex-air force personnel among a vast sea of competing local organizations. Its membership, best placed to do so, supports the Canadian Air Force, no matter what its name may be at any given time. In doing so it absorbs the costs that all ex-RCAF members would logically be expected to share. Various attempts to change this situation and bring all ex-air force personnel together for common cause under one umbrella have had mediocre results which are difficult to explain. Sadly, many of those bled off by local organizations are retired senior officers whose expertise would be most valuable.

The Association, divided between Wing membership and Members-at-large, has had a history of ups and downs. Organized in 1948-49, by 1959 it had a membership of roughly 10,000; from a high of almost 13,000 in 1963 it hit a low of just over 9,000 by 1971. A full attack on the problem from a public relations view was required at the National level. Efforts had to be focussed toward getting the attention of the National media and potential members.

The 1971 Annual General Meeting (AGM)/Convention, which had been set up by Frank Ball and a committee of the local Wing, was held in Saskatoon September 29-October 1. It would be Al Goodwin's last activity as National President. The attendant annual general meeting featured the approval of a revised constitution and bylaws proffered by the Goodwin Committee, which had been set up by Alex Jardine, AFC, CD when he was National President. Members were Al Goodwin, Wally Gryba, George Ault and Sammy Sayle. Their recommendations updated the Association to then current times.

Goodwin was succeeded by Fred Way, a wartime Wellington pilot of 420 (Snowy Owl) Sqn who completed a tour of bombing operations in Europe and North Africa. Hailing from Calgary, Alberta (now resident in Penticton, BC), he was a MOT Designated Civilian Flight Test Examiner on private, commercial, and multi-engine aircraft. Fred practised as a flight instructor for many years and, no matter where he went in Western Canada, there was liable to be a pilot show up who had been one of his students.

Having lived there 16 years before, the visit to Saskatoon presented an opportunity to meet old friends and see the changes in the area. The meeting experience would serve in good stead in preparing updates of the processes in use. It was observed that many questions raised could be precluded by improved distribution of policies and procedures.

Tommy Dowd, who had looked after membership records for many years was about to retire, and Pierre Clermont, hired to replace him, remains in that job today, himself almost ready for retirement. The office manager also retired and was replaced by my daughter Brenda, who had moved to Ottawa with husband Berny, recently transferred to RCAF Station Uplands from previous duty with 5 Service Battalion at CFB Valcartier, Quebec.

Fred Way and I found that we were kindred spirits, thinking alike on the majority of management situations, the need to increase membership and to form alliances with other organizations. The difficulty of communication was solved by a conference phone call every Friday where I, as his staff officer, could report situations and receive direction, and confirm action that would be taken. This worked very well, and enabled progress, notwithstanding the distance, the more primitive communications resources of those days, and the few times each year that we met face-to-face.

Membership of the RCAFA in the National Council of Veterans Associations of Canada, chaired by Cliff Chadderton, Chief Executive Officer of the War Amps, allowed the Association to further its service on behalf of veterans without staffing for that purpose. Accordingly, steps were taken to strengthen the ties represented by that membership.

Recognizing that the production and issue of policies and procedures was a paramount need, a booklet series was developed with 15 individual booklets in the '100 series', covering all aspects of Association activity in which Wings were involved. They were distributed to Wings, Groups and NEC members. The '1,000 series' covered limited distribution subjects such as National Conventions, Guidelines for Convention Hotels, Forming New Wings and Group Convention Guidelines. The issue of these booklets reduced the volume of questions directed to HQ, and resulted in much-improved administration of the matters covered.

A host Wing was responsible for arranging hotels and other resources for a convention within NHQ requirements; however, where convention arrangements had previously been short term, usually beginning one year before a convention, timing was now extended to three years. This improved considerably the choice of available hotels, and the ease with which arrangements could be made.

In the winter of 1971/72 a liaison trip was undertaken to Wings in the United States, not previously visited by anyone from the National level. Bunny travelled with me by Forces scheduled passenger aircraft to Colorado Springs, Colorado where a rental car was obtained to drive via Albuquerque, New Mexico for a visit to 902 (Aero Camino) Wing in Santa Barbara, California where Jim Thompson, an acquaintance from our concurrent postings at Greenwood, hosted us.

After a successful meeting with the Wing, he went with us for a visit the next day to the Aero Spacelines Inc. factory that transformed Boeing B377 Stratocruisers, into Guppy-type freighter aircraft which, with minimum clearance around the load, transported ballistic missiles from factories to Cape Canaveral, Florida for use in the NASA space program. Initially the boosters had been carried by rail, but their diameters had been limited to those of the railway tunnels along the way, then they were delivered by sea, but that was slow. The Guppies answered both problems. Aero Spacelines has disappeared. The Guppies are now a product of Airbus Industries, the Super Guppy being the latest, with a cargo compartment 25 ft (7.6 m) tall, 25 ft (7.6 m) wide and 111 feet (33.8 m) long.

Next, Bunny and I drove up the west coast to San Francisco, California where a successful meeting was attended at 900 (Golden Bear) Wing with Bill Tuttle, whom we had met as a delegate at the convention in Saskatoon, as host. After an enjoyable 3-day visit there, we drove back to Colorado Springs and our return flight to Ottawa.

On April 3, 1972, Bunny said she did not feel well and went off to rest in the afternoon. Two hours later I went to the bedroom to rouse her, but she had died from heart failure. We had spent 22 very happy years together!

Fred Way and I ventured into the Maritimes in the summer of 1972 for liaison visits. We picked up a rental car in Moncton, NB to go to Nova Scotia for visits to Wings along the North Shore and in Cape Breton. We also visited the Alexander Graham Bell Museum and the birthplace of flight in Canada. Upon coming back across the Canso causeway, Fred said, 'I will always remember that Wing (Sydney), they are all very strong leaders. Its too bad this is not a corporation for just one day, there are at least 15 members there that we could post to some Wings across Canada that need real leadership. And I don't think I will ever forget Big John!!' The trip gave us additional time to outline to each other the actions each felt were required to advance the Association, and they matched consistently. The opportunity was also taken to introduce Fred to my home town on the way back to Moncton.

The 1972 convention was held in Ottawa September 28-30 with the Governor General, the Hon. Roland Michener and Mrs. Michener as honoured guests. Fred and I had been instrumental in creating the *Airman of the Year* award. This would be its initial presentation, and Peter Engbrecht, CGM was the first recipient.

Because it was the first convention I had planned, there was a strong desire that nothing should go wrong, as had happened at the 1967 convention in Montreal when George Ault, QC, the National President at the time, after a few drinks was speaking at the podium during the Annual Banquet, with the US Air Force Chief of Staff in attendance as the honoured guest. While speaking, George, already a short person, became shorter and shorter, his head slowly reaching the level of the podium, then he slid quietly under the table and, as another attendee has said, was hardly missed.

The Governor General speaking at the 1972 convention

My problem concerning the banquet in 1972 arose about 15 minutes before the arrival of the Governor General, when it was found that ticket-takers were prolonging the ticket checks, and only half the attendees had been seated. With the prospect that there would still be some unseated when dinner started, hurried instructions were given to dispense with ticket taking, and all were seated with seconds to spare, as the honoured guests approached.

It has been said that a spouse who has experienced a happy married life is liable, after the death of a loved one, to remarry sooner rather than later, and even sooner if the deceased had indicated that such a course should be taken to get on with life.

I met Sybil Molstad, a member of 410 (Ottawa) Wing when on a liaison visit to the Wing in July. She was a financial clerk in the Public Service, part of whose responsibility was the bookkeeping for Canada's bilingual program. She was probably the only one who knew what it *really* cost.

We were married October 20, 1972. The best man was Sammy Sayle, an ex-Sgt Air Gunner who originated in Jamaica, a stalwart member who had kept the local Wing operating through thick and thin over many years, and who also made a valuable contribution at the National level. Unfortunately, he lost the wedding ring in his suit-coat pocket. He could feel it, but for some reason there was a layer of cloth preventing access. Only when we threatened to use a jackknife to retrieve it did he manage recovery.

Sammy became famous at one meeting for his comment at the podium, 'Will someone please turn on the lights back there, so the people can see me', and for his oft-given and stirring solo rendition of the *Airman's Prayer*.

Our honeymoon was spent at Sir Sam's Inn, Haliburton, Ontario, which was well-known through my practise flights from Downsview.

My extended family was now increased by Sybil's two sons, Stan, a manager at Air Canada, and David, a staff officer with the Government of the North West Territories. We moved into Sybil's house on Nanny Goat Hill (38 Primrose Street), Ottawa. She had rented out the upstairs apartment, and wished to continue doing so, because there was a good tenant in residence. This led to us building a ground-floor bedroom as an addition to the house.

The hierarchy of the Association agreed that we should be improving its support of the aviation industry and many overtures were made, directed toward working in partnership with the industry at all levels. A series of individual discussions at this time with, among others, Punch Dickens, OC, OBE, DFC; Claude Taylor, OC, of Air Canada and Max Ward, OC, of Wardair, covered employee organizations and the employers role in them, and the likelihood of them wishing to align with others in the broader aviation community.

Earlier, while at Downsview, talks with Phil Garratt, CM, AFC, Past President of DHC included similar subjects when he talked about employee alliances and organizations, as they applied to employee aspirations. All these discussions led to further consideration of an overall umbrella organization that would cover all current and retired Canadian aviation participants.

Fred Way and Wally Gryba, an ex-RCAF radio officer and an employee of the Federal Department of Indian Affairs who was Association Vice President at the time, discussed the Honorary Presidency of the Association with George Sellars, Chairman of Canadian Pacific Airlines. The Honorary President had traditionally been drawn from the ranks of retired RCAF senior officers; however, Sellars agreed to assume the position. He would later be followed in it by his successor as Chairman at the airline, Jack Gilmer. It was felt that participation from this source would work to the advantage of the Association, but Gilmer was the last, before the position again reverted to retired senior air force officers.

Time was taken up consolidating changes approved at the 1972 convention, and preparing proposed changes for approval at the next meeting, which was scheduled for Moncton, NB October 10-13, 1973. Fred had initiated and received approval for a new trophy honouring Gordon R. McGregor, OBE, DFC, Commander Order of Orange-Nassau with Swords (The Netherlands), Croix de Guerre with Silver Star (France), War Cross 1939 (Czechoslovakia), who was the oldest Canadian pilot in the Battle of Britain (1940). He commanded the Canadian Fighter Wing in Alaska (1942) and 126 Wing in Normandy and Holland (1944-45). Later he was President of Trans Canada Airlines (TCA), the predecessor of Air Canada, and a Past Honorary President of the Association, before his death in 1971.

Ron and Sybil 1973, in a receiving line

Assembly of the trophy was delayed because the design included aircraft models on two pylons: two Hurricanes in formation on one pylon to represent service as a fighter pilot in WWII, and a DC8 aircraft on the other, to represent McGregor's leadership of TCA. The models finally became available just before departure for Moncton (with hammer, drill, screwdriver, wrench and pliers packed), and I assembled the trophy on a hotel room floor at the Beausejour Hotel, with its initial presentation taking place the next day.

Wally Gryba became National President at the Moncton meeting, and the same calibre of cooperation as had been experienced with Fred Way followed. We searched out and actioned many things that would improve the Association in the eyes of both its members and the public. Interactions with the civilian aviation community were given priority based on the initiation of the McGregor Trophy. Good rapport resulted, and we kept searching for additional ways to interact in the civil aviation field, while maintaining good connections with the current air force.

Sybil and I travelled to her home town at Steinbach, Manitoba to visit friends, then on to liaison visits with Wings at Winnipeg, Regina and Edmonton. On the return trip from Edmonton, Air Canada Flight 104 suffered mechanical problems and the aircraft did not go on from Winnipeg. There was an uproar to get seats to Ottawa. Joe Clark, the Federal Conservative party leader and Claude Ryan from Quebec were trying to get attention from desk staff, when I realized there was a phone on the wall beside me. Calling the Air Canada number, two seats were booked on the next Ottawa flight while the people at the counter were still fussing about who was going where and when. Clark and Ryan were not on board. It pays to grasp all the opportunities that life presents!

A new venture began in 1973 when the RCAF Association Trust was created. I had considered that it would be beneficial, and recommended its establishment to NEC. Relevant donations would be tax deductible. It took some time for Wings to recognize the flow-through capability of the Trust (to designate the destination of donations) but, when they did so, funds donated to it increased greatly. The Trust has since been responsible for disbursing more than $780,000.

Looking for something to do in our spare time, Sybil and I purchased a large duplex (5 bedrooms on one side, 4 on the other) of early 1900s vintage on Fourth Ave. It appeared nothing had been upgraded since it was built. The old lady who owned it, and had lived alone on the 5-bedroom side, moved into care accommodation. The other side had tenants up and down. We proceeded to rehabilitate it, beginning with the larger unit. The responsibility for renovation was mine, Sybil did the decorating. Once the first side had been completed we looked at the situation much differently, the tenants had caused all kinds of problems, phoning at all hours of the night. We sensed that they were going to move out because of a perceived rent increase in the future. We were fed up with their attitude, ……. there must be better ways to make a buck. We decided to sell, and the place was purchased by two young newly-married sisters and their husbands, the sisters wishing to live side by side. They would renovate the second unit. Although we bowed out, a good profit had resulted from the venture.

A/M Slemon, fourth from left, led the representative RCAF D-Day veterans at the 30th Anniversary in 1974 (CF photo)

Next came news that a new granddaughter, Holly had been born December 30, 1973, with Jackie and Don the proud parents of their first-born.

In June 1974 Veteran's Affairs included me in the group going to Normandy for the 30th Anniversary of D-Day. The RCAF contingent, comprising five veterans of action in a short period based on D-Day, was led by A/M Roy Slemon, CBE, Legion of Merit (US), Legion of Honour (France), Croix de Guerre (France), CD, BSc. We also went with Air Div representatives to visit the Choloy Commonwealth Cemetery, located at Nancy, France where personnel who died at Air Div are interred.

August 1974 found Sybil with me on a visit to Great Britain, our mission being to search out the graves of our ancestors, mine near Southampton, hers on the Isle of Wight in England, and at Rothesay on the Isle of Bute in Scotland.

The 1974 convention was hosted in Windsor, Ontario by 412 (Windsor) Wing October 9-12. Toronto Region invested me with the *Peculiar Presentation of the Platinum Pig* at the gala dinner. The pig represented Hogtown, a derogatory name for the metropolis. Atlantic Group presented the *Golden Lobster*, which had been initiated by A/V/M Laurie Morfee, CB, CBE, OBE, CD, Legion of Merit (US).

Work had continued on the booklet series, and there were always busy times on interaction with serving air force personnel, many of whom could be found at the RCAF mess for lunch. There was always lobbying to be done, mostly with selected Senators and MPs, on behalf of the Association. Time was also taken up with correspondence, visits by members who were on vacation in Ottawa, and there was always preparation for conventions and three or four NEC meetings each year, either one or two in Ottawa, the remainder before and after each convention at the convention location.

Life membership was obtained in the Canadian Warplane Heritage and the D-Day & Normandy Fellowship. The Dodo Bird Club of RCAF Flight Sergeants, the Canadian Society of Air Force Musicians and the RCAF Eastern Air Command Marine Squadron Association all presented me with Honorary memberships.

In 1975 the 'Professional Manager (PMgr)' designation was granted by the Canadian Institute of Management, and membership was also obtained in the Canadian Institute of Association Executives.

The 1975 AGM was held in Edmonton, hosted by 700 (City of Edmonton) Wing October 8-11, then in 1976 the AGM moved to Hamilton, Ontario October 6-9.

A proposal had been developed for submission to that meeting, covering a proposed new organization to be called *Aviation Canada*. It was developed in conjunction with the Chairmen of some of Canada's airlines and aviation industry companies. The intention was that our Association would join the new organization after a period of incubation. Having been instrumental in creating the organization outline and its responsibilities, an attempt had been made by me to have the aviation companies set aside sufficient of their personnel to organize and establish it, without success. Rather, it would be up to the Association to build it, with civil aviation support and assistance. This required approval at an annual meeting.

Warren Hunt, National President at the time, presented the proposal at Hamilton without any emphasis or emotion, and seemed very reluctant to sell the idea. It was not approved, shot down by delegates who had not been briefed sufficiently to comprehend the many advantages which would accrue. The old boy's network wanted to keep things cosy, and could only perceive a lot of hard work ahead. This brought to mind the old adage penned by Friedrich Von Schiller, 'Anyone taken as an individual is tolerably sensible and reasonable— as a member of a crowd he becomes a blockhead.'

A 'rainy-day fund' had been initiated by Fred Way and I back in 1972 during his tenure as President, and we managed to cloak it within the annual statements in a completely legal way, with the knowledgeable help of the auditing firm. In the event that there might be rainy days ahead, it was an attempt to cushion the effect of any damaging occurrence. It might also be available for a development project the Association might wish to undertake; however, there was no idea at the time what the nature of such a project might be. Although several members of the NEC were privy to its existence, it remained a secret for some time while further funds were found to add to it.

My hearing loss (dubbed Lancaster ear in Britain) was becoming an impairment, particularly when there was difficulty with statements over microphones by delegates at meetings. It was said by one jokester, 'You have 70% hearing in one ear and 30% in the other. That's 100%. What's the problem?' A hearing aid was obtained and expected to improve the situation, but results were much less than satisfactory so, with deep reluctance, I had to leave the Association job in late 1976 before I said 'Yes' to something that deserved a 'No'. I would have liked very much to stay .... the job was always exciting! Now, a second retirement and new challenges were ahead.

Doug Harvey, DFC, CD was my replacement as GM. He was the 408 Sqn pilot who had joined with our crew and others in opening packages from home at Beningbrough Hall, and was now retired from RCAF Public Relations.

His proposed project to improve the status of the Association was the establishment of *Airforce* magazine, although many wondered whether it might be a risky venture, given that it was expected the routine responsibilities of the GM would have to languish in deference to the work required on the magazine. The $30,000 then in the 'rainy day' fund would be used as the seed money for the magazine; otherwise, there were no funds to start *any* project, and there would again be no reserve funds in place. The eggs were now all in one basket!

Although it would probably generate a significant membership increase, it would also change the Association's direction, which had been one of looking outward to civil aviation and others for the last several years. It would now be back to a parochial view based on the Association's original ex-air force back-ground. Many had qualms because of the lack of backup funds, the unknowns involved in the magazine and the checkered and doomed lives of other similar magazines in Canada; however, in the end it was seen as worthwhile to attempt it, and a reluctant decision was made to go ahead. Unfortunately, Doug seems to have been better at PR than at fiscally astute management, and the seed money disappeared in a sudden flurry of activity. As there was no backup in case of crisis, the Association spent many months teetering on the brink of disaster, and the earlier fears that other management duties would be allowed to languish were confirmed.

19

ENTREPRENEUR AND VOLUNTEER
1976-84

which outlines experiences involving the village of Clayton, and Unique Decor

Sybil and I owned a summer cottage on the Mississippi River near Carleton Place, Ontario. As it was within easy access of our home in Ottawa, we had foreseen developing it as our retirement home. Mitigating against that, it was built on a stone bench beside the river where there was little earth cover, and it would be difficult to landscape. We decided to look around the area for something with better prospects. As usual there were lots of places, but the majority were in poor condition and seemed useless for our intended purpose; however one day, exploring in the direction of Clayton, Ontario, we had given up looking at properties advertised in the newspaper and were ready to turn for home.

There, right in front of us, as we went south into Concession Road 2 to turn around, was a sign in front of a riverside property. We fell in love with the property and bought it the next day, eventually receiving the deed on August 30, 1976. We could not move out of Ottawa right away, so we rented it back to the seller, Ralph Monette while he completed a new home he was working on. The move was made from Ottawa in the Spring of 1977, and we settled into village life.

Clayton, a small village on the Indian River, is 40 miles (64 km) west of Ottawa. Located north of Carleton Place and northwest of Almonte, it had been a busy place in the late 1800s until bypassed by the railroad. Then it settled down to be a place that time had passed by. When we arrived there it seemed as if we had gone back 50 years. There was a genuine old-time general store and post office in the most picturesque of settings. Commuting into Ottawa was easy, both summer and winter, to the point that some of our cultural connections remained with Ottawa rather than Almonte, where a wide range of activity was also available.

There was a 3-bedroom bungalow on the property, built in 1967. Because of the sloping land, it was two storeys at the back. It was about 500 ft (152 m) upstream from the Clayton dam, backing up the Indian River system to form Clayton Lake. There was a smaller lake in front of the house then, after negotiating westward along a reach of river, the main lake came into view.

My first volunteering effort in the village was as owner's representative for the construction of the Clayton Community Centre. Eldon Munro had the contract and Clarence Gemmill, the Postmaster, was president of the Clayton Recreation Club, owner of the building. Charlie Rath, a municipal public works employee, was treasurer. The project was 50% funded by *Wintario*, the Ontario Lottery Commission, with the balance raised in the community.

Before long a hue and cry went up from pro-temperance residents. Horrors! Liquor would be available at dances! The Recreation Club asked me to counter the outcry, and this led to several articles for the *Almonte Gazette*. Before long the furore died down. The building completed, it was a welcome and much needed facility in the community.

In the winter, cross country skiing on the river, lake and surrounding bush trails, often with neighbours, kept us in trim. For summer activity, early acquisition of a 16-foot (5 metre) Sports Pal canoe enabled us, with the help at times of an electric trolling motor, to explore the lake system. It was soon found that the Sports Pal was sluggish in relation to other canoes, so a York canoe of the same length was added to our inventory. Now guest couples could join us, the men in the Sports Pal, the women in the York. But it wasn't all smooth sailing.

One day we got soaked by a torrential downpour that had not been forecast. On another occasion I was unceremoniously dumped from the canoe as we tried to disembark. That prompted an immediate start on a floating dock! Flotation was provided by rigid insulation under the deck, but the muskrats liked its taste and would do anything to get to it through the outer boards. A running battle started, attempting several different solutions, but it had not been won by 2001 when the place was sold.

Birds were plentiful. An annual bird list was kept which usually numbered about 120 species each year. There were at least four nesting pairs of Common Loons and several Great Blue Herons on the lake system. Wild animals in the area ranged from bears to deer, beavers, martens, mink, muskrats, otters, rabbits and raccoons.

The soil in the garden was the very best. It grew marvellous crops: tomatoes the size of baseballs, big potatoes and outsized ears of corn. The raccoons always managed to get to the corn first, but it was tall and they had difficulty reaching up to break off the ears. One would climb up until its weight uprooted the stalk, and if it took two or more climbers to topple it, no problem, that also happened.

The house had been heated with oil but, with wood available, it was decided to install a wood/oil combination furnace. Discussion with Ralph Monette resulted in agreement to husband a section of his wood lot in return for any salvaged wood. This enabled most of our heating to be produced at no cost other than gas for the chain saw and the sweat factor.

At the Spring 1977 NEC meeting the Association Distinguished Service Award was presented to me, as was the Queen Elizabeth Jubilee Medal 1977 later that year.

In Fall 1977, a combination workshop, warehouse and carport was constructed and the shop equipped with a full range of carpentry and shop tools. After the second retirement, it was felt there should be more involvement than just community work. Sybil had started a business, *Unique Decor Unlimited*, in the basement garage to make and sell free-form decorative ceramic products.

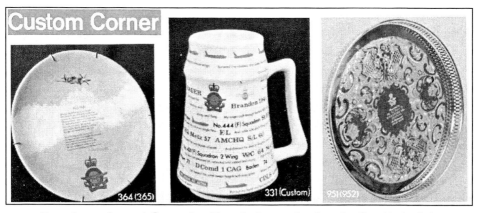

From the catalogue- left to right, 10-inch plate with colour Spitfire, High Flight and RCAF badge, a career mug listing all postings, and an engraved silver tray

Deep concern was felt for the financial situation in the Association. The Association needed financial help in the early period of *Airforce*, and it was doubted there would ever be enough money to float it in the short term. So after discussion, Sybil agreed that we jointly run the company and expand it to include military memorabilia products. The Association already had regalia and a few general RCAF-badged items, but there seemed to be a large unserved market for nostalgia items as veterans aged. Accordingly, arrangements were made with Airforce Productions Limited (AFPL), the Association subsidiary responsible for publishing *Airforce* and selling regalia products, for new items to be developed and advertised in the magazine.

We expanded the *Unique Decor* product lines as fast as possible and, when orders arrived at AFPL, picked them up and provided fulfilment services, with AFPL getting an automatic 20% rebate on all sales arising from an Association source. We were able to provide a turn-around to shipment time of approximately one week.

Initially, simple ceramic items were offered with RCAF and RCAFA badges. A glass decoration company in Barrie, Ontario was soon bought and its resources, which included updated kilns, integrated into Unique Decor. New creations were developed based primarily on the poems *High Flight* by P/O John Gillespie Magee, Jr, RCAF; *Our Ground Crew* (author unknown); *The Airman's Prayer* by W/C G. P. Creed, RCAF; and *An Airman's Grace* by Father John McGillivray, RCAF.

Wooden plaques, pen sets, watches and belt buckles

The initial product was a 6" x 6" (15cm x 15cm) ceramic tile on which a coloured badge was applied, along with a poem. They were also used on any product that had one flat surface the size of the decoration or larger, such as beer steins, vases, and open books. On some products the badges were replaced with service or civilian aircraft or Remembrance text.

Another popular decoration, Sgt. Shatterproof, created by RCAF graphic artist, the late Warrant Officer Ray Tracy[6], and others of Ray's cartoons were used as wrap-around decorations on beer steins, and flat on tiles associated with wood plaques.

There was a series, *Quotes from the RCAF* which provided early and prolonged sales volume as did *Aviation Comicups,* and station and squadron badges. We also listed popular products obtained from other manufacturers, a wide selection of aviation books, *Canadian Skies* calendars and colouring books, aircraft lapel pins, ball caps, belts and several others. Miniature badges for rings and other applications, searched out from wartime end-stocks at jeweller's shops near wartime air force stations in Canada, rounded out the items available.

By 1978 we could provide both ceramic and glassware items with access to decoration involving many full-colour badges. All of these products were included in an AFPL catalogue published by *Unique Decor.* As a volunteer director of AFPL, it was possible to promote both the sales program and the Association in the catalogue.

The combined appeal of *Airforce* magazine, and the increasing size of our catalogue enabled the magazine to weather the early years; however, we didn't rest on our laurels. We kept adding products to keep sales up over an extended period.

---

6   Ray's cartoon "TGIF at the Mess" is shown in one of its applications on page 174, Sgt Shatterproof at page 176.

The next move was to add civilian-badged items and sell them direct to stores and civilian organizations. This helped us make enough profit that we could continue the 20% rebate to AFPL. A *Unique Decor* wholesale catalogue was produced, mirroring the AFPL catalogue, and we soon began wholesale sales throughout Canada, in particular sales to the Forces-wide CANEX stores and aviation supply stores.

On the supply side, we had standing purchase orders with local cottage industry for 300 undecorated ceramic beer steins each month. More new badges were added to our inventory as fast as we could pay for the firing-ready colour decorations. By arrangement with Joe Schwarek, a plaque producer, we were able to advertise his entire line of wood plaques with military badges in both catalogues. These were picked up at his plant, on the route from Ottawa,

A badged carafe set

as orders were received. By 1980, customer response had resulted in the catalogues increasing to 28 pages.

On the sales side, it was not uncommon to have orders for several cases of glassware for a reunion of a RCAF squadron. Customers were located as far away as CFS Alert, North West Territories and CFB Baden-Solingen, Germany. Attendance at air shows and reunions from time to time provided both onsite sales and the opportunity for discussion with show attendees regarding choices for possible future products.

There was one order which was not welcome, from Lahore, India for one of each item in the catalogue. Obviously intended for pirating, it was ignored.

Pat Murphy, owner/partner of Aviation World in Vancouver, BC was one customer with significant purchases. At one point he wrote in a note with his invoice payment, 'It's a pleasure to see an energetic sales promotion such as yours. Blind trust. You must be instrument-rated!'

The NEC invited me to its Winter 1980 meeting, which was held at North American Aerospace Defence Headquarters, Peterson AFB, Colorado Springs, Colorado and its hardened site under Cheyenne Mountain. Again, in 1981, there was an invitation to go to 407 Sqn CFB Comox, BC for the Winter NEC meeting.

Meanwhile, word of Dad's health had not been good for some time, and he died March 28, 1980 at age 87.

Airforce had been steadily gaining in advertising and content over the years, although advertising was very hard to come by, and membership advantages gained by having the magazine took hold slowly; however, by 1989 membership had increased to 12,756 and by 1995, with the Association name changed to *Air Force Association of Canada*, and the help of a National recruiting campaign, it was 15,170. It peaked in 1999 at 16,380.

The black-and-white decoration shown is by Ray Tracy. Combined with a colour badge and lettering it was used on two tiles placed on a wood plaque background, as 'TGIF at the Mess". The lettering at lower right is, "There shall be no discussion of politics, religion or women, KR (Air)" as if that might be considered at a TGIF. Many have recognized their friends around the piano.

It is hard to gauge the PR effect the sales program had on improving the Association's existence, vis-à-vis the magazine. Nonetheless, the eggs were divided among more than one basket. The sales program was of some assistance in keeping the wolf from the door, and Airforce has now become the leading aviation magazine in the country, in no small measure due to the efforts of publisher, Bob Tracy; founding editor Doug Steubing; and the current editor, Vic Johnson.

In Summer 1980, older friends Hilda and Earl Davis, who lived in Ottawa but had a cherished homestead across the river at Breckenridge, Quebec asked us what we knew about auction sales. They had many pieces of antique furniture in the house, left by their forebears, and were experiencing a lot of vandalism. The decision was made to hold an auction sale to dispose of the property and its contents. Sybil introduced them to Charles Hollinger, an auctioneer whose sales we had attended. After he got a license to work in Quebec, planning began in earnest. There were certain things that needed to be done in preparation for the sale, like replacing some rotting verandah posts, and preparing a toilet for auction attendees to use.

A farm tractor with a front-end bucket was used to lift the roof and take out each verandah post in turn, replace it, and lower the roof onto it before nailing. During this process the tractor transmission was acting up, jerking the tractor back and forth each time it moved. As part of this process Earl and the tractor disappeared unintentionally into the shrubbery, and he backed out without his toupée. No problem, he just went back in, pulled it down onto his head, and continued with the work at hand although, without a mirror available, the toupée had a rather rakish tilt for the rest of the day.

The preparation of the toilet seat also caused some laughs. He had been asked to use one from the bathroom in the house, but he thought it a better idea to cut a hole in a piece of plywood with a chain saw, and let it go at that. When we saw it, it was obvious that splinters would transfer if it was sat upon. He eventually got it right by adding the regular seat mentioned earlier, and a successful auction was held.

By 1981 a building permit had been obtained to add to, and remodel our home in Clayton. Ralph Monette contracted to build an extension across the back to the weatherproof stage. This addition would contain a generous lower floor plant room, storage closets and an outside patio. The second floor would allow the size of the kitchen, bathroom and master bedroom to be doubled. We would do the exterior cladding and the interior ourselves but, with everything else we were involved in, it became a slow process. Because of several unforeseen circumstances, it was not fully completed until 2001. Included in the interior changes were the removal of partitions to form a larger living room and to improve the view, parquet hardwood floors throughout, new kitchen cupboards, and updated kitchen and bathroom fixtures.

Sybil, without success, had been telling her doctor for several years that there was something wrong in her body that she could not explain, causing her to be ill at times. She was eventually diagnosed in late 1981 .... inoperable cancer. She had been right in her conviction all along, and the decision was quickly made to fight back.

An assistant would live at our place, and look after essential *Unique Decor* business. We went to the Livingston Clinic in San Diego, California in June 1982, where Sybil was put on an advanced series of treatments. When it was necessary for me to return home on business, her son David took my place to provide company until my return two weeks later. Eventually, after three months there, she was informed that the treatments were improving the situation, but certainly not fast enough for lasting effect. She was advised that she should abandon the treatment, that continuing would be fruitless.

Six months later she was supposed to go to palliative care, but chose to stay at home. She would be looked after by me up to the point when there was no alternative to going to hospital. She promised that she would go there when I decided it was time to make the move. On March 24, 1983 it was decided she should let me take her to the hospital. The decision had been made just in time, she died the next day.

There did not seem now to be much point in finishing the house. For months there was tar paper and battens on the outside, and only half the inside work completed. Keeping busy with other activities, it seemed impossible to get beyond them.

Sgt. Shatterproof, by Ray Tracy

20

CHINA, AND ELSEWHERE
1984-2000

which covers early retirement and travel

Unique Decor experienced continued growth and there were requests from several people to buy it. At the time, finishing the house had priority, but there was no desire to give up the company yet, even though it was being run down to some extent, no new products were being added.

And, by the way, did someone say retirement was not a busy time? Complaints are often heard from seniors that they have nothing to do. There was reason to think it was busier now than when working. There was always lots to do, and always someone wanting help to do ..... *their* ...... thing.

In 1984 I met Geraldine Knight of Ottawa, who had been in the WAAF in a short postwar period, and was retired as a technician in wood anatomy with the Federal government. Her post-employment venture was as an artist. She had taken arts training and was an alumnus of Algonquin College, where the Arts faculty is located beside the Rideau Canal in Ottawa. This became the inspiration for the name of a group of artists trained there, who formed the *Canal Art Group* at Geraldine's behest.

We both liked travelling so, considering the many advantages of travelling as a couple rather than as singles, we decided to pool our resources and become travelling companions. Our intention was to travel widely, and often, throughout the world, becoming part of the renewable resources of many communities worldwide. We also considered that it was time for me to retire (the third time), so that we could take advantage of discounted last-minute travel.

We soon developed a routine, that of her arriving at Clayton on Fridays to a prepared dinner, then spending Saturday and Sunday in mutual village activities. She usually returned to Ottawa after dinner on Sunday. In turn, I was usually in Ottawa overnight on business or errands at least once each week.

Later on, when marriage was discussed, she reminded me that God had not blessed her first marriage (to a Swiss national) and that she did not anticipate that He would bless a second. She had experienced significant problems in her marriage and would not take the chance. We would continue to maintain separate homes but my extended family now included her two sons, Jean-Pierre, of Zurich, Switzerland, a computer technician who ran a distribution and training firm, and Laurence, of Woodbridge, Ontario, an Ontario Land Surveyor.

The Great Wall through an archway

We became avid globe trotters usually doing one or two major trips each year. The first of these was a long trip beginning September 1985, intended to break the syndrome that kept me working instead of taking it easy. Our primary destination was Beijing, China where our friends, Tom and Millie Clark were employed at the Canadian embassy, but we intended to make the most of the trip by including stops along the way. Geraldine found that a trip around the world was cheapest. She departed September 25, ahead of me, and went West with a scheduled break in Vancouver (to see her brother); then to Beijing via Tokyo, Japan; Bankok, Thailand; Bombay, India; and London, England via Dubai, United Arab Emirates.

On the other hand, I departed Ottawa October 3 going West to Toronto, then East to Singapore's Changi Airport via London and Bombay, using an Air Canada parent's pass provided by stepson Stan. On arrival at Changi a flight was found to Beijing via Hong Kong. By the time I arrived Geraldine had been in Beijing for three days, and was almost acclimatized. We stayed in Beijing for about three weeks, did all the tourist attractions, and purchased rugs for our homes at the Peoples Rug Factory No.1.

There were rugs in piles throughout a massive warehouse, but there was only one in one of the patterns we liked. It was on the floor, obviously with one corner run over by a loader, its corner being dirty and heavily tread-marked. We ordered several rugs in different designs, including one of the design on the floor, but said categorically that it was to be a newly manufactured one, not the one on the floor.

It was time to leave Beijing. Tom and Millie had been wonderful hosts, ensuring that any help we needed was provided through their resources, and we would visit them again in 1987........ but be greeted in another place, Moscow, Russia! And we would visit many interesting places in that country.

Next, we went on October 19 (Day 1) on a 24-day escorted tour with the China Tourist Service in which, for the first part, we would board a plane for a destination, land there and be met by a guide and driver, taken on a local tour, stay at a hotel for one or two nights, visit local attractions, then repeat the process again the next day at a new location. We flew to Xian in a DC-6. The Terracotta Army (Day 2) was the primary attraction but next day the Small Goose Pagoda provided a challenge and a good laugh with its 184 steps. The guide decided not go up with us, probably expecting that those old people would not go up very far. We fooled him, and went all the way to the top. He ended up there right behind us, puffing and perspiring. He had not lost face after all, but sure came close!

Map 3- Partial map of China showing the tour route (R. Diment VRG)

Day 4 was a stop in Kunming and a 125-mile (200-km) drive by car to the Stone Forest of Lunan, 64,000 acres (25,600 ha) of eroded limestone, which was really an inspiring sight. The driver on this trip blew his horn at almost everything that moved, even vehicles coming in the opposite direction, on a long section of road converted to a single lane by rows of rice laid out to dry on half the width of the pavement. There were several times that he had to cut out into the rice to save us. He was relatively young, so when I buy rice even today it comes to mind that he may have run over it. Our overnight hotel at the Stone Forest was ancient. Smoke poured out around the eaves of the kitchen annex and made us wonder if we would be served double-charred Chinese food. The next morning we were driven back to Kunming and given a city tour, before leaving for Guilin. Oh! Almost overlooked, ... the food at the Stone Forest hotel was excellent!

We were to leave Kunming from the military airport, where we were unloaded from a bus at the furthest distance possible from the airport buildings (Communist security, I suppose) and stood in the field surrounded by our luggage. The aircraft, a Hawker-Siddeley Trident, taxied up and refuelling was started. It did not take long for most of the 90 or so passengers, mostly Caucasions, to retreat in a hurry, moving a considerable distance away with their baggage. The fellow doing the refuelling had the nozzle in one hand, nonchalantly holding a lighted cigarette in the other, but the aircraft lived to fly another day .... and we all had to carry our own bags back to the aircraft before boarding the flight.

Guilin was the next stop (Day 8), where the main attraction was a 2-hour boat trip on the River Li to Yangshuo, through some of the most glorious scenery ever viewed. On the way back by van, a 1,000 year old banyan tree provided a place to stop, and then we encountered a Chinese funeral procession of at least 200 people en route to a grave site. Our conclusion was that the deceased must have been very important, or had hordes of relatives. On Day 9, we arrived in Shanghai where we met guide Xu Goo Ting, and over-nighted at the Seagull Hotel. Day 10 included a Shanghai harbour cruise.

Then we changed to railway travel with escorted day tours, and over-nighting at a local hotel in each city. The first train trip, on Day 11, was to Hangzhou, a resort famous for scenery, scenery and more scenery. We visited a Tea Commune to learn how tea leaves are grown and dried, and then met young children in their school. A visit to West Lake was next, then to the largest silk factory in China, with 400 computer-controlled looms in one large room, using 1970s technology.

The Day 12 train journey was to Suzhou, the Venice of the East, for wonderful scenic views and several visits to industrial plants. The next day we visited the Wangshi

(Fisherman's) Garden and the Humble Administrator's Garden where our guide, a very small teenager with a big pennant for us to follow, got lost. A TV crew from Hong Kong was filming, and her route had to be changed. We got her back on track and taught her some navigation, showing her how she should look up above the fence to see the buildings outside, where she could identify the spot where we entered the garden.

On Day 14 we took a 40-minute train ride to Wuxi. There were several opportunities during a tour of the city to see the Grand Canal and its many convoys of linked barges. We were treated to a wonderful boat trip (Day 15) on Lake Wei Hi. We also went to another silk factory, and visited a pagoda

Linked barges on the Grand Canal, through the smog

high on a hill above the city plain. The next day included a visit to a clay figure factory, a short cruise on the Grand Canal, and departure by train for the return to Shanghai, where the evening entertainment was a performance at the Shanghai Acrobatic Theatre to finish the tour. Boy, were they good!!

We overnighted again in Shanghai and left (Day 17) by air for Wuhan where we did a city tour, and then joined *MV Emei* for a Yangtze River cruise through the Three Gorges to Chungking. After the captain's welcome cocktail party that evening, one of the *hors d'oeuvres* served at dinner was turnip slices topped with sugar .... a new one to us! We were the only Caucasians at our table but one of the Chinese men was from San Francisco, California. He became the interpreter, and spoke very good English. Food was served on a large Lazy Susan at the centre of the round 10-chair table. It was obtained by spinning the turntable, stopping where you wished and using chopsticks to retrieve a portion of hot food for your plate, then it was spun off to someone else. The only utensils on the table were chopsticks. We had fears of starving, because the other diners were much more adept at spinning and retrieving than we were, but they were kind to us, and gave us a chance. After dinner we danced on the Yangtse as we progressed upriver.

The next morning we attended a briefing about the Gorges, and noted that weather conditions were not the best. There was very low-lying cloud and a threat of rain. We were scheduled to stop at Sashi City for a shore excursion, but it was cancelled because the ship was late, having had to stop overnight because of thick fog. Most passengers stayed out on deck all day where the temperature was about 20C (68F). Although the scenery was wonderful and life aboard ship was good, it was somewhat tempered by the low cloud and haze. Day 21 we were embarked in small, and definitely flimsy, 14-passenger flat-bottomed motorboats to go for an hour's run up the Da Ling river to lunch at Double Dragon's Town. Several of the boats had to be towed off the rocks, in some instances by other boats that just happened along .... or did they? It emphasized to me the extreme risks tourists subject themselves to, when they are not fully briefed before going on an adventure.

This trip was amongst the greenest of green foliage, and monkeys were expected to be seen on the hillsides but none showed up. Although I had serious reservations about the risks, my notes say that the event was worth it, and the lunch was excellent!

Early on Day 22 there was another silk factory to see, on a morning that included a visit to Wanxian. There was also a visit to Shibao in the afternoon. The captain's farewell dinner was held on the last evening and we were pleased to receive a standing ovation from our table mates. It must have been for holding our chopsticks correctly! The cruise finished with a good talent show by the crew, which took up most of the evening.

The next morning (Day 23) we arrived in Chungking and went on an extensive tour of the city. In the evening our guide insisted we must see a famous Hard Rock troupe from Guangzhou (Canton), because they were so good! It was obvious he wanted to attend, but could only do so without paying if he was escorting us. We sat for 30 minutes, but there was so much noise and smoke that we had to give up, and he bowed deeply as he saw us leave. Our room was in a section of the Remini Grand Hotel that had not yet been renovated, ... not as 'grand' as advertised, ... where the racket seemed louder than when seated in the theatre. During the night, on a visit to the washroom, stars could be seen through bullet and other holes in the ceiling. They had probably been there since the revolution in 1949, when many troops were billeted there.

We went by air November 11 (Day 24) to Guangshou where we stayed overnight at the Garden Hotel, the largest in Asia at that time, and this ended our tour with the China Tourist Service. The next day (November 12) we went to Hong Kong where we were tourists until November 21. Then we went by air to Bangkok, Thailand and booked in at the Siam International Hotel. We acted like tourists until leaving Bangkok on an early morning flight November 26. The flight took us north to Chiang Mai where we visited an open-air jewellery workshop a short distance from the city, and shopped for sapphires. We were successful in getting some very good specimens at a reasonable price.

We had arrived at the right time for an annual Thai holiday, Loy Kathong (Festival of Lights), in which miniature decorated paper boats are equipped with lighted candles and joss sticks and, as a prayer is said to thank the water spirits for sustaining life, cast upon the river to float away. Imagine the entire population of a city participating and, also imagine the mess on the river banks the next day! It is a very moving ritual, and the myriad of lights on the water presents a wonderful display.

The Temple of Dawn, Bangkok

It was back to Bankok on November 28, then the next day we went north-west of the city by bus to visit Kanchanaburi War Cemetry on the way to the River Kwai, where we settled in at the River Kwai Village Guest House. First we were taken up-river to visit a deep cavern. Then, upon return, we rode down-river in a long-tailed boat, and boarded a train to ride back along the Death Railway and over the bridge. Walking back over the bridge, we felt just as we had when viewing the movie, *Bridge on the River Kwai*, ... rather an eerie feeling to actually be there!

Back in Bangkok to overnight again, we left by air for Bombay, India the evening of December 1 for a late arrival at the Airport Plaza Hotel. We discovered that our reservations had not arrived and we were offered accommodation at a sister hotel, but found that we were sleeping in sheets washed in gasoline. Phew! Our response? .... to hell with the expense, move the next day to the Taj Mahal International Hotel across from the Gateway of India in the Colaba district. Allotted a room on the 25th floor of the tower, we were surprised to be able to watch a Navy air show .... *from above*!

December 4 we visited both the Cathay Pacific and Gulf Air offices to sort out flight schedules for the rest of our original itineraries. As we walked past the Prince of Wales Museum, begging mothers were seen wiping mud on babies' faces to entice more donations because a tour bus was due to arrive.

On the way back to the hotel we walked through some of the wildest slums imaginable, including a fence draped with piles of rags that were laid out each night as shelter. Also seen was a truck just finishing the unloading of large-diameter sewer pipe. Before the truck was gone, homeless people had begun moving into what they probably considered choice accommodation.

December 8 it was off on evening flights to London on different airlines. We met in London and, on December 11 visited sister Betty and her husband, Peter Dawson, living there at the time. We visited Sylvia, an air force friend of Geraldine, went to Broad Marston Manor south of Stratford-on-Avon for two days and then on to the Falcon Hotel in the city, from where we visited Shakespeare's birthplace and saw a performance of Charles Dickens' play, 'Nicholas Nickleby'. The last day there we took a bus ride to visit Coventry Cathedral and Warwick Castle.

We then overnighted by train to Paris, France December 20, arriving at a hotel operated by the Mallet family. Dominique Mallet, a geographer friend who had worked in Ottawa, had invited us for a very enjoyable Christmas with a seven-course dinner, and a most enjoyable visit that will long be remembered. December 27 we were off by train to Zurich, Switzerland where we were met by Geraldine's son, Jean-Pierre, and stayed at the Hotel Lindenhof in Baar. Generally, we visited places in the area with J-P until January 1 when we went to his home for New Year's dinner.

Dancing with Geraldine aboard Grand Princess 1998, on a Mediterranean cruise after her chemotherapy treatments

We travelled with him to Lucerne January 2 to see the Transport Museum and, on January 4, went with him to the Migros' Shopping Centre in Zug. Then, after a few days visiting friends in the area, we left by train January 12 to return to London. We spent the rest of our time with Betty and Peter, and going up to London on our own to see *Starlight Express* at the Apollo Victoria Theatre. January 17 Geraldine returned to Ottawa on her 'around-the-world' ticket.

Having been informed by Betty that Mom was in hospital, and wishing to see her, I tried to make arrangements to fly to Halifax, NS but ended up leaving London January 20 for Toronto, then East to Moncton, NB. Brother Charles and his wife, Audrey met me in Moncton and took me to Sackville. I was able to visit Mom in the Sackville Hospital twice before leaving for Ottawa and home. It had been a wonderful 3½-month vacation, marred only by Mom's sickness, but it was nice to be home in familiar surroundings.

About two months after the trip was over the rugs purchased in China arrived, the *dirty* rug being one of them! We wrote to the People's Rug Factory No.1 to tell them what had happened, and our disappointment at the result. We also mentioned that we wouldn't like to see the excellent relations between our countries harmed by a little problem such as a soiled rug. In due course a reply arrived. Its opening statement was, 'And the same to you.' Even though it was known that different ethnic approaches to writing could cause problems, was I reading it correctly? I hurried to read the rest of the letter, and found that they were merely agreeing with our comment about relations between our countries. They were prepared to replace the rug, and we could keep the soiled one if we wished, it should clean up easily. They also asked us to visit the factory on our next trip .... what next trip? In six months the replacement rug arrived, and the initial one cleaned up fairly well. We were the only ones that knew it had been subjected to the insult of being run over by a loader.

The outside of the house in Clayton was soon completed, and the assets of *Unique Decor* sold. Several buyers wanted various specialties, so it was broken down into packages of items: ceramics and high-fire decorations, glassware and low-fire decorations, kilns, and a mail order library and literature. Each package sold quickly. The carpenter shop machinery and tools were kept intact. There were still some furniture items to be made, and more nails to pound!

After selling the company assets, the expertise built up in operating it was put to use as a Marketing Consultant to people who planned to start mail-order businesses. I also took on the provision of support services for the artists in the Canal Art Group, and published newsletters for several volunteer organizations in Ottawa, Almonte and Clayton. Word from home regarding Mom's health continued to be disappointing, and she died March 21, 1986 at age 86.

Every traveller's nightmare is to miss an important flight. March 6,1987 Geraldine and I were en route Ottawa-Montreal-La Guardia, New York-Manaus, Brazil to connect with a Caribazon Cruise aboard the Eperotiki Line's *SS World Renaissance*. Flights became tangled up because of bad weather, leading to a terrible situation, and it appeared we might not make the ship on time. Nothing was available out of La Guardia, but Kennedy airport looked promising so we went there by taxi.

The only flights available to Manaus, were via Rio de Janeiro and Sao Paulo, Brazil. Desperate, we booked and arrived in Manaus at 0530 hrs (5:30 am) where a sleepy room clerk at the Hotel Amazonos asked if we wanted tickets to see the *Parting of the Waters* at the confluence of the Amazon and Negro Rivers at 0900 hrs. The delays and rerouting had not been his fault, but the tone of our negative response probably made him feel like a co-conspirator.

We made it to the ship on time but had travelled an estimated additional 2,600 miles (4,160 kms) out of our way to do so .... ; however, the long-scheduled cruise was excellent. One day we went ashore to swim in the Amazon, and sent an 80-year old lawyer from San Francisco into the river to test for piranhas. It wasn't the season for lawyers! ....or for piranhas!

We were developing an even deeper interest in the travel industry, and now made a major investment in *The Travel Machine*, an Ottawa travel agency, and escorted small groups to locations in our home country and the Carribean. Our attempts at getting Federal government business were not fruitful, we did not have the influence of the larger travel companies. As time went by we found that we were not in agreement with the management approach and procedures used by the company management in dealing with their customer's problems. Accordingly, we sold our shares after 11 months, and set our minds to other things, one of which was the installation of parquet hardwood floors throughout Geraldine's condominium, along with an upgrade of her kitchen and the creation of a studio in her basement.

The family doctor, Peter Davison, MD, an ex-RCAF pilot and aviation medical specialist, told me that my hearing loss should be pensionable and a subsequent application resulted in a 10% pension.

Davison's office was a great place to meet old air force guys. Another place for such meetings was at Legion Headquarters where one day I met LCol Jean Boulet, when visiting to see my pension counsellor. Later, in the hall, the counsellor said to him, 'Jean, you flew as a navigator in Lancasters didn't you (he was on post-war duty)?' Quick on the uptake, Jean replied, 'Eh?, Eh?'.

Son Don, transferred to CFB Borden, Ontario since 1984, died in his sleep from heart failure, February 24,1990 at age 49, survived by his wife, Jackie and daughter Holly. It seems he had inherited Bunny's family malady. At the time he was very active in his volunteer job of Ontario Vice-president of the Union of National Defence Employees.

Tom and Millie Clark, who had been our hosts in China and Russia, were living in Ottawa by 1990, and Tom had a strong urge to purchase a new computer. As I did not have one, he proposed that we buy two, he could get us a discount. Not having been involved with computers since the 1960s, the vastly changed technology provided many challenges to self-instruction. At one point there was so much frustration while using an early graphics program, that I said to myself, 'This is all Greek to me!' ...... then hit a key ...... and the Greek alphabet appeared!

Geraldine maintained a studio, *Indian River Studios* in the space that was initially used for *Unique Decor* and promoted a strong sense of the arts in the village, particularly enjoining painters and other artisans to improve both their work and promotional advertising. There was also a need for improved community activity to support a housing proposal in which we were involved. We developed enough interest to formalize *Clayton Capers*, advertised as 'a Gala Weekend of Family Fun at the Best Little Village by a Dam Site', which produced funds for many projects. Part of *Capers* was the *Indian River Studio Tour*. It continues to be held annually, but now in the fall, and the name has been changed to the *Crown & Pumpkin Studio Tour*, the 'crown' taken from the logo of the local municipality, pumpkin from the Fall season in which it is held.

There was now news of a second granddaughter, Rebecca, born April 26, 1988 to Evelyn and Rod.

Very strange things happen when you travel. On a trip to Texas in 1994, having been out to dinner at a restaurant in Houston and on the way back to the hotel, we were in the on-ramp trying to meld with freeway traffic. Up to and past the highway speed limit and still not at the main lane speed, a police whistle was heard. The lady officer who gave me a USD100 speeding ticket admitted on questioning that she was afraid to tackle speeders in the through lanes, so she picked them off in the entry lane. Technically speaking she was right, but what a way to run a highway!

And driving a strange rental car in a land like Germany, France, and particularly England, with its historical tradition of driving on the left, can test even the best of relationships, but we weathered it. Discussions with others have convinced us that our experience was an exception, there were others who almost parted because of it.

Geraldine belonged to a single's dance club in Ottawa which, by coincidence had been started by Sybil and another friend some years earlier. A mutual friend of all of us was Boris Malkov, a White Russian born in India, who had been a captain in the Canadian Intelligence Corps. Discussion with him usually centred on a roughly 1,000-page manuscript he had written on philosophy. He offered it to local publishers without success, so decided to take it to India to be self-published, and to visit his birthplace.

On arrival in Calcutta, he visited the toilet before leaving the airport. With no clothes hook on the door of the cubicle, he tossed his coat over the door and settled down to serious business, only to see the coat tail disappear over the top of the door. Caught with his pants down, by the time he became mobile, the thief had disappeared along with the coat. It, and the rupees sewn into its lining, representing about ten thousand dollars Canadian, were long gone and so was his dream of publishing his book and visiting his old home. Destitute, he asked the Canadian Embassy to advance money to get him home.

The 50th Anniversary of VE-Day (1995), the end of WWII in Europe, led us to go on a personal anniversary trip. We travelled to England, then to France and Switzerland. Return to England was via the *Eurotunnel* which had been completed the year before. We bought the tickets at the railway station in Zurich, where the clerk asked us to come back the next day because he had not yet used the required procedure and wished to check it. Once back in England, laying on our backs on the lawn, at Joyce and Walter Weisflog's home in Brighton, was a great way to watch an air show, which included Britain's only Lancaster still flying and the RAF *Red Arrows* demonstration team.

A usual procedure when in England was to select a hub city from where we could radiate for sightseeing. We would stay for a week visiting selected places in the local area. On this occasion we had selected Cambridge as the hub, which allowed us to visit Ely Cathedral, the Imperial War Museum aviation displays at Duxford, and Newmarket, along with other local points remembered from earlier days.

Some residents in Clayton had heard complaints that seniors had to move from their home villages to get into senior's accommodation in urban locations. From this idle chatter the *Clayton Seniors Housing Corporation* evolved, with me as president. It took seven long years to convince the Ontario government of the merits of seniors staying in an environment with which they were familiar. Marion Vallentyne had become president well before approval occurred. Once the idea was accepted and approved, 25 apartments were built in a complex named *Linn Bower on the Indian River*. When they were occupied, it practically doubled the village population in one fell swoop. My participation in the official opening by representatives of the Government of Ontario, held June 22, 1996, included the preparation of the program.

In 1997 Geraldine tried to tell the doctors that she was ill, not feeling as usual, but could get no one in the medical community to listen .... deja vu. Eventually, after a lot of haranguing the doctors, cancer was diagnosed in December, and she started chemotherapy, going through such difficulties that a person had to wonder whether it was worth the trauma.

Meanwhile the massive Ice Storm of January 1998, which left four million Eastern Canadians in the cold, had struck while she was scheduled for chemotherapy treatments. Although power was not lost in Ottawa, it was out for ten days in Clayton. Wood was available for the furnace but, without its electrical fan to distribute it, the temperature in the house hovered around 12 dC (about 55 dF). Without power to operate the well pump, a hole was chopped in the lake ice to obtain water. My emergency generator was hooked up to run the refrigerator and one light. Unfortunately, I hadn't considered putting a few other important items on the separate circuit for use with the generator in emergencies.

The crackling of boughs breaking from trees, and ice crashing to the ground, was heard on each venture outside. Even with such a chaotic situation, it was possible to visit Ottawa daily throughout the period of the storm to take Geraldine to her appointments. By summer the cancer was in remission.

In 1998, several veterans decided that Clayton should have a Cenotaph. One of the primary instigators was a mason who had rescued a very large brass eagle somewhere in his travels. Incorporated into the design for a stone cairn, the eagle would sit on top. Everything was looked after except the digging for the base. Nick Patafie (ex-Navy, ex-RCAF) volunteered with me to do that, with the result that two old codgers spent several hours digging. The cenotaph was completed for Remembrance Day, a worthwhile addition to the community.

August 23, 1998, my son Rod was killed at age 55 when he stopped at the approach to the Sackville, NB on-ramp of the Trans-Canada Highway to transfer a coffee he had just purchased at a fast food stop into a thermal cup, before going onto the highway. A van from Cape Breton, NS, travelling at highway speed, veered off the road and hit Rod's car. Apparently the driver had fallen asleep after many hours on the road. Although everyone was distressed to lose him, Rod's death may have been a blessing in disguise. He had told me a few days earlier that *lupus* symptoms, that earlier had required a bone marrow transplant, were back and he expected additional problems. He was survived by his wife Evelyn, and daughter Rebecca (Becky), age 10, who was in the front passenger seat in the accident, but was unhurt.

A traditional view of the Great Wall, left (also on front cover), and the Trinity Cathedral in Zagorsk, Russia, taken during a visit in 1987

By 2000 Geraldine was again suffering seriously from cancer, and was hospitalized in July. By early August she was in bad shape. Both her boys arrived to stay with me at her home. By August 8 she had descended into delirium and, after a difficult period, died August 11. Her funeral was held at the Anglican Church in Clayton and many, the local people in particular, demonstrated that they appreciated what she had done for the community. She was very fond of Clayton and her ashes were spread on the lakeshore as she had requested. She had named me Executor of her will. It was complicated because of assets held in Switzerland; however, with the help of lawyers in both countries, it was possible to pass administration over to her son, Laurence by September 2002.

21

A MOVE, A MARRIAGE, AND MARCHING ON
2001- 2005

which covers subsequent retirement, marriage and travel

Berny, Brenda's husband, had died December 5, 1977 while a Sgt Supply Tech with a Service Battalion in Egypt on a Peacekeeping mission.

Later, Brenda worked as a paralegal in Barrie, Ontario and married Gary Greenfield, BSc, PEng, LLB, CD, a lawyer who had been a Capt in the Royal Canadian Electrical Mechanical Engineers.

In the year 2000, by now retired and living in Sidney, BC, Brenda and Gary were concerned that I was aging in a small village, without relatives or handy medical resources. Lack of bus service, in case I should become unable to drive, was also a concern. They felt that I should move to be near them and, after considerable thought and nothing to keep me in the village, plans for the move were begun. It would also place me near sister Betty and her husband Peter, now in Victoria after retiring from Cairo, Egypt.

Travelling to Edmonton, Alberta May 18, 2001, I met Brenda, who had journeyed from Sidney and, together, we attended a 408 Sqn Reunion. The reunion was very pleasant and we concluded when parting that I would move, and live in an apartment in the home that she and Gary occupy.

It was not difficult to sell my property at a good price, and a sale, with Charles Hollinger as auctioneer, was successful. My intention for the move was to travel alone by van, driving short legs, and taking a day at each stop for local sightseeing. Trying to avoid Chicago, the route would be through Kansas City, Kansas, a route not previously driven. My Ford Windstar was loaded with the things which could not be parted with and, after saying goodbye to the village and other friends, the trip was begun July 2, 2001.

Friends and relatives in the Toronto area and at Leamington, Ontario were visited first. Crossing the US border at Detroit, Michigan, my route took me to Indianapolis, Indiana; then through St. Louis, Missouri; and on to Kansas City; then Lincoln, Nebraska; Cheyenne, Wyoming; Salt Lake City, Utah; Boise, Idaho; Pendleton, Oregon; Anacortes, Washington; and by ferry to Sidney, BC, for arrival July 21 feeling just as fresh as if the trip had only been around the block.

The most interesting visits were at the new Great Platte River Road Archway

Spanning Highway I-80

Monument, located astride Route I-80 near Kearney, Nebraska (actually a pioneer museum celebrating the Oregon Trail), and the Strategic Air & Space Museum in Ashland, Nebraska. Another Oregon Trail site was on Route 78 at Walter's Ferry on the Snake River in Idaho, where there was Indian and wagon train history.

With the move to BC, 8 of the 10 Canadian provinces have been called home, Alberta and Newfoundland being the only ones missed. I moved into the lower apartment in Brenda and Gary's home near Sidney, and started walking for exercise on excellent local trails, including one of 6 miles (10 km) around Elk and Beaver Lakes. While the area was enjoyed and Brenda and Gary made sure I met and associated with their friends, I soon purchased a condominium in Victoria, because it would probably result in being closer to more things to see and do.

But I got into a rut, a really deep one, in which each day was exactly the same as the one before. Ladies had been met in my condo building, all ten or more years younger, but there seemed to be nothing in common with any of them. Each of several dates for dinner ended with the thought that if it had not occurred, it would not have been missed! But still, although Gary and Brenda continued to keep me involved in their social activities and there was access to friendship with many younger people in their circle, deeply missed was female companionship with someone from my era.

Working on my computer the evening of May 27, 2002, a popup showed on the screen advertising a singles site. 'What the hell!, I might as well see what it is'. There was an entry which included, 'Veronica Bennett, ex-WAAF, interested in travel and cruises'. Curiosity got the best of me and my reply was sent using *Cruise Nut* as my signature, ... Veronica, slightly earlier, had the same popup appear, she too had been curious, and had originated what I later read. My response arrived on her computer so soon afterwards that she was suspicious, and emailed the site saying in effect, 'If this is a method of getting me to pay a fee, you are not getting it, but if it is genuine here is my phone number, etc, etc.'

When the phone number was relayed to me from the site it appeared to be local, so it was looked up in the reverse number portion of the phone book. Lo and behold, the location was a few minutes from my condo. We had a long chat on the phone, and arranged to meet May 30. Our ages were within a few years of each other, and the first meeting showed that there was more than above-average compatibility. We had morning coffee, a walk around the inner harbour, a very long lunch and parted at about three in the afternoon. Flowers were quickly sent as it had been learned the next day was her birthday. When you are older you have to move faster, much faster!

The marvel of the 'happening' was that the 'popup' never showed again on either of our computers. Veronica had recently moved back to Victoria after 40 years in the USA, and I was not long in Victoria from Ontario. We had been stationed seven miles apart in WWII, she as a WAAF aero-engine mechanic, and we had frequented the same pubs in Stratford-on-Avon.

If the qualification to be a Cockney is to be born in London within the sound of Bow Bells she qualifies, having been born in Charing Cross Hospital; however, her father was a Canadian from Vancouver and her mother an Irish lass. Our backgrounds had a lot of common elements regarding the war, she had worked in London at the time of the blitz and, on more than one occasion, had travelled into London to work, to find that the building where she was employed had been made derelict by bombing. She had seen first hand what happens when shrapnel hits people, and also experienced the buzz bomb (V-1) attacks.

When I first visited her condo, her Missy, a smallish Maine Coon cat who normally ran for cover at the sound of the door bell, came out to visit with me and gave her necessary and unqualified 'seal of approval', so Veronica and I started dating. It could be said I had been in the doldrums but, from then on, there hasn't been a dull moment, its back to the life tempo which was formerly familiar. We started to travel, go to dances, and join day trips and other activities at the Monterey Senior Centre in Oak Bay.

We were married October 24, 2002 by the Reverend Glenn Sim, CD, a former air force padre, at St. Mary's Anglican Church in Saanichton, BC, with guests from as far away as Ontario, NB and Florida. The reception was held that evening at McMorran's seaside Beach House at Cordova Bay. The bride and groom traditionally leave part way through such an event, but we were still there when it was over, helping to load leftovers into cars and making sure everyone had a ride home with a sober driver.

Our wedding contained one unique addition though. Having all the material things we thought we needed, we asked guests to donate to the Royal Canadian Air Cadet Continuation Flying Training program if they desired, in lieu of gifts, through the RCAFA Trust. Few weddings are able to offer tax deductions!

We had arranged a cruise to Australia and New Zealand before the decision to marry, so we delayed our honeymoon until the cruise date. We flew to Los Angeles, then by Qantas for an overnight flight to Sydney, Australia to board the Princess

Rover's Return Pub, Dunedin, New Zealand

Cruises' *Regal Princess* January 8, 2003 (Day 1) for a cruise which included South-Eastern Australia and New Zealand. The next day was spent at sea, then we were in Melbourne where our day trip was a city tour and a visit to the Kangaroo/Koala Wildlife Park. After another day at sea we arrived at Hobart, Tasmania on Day 5, where we visited Bonorang Wildlife Park, and saw kangaroos, wallabees and Tasmanian devils. We departed Hobart to the skirl of bagpipes, spending another day at sea en route to Fiordland, New Zealand. Day 7 was spent cruising three fiords, each very beautiful, then next day (Day 8), we were at Dunedin where we toured a brewery and visited the *Rover's Return* pub. It was here that we found we were not the only honeymooner's on the cruise, we met a pair of relative youngsters from Alaska.

Then we cruised on to Christchurch for Day 9, where we were amazed at the scenery. Our day trip took us to the Royal New Zealand Air Force Museum, then a wine-tasting party, and a city tour before returning to the ship. Wellington was visited the next day, where another city tour was enjoyed. After another day at sea, we disembarked in Auckland on Day 12 for a city tour, by bus, which then took us to the airport where we boarded an overnight flight to Los Angeles.

Unfortunately it was an hour late reaching Los Angeles and we were misdirected. As a result we missed our connecting flight. It took most of the day to get things sorted out. We had to overnight in Vancouver, and arrived back home January 21, very happy, but also very tired!

Later on in 2003 we both joined in the Dominion Institute's Memory Project, doing school visits to talk to students about War, in advance of Remembrance Day. My subject was Bomber Command and Veronica's, life as a teenager during the London Blitz, and both became convinced that we should write our memoirs. Our first school visit included two presentations to high school classes at Claremont High School, near our home. During the subsequent question period, one young lady innocently asked, 'How long have you two been married?' She was probably expecting the answer to be a large number of years. The response was, 'Thirteen months.' While her jaw dropped, the rest of the class clapped enthusiastically. Next question?

We enjoyed a two-week visit in Florida with friends in early 2004 followed by a Panama Canal cruise. Later, we spent Christmas in Hawaii.

With the proclamation by Veteran's Affairs Canada that 2005 would be the Year of the Veteran, we became involved in several activities. There was a military tattoo on May 7 which was well-attended, and a musical treat. It was followed on May 8, the 60th Anniversary of VE-Day, by a parade. We marched to the Cenotaph for ceremonies, and a street dance to commemorate the dances which started spontaneously in England and

Puerto Vallarta, Mexico harbour 2004,
(also on front cover)

Holland upon the declaration of peace. Of course Veronica and I participated whole-heartedly, just as we had done individually 60 years before.

My participation then was around Yorkminster in the city of York, Veronica's at RAF Wigsley, Lincolnshire. She also marched in the Wings for Victory parade in Lincoln the following week.

A small fireworks display was included at York. Fireworks make wonderful displays but, even today after so many years, a twinge of disorientation and stress is felt when I watch them, and cannot help but compare the pyrotechnics with those surrounding bomber targets. Remembered are the FLAK explosions, searchlights, reds, yellows and greens of target indicators, exploding bombs, exploding bombers, and tracer shells all adding colour, with all this outlined by fighter flares almost making day out of night. The memories persist, and we are very thankful that we can still keep marching on.

Aboard MS Zaandam at San Juan del Sur, Nicaraugua
2004 with another cruise ship in the background
(also on the front cover)

22

WHAT IT ALL MEANT

which provides an epilogue to summarize a most enjoyable life

An ounce of experience can sometimes outweigh a whole pound of theory!! That, along with tradition, habit, and custom largely rules a life. Although nourished in apprenticeship as a carpenter by my father, later employed as a construction engineer of senior rank in the RCAF and the CF, and granted the designation 'Professional Manager' by the Canadian Institute of Management, there had not been formal training other than High School, and as RCAF aircrew.

There is still so much I'd like to do and, although there is currently reasonably good health, no guarantee of time left in which to do it.

This life has encompassed slightly more than 75% of the 20th century and a reasonable start into the 21st, during all of which dramatic changes have occurred. We have seen the replacement of human muscle by machinery in doing work, space exploration, and the dawn

At Waikiki, Hawaii 2004 (Photo: Martin Cohen)
(also on back cover)

of the *cyber-age*. From horse-drawn carts and roads being built by hand by gangs of labourers, we have come to the point where we can order almost anything through the Internet.

Folks in single career lives must miss a lot. I have been most fortunate to experience so many different vocations, hardly a similar one as they developed, and to meet so many wonderful people. Of course there were a few of that other type, and notorious ones too, but very few of them indeed!

A report in 2001 said that short people (my 5' 6", or 168 cm qualifies) may be programmed to live longer. Living longer of course depends on many things. Fate deals out problems that may arise from stress or other factors. For instance there was scarlet fever, a diagnosis of colitis and a hearing impairment. The last two probably arose from WWII operational experiences and, although the colitis finally was brought under control, the hearing loss has become profound. A hiatus hernia, shingles, skin cancer and several allergies serve to round out the factors which may be added to 'programming' in my case.

The friendship of former air force personnel means a lot. Meetings of two ex-air force people for the first time for any reason, be they millionaires or paupers, judges, dieticians, mechanics, farmers, or any number of other backgrounds, quickly results in reminiscence. Just find out that each other is ex-air force and the climate changes, back to the compatriots we once were. Not having been acquainted with each other previously doesn't matter much either. There is a common bond from a similar ethos and perceived common experience.

As you may have gathered, travel has been a very large part of my life and, in addition to the many freebies that came along, roughly a quarter-million dollars has been invested in that initiative. St. Augustine said, 'The world is a book, and those who do not travel read only a page.' He would certainly agree that it was all a good investment. Lots of memories of travel experiences have evolved to be shared. Here are some that have impressed me most, listed in no particular order.

In Russia, the beauty of the art in the Hermitage Museum stirred me, as did the decorations in the Moscow Metro, seen in a circle tour that cost *ten cents* Canadian, and those decorations had mostly been done while WWII raged in the country. We usually see semiprecious stones in small trinkets, but in Zagorsk, there were buildings with massive columns of green malachite and blue lapis lazuli, awesome!

The Opera House in Sydney, Australia is a striking example of modern architecture. Visiting native villages along the Amazon River area reminded me that people can be happy while living simple lives. In China, the Forbidden City appears architecturally perfect, the Great Wall a symbol of strength past.

In Hawaii, the most haunting thing was the primal beauty of the big island but Maui was the most beautiful island seen. And the road to Hana, although through beautiful country, was not the smoothest bus ride.

Experiencing the first hurricane in London (1987) in 500 years showed what garbage day in the modern age could be after the cans were strewed, and how plane trees could be uprooted by the hundreds. In the Caribbean, St. Thomas has a romantic viewpoint at every turn. Cabo San Lucas, Curaçao and Guadalupé are places that should be revisited. White water rafting at age 65, and hot air ballooning at 70, were invigorating to say the least. Watching an air show centred on the Gates of India from a 25th floor hotel balcony was not as good as looking into the sky to see one!

In England, the coasts of Cornwall and Devon from Lands End around to Clovelly, North Devon, and Clovelly itself, are very scenic, as is the Cotswolds area, in particular the village of Lower Slaughter. There is nothing to match a donkey safari in Egypt, especially when a horny donkey stallion kept chasing bicycles; and a taxi ride from Luxor to Hagarda on the Red Sea was both bumpy, lonely and yet entertaining. There were plenty of sheep and goat herds tended along the way by women, one with gold bracelets from wrist to elbow, carrying the family wealth wherever she went. In Italy the historic site of Pompeii was most interesting, even though seen in pouring rain in a sea of 132 blue and white umbrellas. And the island of Mykonos is a jewel in the Aegean Sea. Inca ruins in Mexico are majestic. It is not difficult to imagine the sights at the peak of the Incan empire. In Malta, you have to stop and think, 'How could this little island have survived in WWII, with almost incessant bombing? And you have to wonder how the few aircraft and pilots available could defend it.'

Standing in Florida in a sheepskin coat on a cold Cocoa Beach in January, after two cancellations because of extreme temperatures, watching a space launch was a glorious sight. Closer to home, recollection of the majesty of the Rockies brings good feelings, as does the rugged lines of the Western Peninsula in Newfoundland, and the Cape Breton Trail.......... all these, and much more, have been carefully tucked away in the memory bank!

I have been fortunate to travel the world. Cruises on the Atlantic and Pacific Oceans, the Mediterranean and Caribbean Seas, and the Amazon, Yangtze and Nile Rivers, as well as a lot of land-based travel have provided much excitement and enjoyment.

It is great to be survivors and to know that we were born before television, polio shots, Xerox, penicillin, frozen foods, videos, contact lenses and the pill. We were there for the beginnings of credit cards, radar, split atoms, ballpoint pens and laser beams; well before dishwashers, tumble driers, electric blankets, air conditioners and drip-dry clothes .... and were here before man walked on the moon.

We thought *fast food* was what you ate in Lent, a *Big Mac* was an over-sized raincoat and a *crumpet* was on the menu for tea. We existed before house husbands, computer dating, and *sheltered accommodation* was where you waited for a bus. We got married *first* and then *lived together*.

Our cars and trucks had no turn signals, seat belts, four-wheel drive or radial tires, inner tubes were required. The windshield wiper had to be operated by hand from inside when it rained and, just to make things worse, there were few paved roads to drive on. Older vehicles had to be cranked, new-fangled ones had a start button on the dash.

We were before day care centres (mothers tended families at home), group homes and disposable diapers. We had to wait for FM radio, tape decks, artificial hearts, word processors and young men wearing earrings (we knew that body piercing was the initial step in a surgical procedure). For us *time sharing* meant togetherness, a *chip* was a piece of wood or a fried potato, *hardware* meant nuts and bolts, and *software* had not yet become a word, because there had been no need for it.

It was when the term *making out* referred to how you did in your exams, *stud* was something that fastened a collar to a shirt and *going all the way* meant staying on a bus to the terminal. In our day, cigarette smoking was *fashionable*, you mowed *grass*, *coke* was kept in the coal bin, a *joint* was a piece of meat you cooked in a *pot* for Sunday dinner. *Rock Music* was a mother's lullaby. *Eldorado* was an ice-cream, a *gay* person was the life and soul of the party, while *aids* just meant beauty treatment or help for someone in trouble.

We must be a hardy bunch when you think of the way in which the world has changed and the adjustments we have had to make. No wonder there is a generation gap today ..... but ...... by the grace of God ..... we have survived! Survived to experience progress, and become slaves to the material objects we own .... please define progress.

There are several credos I have tried to respect: Life is change, best prepare for it, those who don't get lost by the wayside .... Normal people worry me, but how do you describe 'normal'? .... Life is a collection of memories, try to make them good ones and, if you are making a presentation and some doubt exists, go out of your way to make it sound convincing! And have tenacity, be honest with yourself and others, and commit yourself to doing a good job: .... all the while challenging conventional thinking!

I had always wondered about the mystery of why I was rushed to Greenock to board the Ile de France, and I had also heard rumours from North York personnel of an Order of Canada recommendation, so I applied October 19, 2003 for a copy of my military records under the Freedom of Information Act. 1,000 pages of material, containing many duplicates, were received July 16, 2005. While a lot of information was confirmed for me, there was nothing about the Ile de France incident, and certainly not many pieces of paper regarding my 2 1/2 year experience in England. There was, however, a letter from ATC confirming receipt of an Order of Canada recommendation, but the recommendation itself was not in the file. Apparently the submission, which was not successful, was a joint one between the Base and North York. It was nice to know though, that there was a group of people who thought enough of my efforts to consider such an award.

And as far as human altercations go, the ravages of War prevent many people from reaching their full potential and leave much grief and suffering in their wake. Is it not time that humans found more peaceful ways to coexist on this Earth, and to settle their real or perceived differences? Many young people who go to war with a sense of adventure find that their efforts will likely end in disaster, like the loss of so many boys from my home town. Ten aircrew boys departed, only two were fortunate enough to come home at war's end.

> "The moving finger writes;
> And having writ, moves on."
>
> The Rubaiyat by Omar Khayyam

Left to right- Distinguished Flying Cross, 1939-45 Star, Aircrew Europe Star with France Germany bar, Defence Medal, Canadian Volunteer Service Medal with Overseas bar, War Medal, Canadian Centennial Medal 1967, Queen Elizabeth Silver Jubilee Medal 1977, Canadian Forces Decoration and bar (also on front cover)

On the way to Germany

Often during the daylight first legs of an operational trip, when joining the bomber stream en route to a target, other Lancasters and Halifaxes would follow along behind us. They could be from stations farther to the south in England, far distant from ours. They didn't know us, nor did we know them. We were all just going in the same direction together.

ANNEX A

The aircrew boys from the Sackville, New Brunswick area
who gave their all in World War II.

JOSIAH ANDERSON

Captain James Josiah Anderson, a farmer's son from Middle Sackville, NB was well-known in the community as the first village boy to consider a career in aviation. As a civilian member of RAF Ferry Command he was killed in August, 1941 at age 24, when his Hudson aircraft hit a hill in Scotland in very bad weather at the end of a Trans-Atlantic ferry trip. Joe is buried in Buteshire, Scotland. His brother, Donald and the author were in the same class at school, Joe was 4 years ahead of us..

••••••

STAN BICKERTON

F/S George Stanley (Stan) Bickerton, 24, a pilot from a farm family in Upper Sackville, NB was killed September 14, 1942 during his final operational training course when his Wellington went missing in action from 22 OTU. Stan is buried in Amersfoort, Holland. He had potential romantic intentions in the high school years toward the author's cousin, Kathleen but was chased away by Grandfather in the very early stages.

••••••

BILL DIXON

F/O William A. (Bill) Dixon, 24, a navigator from a farm family in Aulac, NB and a casual friend of the author, was a member of 578 Sqn based at Snaith, Yorkshire. He was killed when his Halifax bomber was shot down in action against Nuremberg March 30/31, 1944, the raid in which 95 bombers were lost. Bill is buried in Durnbach, Germany. The author also flew on that raid but was unaware that Bill was also out there somewhere in the moonlight. It is noted that a member of Bill's squadron, P/O C. J. Barton was awarded a posthumous Victoria Cross for his actions that night.

••••••

GEORGE FAWCETT

Sgt George H. Fawcett, 23, another farm boy from Upper Sackville, NB, was killed in action as a pilot with 126 Sqn November 10, 1942 when his Hurricane fighter had an engine failure and crashed into McDonald Lake soon after takeoff from the Dartmouth, Nova Scotia airport. George is buried at the Upper Sackville Cemetry, Upper Sackville, NB.

AUSTIN MAXWELL

F/O Austin V. Maxwell, 22, the son of a Sackville, NB grocery supermarket proprietor, and a pilot in 102 Sqn based at Pocklington, Yorkshire, was killed when his Halifax was shot down on a raid to Sterkrade, Germany June 17, 1944. Austin is buried in Kleve, Germany. The author can remember Austin bagging groceries in his father's store during the early school years.

••••••

ALBERT RICHARD

P/O Joseph Albert Richard, 20 was born into an Acadian family in Middle Sackville, NB. He was a classmate of the author and the second village boy to be involved in aviation. As a member of RAF Coastal Command, stationed at Bircham Newton, England with 407 RCAF Sqn, he was a Wireless Op/Air Gunner on Hudson aircraft, and was lost in action April 28, 1942 on a night patrol in the North Sea area. A senior member of the squadron, he had done 26 toward his tour of 30 operations. Albert has no known grave; his name is inscribed on the Runnymede War Memorial at Egham, England where the author has seen it.

••••••

DICK TRITES

F/L Richard Murray (Dick) Trites, 25, the son of a Sackville, NB lawyer who did the author's family's legal work, was a pilot with 464 Sqn in the Second Tactical Air Force RAF, flying twin-engined Mosquito fighter-bombers on night intruder operations. He was lost in action January 18, 1945 when his aircraft crashed after the failure of an engine. Dick is buried at Merville, France.

••••••

LAWRENCE WRY

P/O Lawrence A. Wry, 21, a navigator from Sackville, NB and a member of 514 Sqn, was killed in a raid to Stuttgart, Germany on the night of March 15/16, 1944 when his Lancaster was shot down. He is buried at Villars-le-Pautel, France. By coincidence, Lawrence flew in the Lancaster II and his pilot's name was Sutherland, both the same details as enjoyed by the author. What are the chances of the four similarities, same home town, both navigators, both same rare aircraft mark, and both with pilots of the same surname?

BIBLIOGRAPHY

408 Squadron	408 Squadron History. Belleville, Ontario: The Hangar Bookshelf, 1984.
Allison, Les & Hayward, Harry	They Shall Grow Not Old, A Book of Remembrance; The Commonwealth Air Training Plan Museum, Brandon, Manitoba, 1992, 1996.
Collins, Robert	The Long and the Short and the Tall: An ordinary airman's war. Saskatoon: Western Producer Prairie Books, 1986.
Dunmore, Spencer & Carter, William, Ph.D.	Reap the Whirlwind. Toronto: McLelland & Stewart,1991. Crecy Books, 1992.
Garbett, Mike & Goulding, Brian	Lancaster at War-3, Ian Allen Limited, England, 1984.
Harvey, J. Douglas, DFC, CD	Boys, Bombs and Brussels Sprouts, McLelland & Stewart Limited, 1981.
Hastings, Max	Bomber Command. England: Michael Joseph Ltd, 1979.
Messenger, Charles	Bomber Harris, Arms and Armour Press, England, 1984.
Middlebrook, Martin	The Berlin Raids. Harmondsworth: Penguin Books Ltd., 1988.
Middlebrook, Martin	The Nuremberg Raid. London: Allan Lane, 1973; rev. ed. Harmondsworth: Penguin Books Ltd, 1980.
Middlebrook, Martin & Everritt, Chris	The Bomber Command War Diaries. Harmondsworth: Penguin Books Ltd for Viking, 1985.
Milberry, Larry	Canada's Air Force at War and Peace, Vol 1, 2 & 3 CANAV Books, Toronto, Vol 1 & 2, 2000; Vol 3, 2001.
Searby, John, DSO, DFC	The Bomber Battle for Berlin, Airlife Publishing, England, 1991.
Starkey, Richard	A Lancaster Pilot's Impression on Germany, Compaid Graphics, England, 1999.
Wheeler, William J.	Flying under Fire, Fifth House Limited, Canada, 2001.
Yates, Harry, DFC	Luck and a Lancaster, England: Airlife Publishing, 1999. Wrens Park Publishing, 2001.

SELECTED GLOSSARY

ABC- ABC Construction Company

A/C- Air Commodore

a/c- aircraft

Air Div- No.1 Air Division

AFAC- Air Force Association of Canada

AFC- Air Force Cross

AforP- Authorization for Project

AFPL- Air Force Productions Limited

AFS- Advanced Flying School

AFU- Advanced Flying Unit

AGM- Annual General Meeting

A/M- Air Marshal

AMB- Air Materiel Base

Aldis- a directional hand-held signalling lamp

AOS- Air Observer's School

ATA- Air Transport Auxiliary

ATC- Air Transport Command

A/V/M- Air Vice Marshal

Avro- AV Roe & Co, Ltd

BAC- British Aircraft Corporation

BC- British Columbia

BBC- British Broadcasting Corporation

BCATP- British Commonwealth Air Training Plan

BComd- Base Commander

Block buster- 8,000 lb (3,629 kg) bomb

bobby- English policeman

BSc- Bachelor of Science

BTSO- Base Technical Services Officer

CAdO- Chief Administrative Officer

CANEX- Canadian Forces Stores for CF personnel

CAP- Canadian Air Publication

CAS- Chief of the Air Staff

CB- Commander of the Bath

CBC- Canadian Broadcasting Corporation

CBE- Commander of the British Empire

CCE- Chief of Construction Engineering

CE- Construction Engineering

CD- Canadian Forces Decoration

CF- Canadian Forces

CGM- Conspicuous Gallantry Medal

Chevy- Chevrolet

CHMC- Canadian Housing & Mortgage Corporation

Clag- generous amounts of low cloud and fog

CMM- Companion of Military Merit

CMU- Construction & Maintenance Unit

CNE- Canadian National Exhibition

CNR- Canadian National Railways

CO- Commanding Officer

Col- Colonel

Cookie- 4,000 lb (1,814 kg) bomb

Cpl- Corporal

CTSO- Chief Technical Services Officer

DCEM- Director of CE Maintenance

DM- Deputy Minister

DND- Department of National Defence

DOT- Department of Transport

DCL- Defence Construction Ltd

DFC- Distinguished Flying Cross

DFM- Distinguished Flying Medal

DH- DeHavilland Aircraft Company

DHC- DeHavilland Aircraft Company Canada

drogue- a cone-shaped device towed behind an aircraft as a target

DSO- Distinguished Service Order

Elsan- a chemical toilet

FIDO- Fog dispersal system at an emergency airfield

F/L- Flight Lieutenant

FLAK- anti-aircraft fire from the ground

F/O- Flying Officer

FLQ- Front de libération du Québec

FTR- failed to return

FTTU- Field Technical Training Unit

gaggle- A loose formation of aircraft

G/C- Group Captain

Gp- Group

GEE- see page 54

G-H- see page 50

GM- General Manager

ha- hectare

H2S- see page 60

HCU- Heavy Conversion Unit

Hon- Honourable

HQ- Headquarters

hrs- hours

IBM- International Business Machines

ITS- Initial Training School

Jointer- a small fixed mechanical device for planing lumber

KIA- killed in action

LCL- less than carload lot

LCol- Lieutenant-Colonel

LLC- limited liability company

LMF- Lack of Moral Fibre

Link Trainer- an early type of aviation synthetic trainer

Mae West- a personal flotation vest device

Maj- Major

meat wagon- ambulance

Met- Meteorology

MiD- Mention in dispatches

Minquire- Ministerial Inquiry, usually by telegram or mail

Monica- a British onboard fighter detection device

MSEO- Mobile Support Equipment Officer

MTA- Mount Allison University

nav- navigation, navigator

NB- New Brunswick

NCO- Non-commissioned officer

NEC- National Executive Council

NHQ- National Headquarters

Nos- Numbers

NPF- Non-public Funds

NAAFI- Navy, Army, Air Force Institute

NS- Nova Scotia

OBE- Order of the British Empire

OBOE- see page 61

OTU- Operational Training Unit

Pitot head- a device fixed into wind at the front of an aircraft to pick up the speed of flight

PEI- Prince Edward Island

PEng- Professional Engineer

Petrol- gasoline

P/O- Pilot Officer

PMQ- Permanent Married Quarters

PR- Public Relations

PTSD-Post Traumatic Stress Disorder

QC- Queens Counsel

RAF- Royal Air Force

RCAF- Royal Canadian Air Force

RCAFA- Royal Canadian Air Force Association

RDF- Radio direction-finding

RCE- Royal Canadian Engineers

SBA- Standard Beam Approach

SERRATE- radar to detect German night fighter transmissions

Sgt- Sergeant

SI- Social Insurance

SCEO- Station CE Officer

Schrage Musik- upward firing 20 mm guns in German fighters

Screened- completed a tour of operations

SOCE- Staff Officer CE

S/L- Squadron Leader

SN2- German airborne radar

SNIN- Staff Navigation Instructor (Navigator)

Sqn- Squadron

Standard- A. E. Wry Standard Ltd

TCA- Trans Canada Airlines

Tech- technician

TI- Target Indicator

TTS- Technical Training School

UNDE- Union of National Defence Employees

US- United States

USAAF- United States Army Air Force

USAF- United States Air Force

VC- Victoria Cross

VE-Day- Victory in Europe Day 1945

WAAF- Women's Auxiliary Air Force (British)

W/C- Wing Commander

WD- a member of the RCAF Women's Division

WINDOW- see page 51

WO1- Warrant Officer, First Class

WO2- Warrant Officer, Second Class

WOP/AG- Wireless Operator/Air Gunner

WW II- World War II

INDEX
with *references for bombing trips

NUMERAL

4 Air Observer School, 30
4 (Observer) Advanced Flying Unit, 40
6 Elementary Flying School, 39
6 (RCAF) Bomber Group, 46, 76
6 Initial Training School, 28
408 Squadron, 46-9, 57, 64, 91-3, 97, 125, 131, 167, 191
426 Squadron, 46, 57, 96
1659 Conversion Unit, 95
1664 Conversion Unit, 92

A

Aachen West, Germany, 87*
ABC Construction Co, 123
Airfield height clearances, 146-7, 153
Air Force Headquarters, 115, 120, 125, 127, 134, 137, 141-5, 153
Air Force Association of Canada, 157, 174
Airforce Magazine, 172
Airforce Productions Limited, 171
Air Position Indicator, 70
Air Transport Command, 145, 148, 151-2
Almonte, Ontario, 169-70, 185
Antique Aircraft Fly-in, 153
Argus aircraft, 132-3, 139
Armco Steelox buildings, 116-8
Astro-navigation, 32, 53-4
Atherstone-on-Stour, England, 43, 86
Augsburg, Germany, 74*
Au Fevre, Normandy coast, 87*
Aviation Canada proposal, 166

B

Base consolidation, CFB Toronto, 149
Base/Station fund, 125-7, 136-7, 147, 156
Battle of Berlin, 51, 60, 84, 89
Battle of Britain, 101, 103, 163

Berlin, Germany, 51, 53, 55-6, 60*-1, 65, 68*, 69*, 70*, 71*, 72*-4, 84, 89, 105
Bomber base, WWII, 47, 68, 73, 105
Bomber Command, vii, 30, 41-2, 45-7, 54, 67-70, 74, 82-4, 89, 91, 93-6, 101-4, 103 107-8, 194
Bomber Force, British, 45, 69
Bomber Harris Trust, 107
Bomber stream, 54, 57, 68, 77, 84, 202
Bombing Offensive
  British, 45, 94, 96, 104
  German, 45
  Far East, 96
Booklet series, RCAFA, 160, 166
Brunswick, Germany, 65*, 69, 71
Bullseye exercise, 44, 60, 72, 75
Butcher,
  A. F & Sons, 109
  Arthur F.(Dad), 3, 5, 7-9, 12, 15-6, 19-20, 23-5, 109, 113, 173
  Bunny, 111, 120, 123, 130, 157, 160-1, 186
  Doris, 24, 32-3, 75, 96, 111
  Stella (Mom), 3, 5, 7, 17, 75, 184
  Sybil, 162-5, 171, 174-5, 187
  Veronica, 192-5
  Wilf (padre), 59
  William T.(Granddad), 3-6, 9

C

C45 Beechcraft Expeditor aircraft, 122, 130, 139, 144, 150
C119 Packet, 145
C130 Hercules aircraft, 97
CAP 209, CE Manual, 141-2
Canadian Broadcasting Corporation (CBC), 91, 104, 107-8, 110
Canadian Forces Base
  Baden Solingen, 173

Toronto, 148, 152, 154

Canadian Forces Station
  Alert, 173
  Chibougamau, 139
Canadian Warplane Heritage, 166
Canal Art Group, 177
CANEX, 155, 173
Canso aircraft, 97, 139
Catalogues
  AFPL, 172
  Unique Decor, 173
CE Branch, 115-6, 156
CE News, 142
Churchill, Sir Winston, 84, 94, 101-2
Classification Test, 29
Clayton Capers, 187
Clayton, Ontario, 169-70, 175, 177, 185, 188-90
Controllers, German, 61, 68-9, 74
Crewing up, 42
Cross-country exercise, 31, 42, 60, 122, 150
Coutances, Normandy, 89*

D

DC3 Dakota aircraft, 42, 97-8, 115, 130, 132, 134, 144, 150
D-Day and Anniversaries, vii, 87-9, 104, 165-6
DeHavilland Aircraft Canada, 145, 147, 148, 153, 163
DH 82, Tiger Moth aircraft, 39
Downsview, 144-5, 148, 152-7, 162-3
Düsseldorf, Germany, 85*-6

E

Enamel & Heating Products Ltd, 110, 112
Engine performance and handling, 88
Enlistment, 25, 115
Enterprise Foundry Company, 110, 112
Essen, Germany, 75, 77*

F

F104 Starfighter, 155

Ferrying aircraft
  in England, 63, 65, 92
  in Canada, 96-7
Fighters, FW 190, 38
Fighters, night, German, 45, 54, 58, 62, 67, 74, 86
Fire Prevention, 116, 135
FLAK, 53-4, 58, 61-2, 77, 81-4, 86, 195
Fog dispersal system (FIDO), 76
France, 44, 76, 84-5, 88-9, 98, 117, 142, 165, 184, 187-8, 200
Frankfurt, Germany, 62, 72, 76*
Freidrichshafen, Germany, 86*

G

GEE, 54, 65, 81
General Manager, RCAFA, 157-8
George VI, HM King, see King George VI
Germany, 38, 45, 53, 55, 57, 60, 67-8, 71, 75-6, 80, 84, 88-9, 92, 102, 103-4, 117, 142, 173, 187
G-H, 50, 59-60, 65, 86
Greenwood, NS, 96-8, 130-6, 138-9, 145, 158, 160
Guppy aircraft, 161

H

H21 Vertol Helicopter, 139
H2S, 47, 60, 69
Halifax aircraft, 45, 47, 68, 76, 92, 95
Hearing impairment, 167, 186, 197-8
Hurricane aircraft, 47, 76, 164
Hurricane in London, England, 198

I

Ile de France, see SS Ile de France
Industrial Air Park, Downsview, 153
Integration, 145, 147-8, 153

K

Karlsruhe, Germany, 86*
King George VI, HM, 92

Knight, Geraldine, 176-8, 184-9

L

Lack of Moral Fibre, 106

Lancaster aircraft, generally, 45, 47, 49, 60, 63, 69, 72, 91-2, 101, 118, 167, 186, 188

   Mark II, 46-7, 92

   Mark VII, 96

   Mark X, 96-8

Lancaster specifications

   English Measurement, 48

   Metric measurement, 49

Lancaster II performance, 47, 49, 88

Langar, England, 118-20

Laon, France, 85*

Leipzig, Germany, 55*, 56, 58, 69, 73*

Le Mans airfield, Normandy, 89*

Linn Bower senior's apartments, 188

London, England, 39, 42, 53-4, 72, 74, 90, 92-4, 118-9, 178, 184, 193-4, 198

London, Ontario, 28, 30, 32-3, 114

Longues-Caen, Normandy coast, 88*

Luftwaffe, 39, 106

M

Magdeburg, Germany, 68*-9

Manning Depot, 25-6, 29, 37

Master Bomber, 65, 90

Memory Project, 194

Merville, Normandy Coast, 87*

Middle Sackville, NB, 1, 3, 5, 20, 43, 109

Moncton, NB, 6, 24-5, 33, 97-8, 110, 113, 157, 161, 163-4, 184

Morale, British, 39, 45, 59

Morale, German, 45

Mosquito aircraft, 60-1, 69, 70-3

N

Nazi party, 105

Nissen huts, 41-3

Noisy-le-Sec, Paris, France, 85*

Normandy, France, 35, 86-9, 98, 104, 163, 165

North York concerns, Downsview, 150

North Sea, 38, 44, 68-9, 79

Nuremberg, Germany, 79*-83, 89, 104-5, 132

O

Ottawa, Ontario, 9, 115-7, 122, 141, 143, 145, 147, 157, 160-4, 166, 169, 173-4, 177-8, 184-9

Otter aircraft, 139, 150

Oxygen, 44, 73

P

P2V Neptune aircraft, 136, 139

Pathfinders, 50, 56-7, 60-1, 65, 67-9, 74, 79, 81, 84, 92, 102

Pittsburgh Glass & Paint Ltd, 24, 110

Poems

   Airman's Prayer, 114

   An Airman's Grace, 120

   High Flight, 52

   Our Ground Crew, 99

Post Traumatic Stress Disorder, 106

R

Radio aids, 53

RAF Stations

   Burn, 75

   Long Marston, 89

   Manston, 76

   Sywell, 39

   West Freugh, 40-2, 44, 86

   Woodbridge, 76

RCAF Station

   Baden-Solingen, 126, 142, 173

   Calgary, 97-8

   Centralia, 142

   Crumlin, 30

   Downsview, 144-5, 148, 152-7, 162-3

   Gimli, 97-8, 129

   Greenwood, 96-8, 130-6, 138-9, 145, 158, 160

   Gros-tenquin, 142

Linton-on-Ouse, 46-8, 63-4, 80, 86, 89, 92, 131

MacDonald, 129

Marville, 142

Middleton St. George, 96

Moose Jaw, 129

Penhold, 129

Pierce, 97

Portage la Prairie, 129

Rockcliffe, 144

Saskatoon, 120-3, 127, 129, 132, 145, 159, 161

St. Hubert, 97

Summerside, 115,125,130, 139

Topcliffe, 94-6

Winnipeg, 129

Zweibrücken, 142

RCAF Association, vii, 111, 147, 153, 156-7, 174

RCAF Association Trust, 164, 193

Rationing, 64, 95

Roe, AV & Co Ltd, AVRO, 47, 118-9

S

Sabre aircraft, 119

Sackville, NB, 1, 3, 5-6, 8-9, 15-16, 18, 20, 24, 109-12, 115, 151, 184, 189

Scarecrows, 58, 68

Schrage Musik, 49, 62, 76

Schweinfurt, Germany, 74*, 81

Searchlights, 44, 56, 58, 61-2, 68, 71, 80, 95, 195

Sheppard Avenue alignment, Downsview, 150

South Lancashire Regiment, 2/Bn, 40

SS Bayano, 35

SS Ile de France, 96, 200

Stadium, domed, proposal, Downsview, 153

Storm

Ice storm, Ontario Jan 1998, 188

Summer storm, Ontario June 1971, 154

Stratford-on-Avon, England, 43-4, 184, 193

Stuttgart, Germany, 74*, 76*, 91

T

Tame Boar (see Zahme Sau)

Tiger Force, 96

Toronto, Ontario, 25, 28, 33, 107, 145-8, 152, 154-6, 178, 184, 191

Training, flying

Navigator, initial, 28, 30

Refresher, 38-9, 41, 115

Sqn conversion, 44, 46, 48, 51-2, 86

Twitchy, 62, 131

U

U-boats, 34-5, 96, 103

Unique Decor Unlimited, 171-3, 175, 185-6

USAAF, 45,86

USAAF bases, England

Horham, 73

Newmarket, 68

V

V-1s (flying bombs), 90-1

V-2s (missiles), 93

V-E Day & anniversaries, 95, 188, 195

W

Wellington aircraft, 43, 45, 47, 92, 159

Western Development Museum, 128

Wilde Sau (Wild Boar), 65

WINDOW, 51, 65, 69

Women's Auxiliary Air Force, 37, 131, 177, 192-3

Women's Land Army, 50

Y

Yukon aircraft, 142

Z

Zahme Sau (Tame Boar), 65

ISBN 1-41205797-3